# Social Impact, Organizations and Society

*Social Impact, Organizations and Society* represents endeavors to comprehensively explore the essence of social impact. The editors aim to elucidate its definition, scope, measurement and implementation. Delving into how organizations integrate social impact into their core missions, decision-making processes and operational frameworks, this monograph strives to identify avenues for enhancing social impact generation. Furthermore, its focus lies on fostering effective relationships with diverse stakeholder groups and providing empirical evidence of social impact practices across industries and sectors. Through an in-depth examination of the latest research, this monograph sheds light on the evolving role of corporate social responsibility and its significance amidst contemporary challenges.

**Katarzyna Bachnik, PhD**, is a Professor of Marketing and Innovation at Hult International Business School, Cambridge, MA. She used to be affiliated at the Institute of Management, Warsaw School of Economics (SGH), and has collaborated as Visiting Professor with several universities worldwide. Her research interests include innovation and design thinking, higher education, international marketing and sustainability, and she is an author of several publications and expertise papers in the aforementioned areas.

**Magdalena Kaźmierczak, PhD**, is an Associate Professor in Quality Management Department in the Institute of Management at the Poznań University of Economics and Business (PUEB). Her research interests include corporate social responsibility, sustainability and standardized management systems.

**Magdalena Rojek-Nowosielska, PhD**, is an Associate Professor in the Strategic Management Department at the Wroclaw University of Economics and Business. She is a member of Technical Committee for Social Responsibility in Polish Committee for Standardization and editorial assistant of Research Papers of Wroclaw University of Economics, EBEN Poland, PTPS (Polish Society for Social Policy).

**Magdalena Stefańska, PhD**, is an Associate Professor and Head of Strategic Management Department in the Institute of Management at the Poznań University of Economics and Business (PUEB), Poland. Her areas of interest are corporate social responsibility, sustainability and sustainable development.

**Justyna Szumniak-Samolej, PhD**, is an Assistant Professor at the Department of Management Theory, Warsaw School of Economics (SGH), Poland. She works as a researcher, trainer, lecturer and conference speaker. Her key research areas are management in the new economy, corporate social responsibility, social media and innovative business models.

# Routledge Studies in Management, Organizations and Society

This series presents innovative work grounded in new realities, addressing issues crucial to an understanding of the contemporary world. This is the world of organized societies, where boundaries between formal and informal, public and private, local and global organizations have been displaced or have vanished, along with other nineteenth-century dichotomies and oppositions. Management, apart from becoming a specialized profession for a growing number of people, is an everyday activity for most members of modern societies.

Similarly, at the level of inquiry, culture and technology, and literature and economics, can no longer be conceived as isolated intellectual fields; conventional canons and established mainstreams are contested. *Management, Organizations and Society* addresses these contemporary dynamics of transformation in a manner that transcends disciplinary boundaries, with books that will appeal to researchers, students and practitioners alike.

Recent titles in this series include:

**Transcending Equality, Diversity and Inclusion at Work**
A Self-Critical Engagement
*Marguerite L Weber and Hugo Gaggiotti*

**Sustainable Human Resource Management**
Strategy, Organizational Innovation and Leadership in Industry 5.0
*Edited by Mariusz Sołtysik, Małgorzata Tyrańska, Katarzyna Piwowar-Sulej, and Tri Siwi Agustina*

**Organizations and Industry 4.0**
Management Solutions Beyond Technology
*Vojko Potočan, Kornélia Lazányi and Zlatko Nedelko*

**Social Impact, Organizations and Society**
The Contemporary Role of Corporate Social Responsibility
*Edited by Katarzyna Bachnik, Magdalena Kaźmierczak, Magdalena Rojek-Nowosielska, Magdalena Stefańska and Justyna Szumniak-Samolej*

# Social Impact, Organizations and Society

## The Contemporary Role of Corporate Social Responsibility

**Edited by**
**Katarzyna Bachnik,**
**Magdalena Kaźmierczak,**
**Magdalena Rojek-Nowosielska,**
**Magdalena Stefańska and**
**Justyna Szumniak-Samolej**

Routledge
Taylor & Francis Group
NEW YORK AND LONDON

First published 2024
by Routledge
605 Third Avenue, New York, NY 10158

and by Routledge
4 Park Square, Milton Park, Abingdon, Oxon, OX14 4RN

*Routledge is an imprint of the Taylor & Francis Group, an informa business*



ISBN: 978-1-032-76354-5 (hbk)
ISBN: 978-1-032-77036-9 (pbk)
ISBN: 978-1-003-48095-2 (ebk)

DOI: 10.4324/9781003480952

Typeset in Times New Roman
by codeMantra

# Contents

# Figures

# Tables

# Editors

**Katarzyna Bachnik**, PhD, is an expert with 19 years of experience in management, innovation and design thinking, international marketing and sustainability. She has worked as a lecturer, a trainer and an editor, and she is an author of several publications and expertise papers in the aforementioned areas (including being an author of "Cultural context of management processes. Case of Scandinavia" and co-author of "Business potential of social media"). Affiliated at the Institute of Management, Warsaw School of Economics, she has been granted several international scientific scholarships, including prestigious Fulbright Senior Advanced Research Award, which allowed her to conduct the research project "Social media in shaping a new business model against the background of cultural changes" at Haas School of Business, Berkeley. She collaborated as Visiting Professor with ESADE Business School, Barcelona, Cass Business School, London and Burapha University, Thailand. Katarzyna's academic engagement is backed by business experience. She has worked for enterprises in marketing and consultant jobs. Thanks to extensive knowledge and international exposure, she can take a holistic and analytical approach to management and marketing issues. Now, she serves as Professor of Marketing and Innovation at Hult International Business School, Cambridge, MA.

**Magdalena Kaźmierczak**, PhD, is an Associate Professor in Quality Management Department in the Institute of Management at the Poznań University of Economics and Business (PUEB). Since 2005, she has been scientifically connected with the subject of corporate social responsibility. Her research interests include corporate social responsibility, sustainability and standardized management systems. Her academic engagement is backed by business experience. She is the author and co-author of many publications in the field of CSR. She is a member of the Working Group for University Social Responsibility at the Ministry of Funds and Regional Policy of the Republic of Poland and a member of Technical Committee no. 305 on Social Responsibility set up by the Polish Standardization Committee. She is also a member of the Social Responsibility Rector's Committee at PUEB and Committee of Ethical Science Research conducted with participation of humans.

**Magdalena Rojek-Nowosielska**, PhD, is an Associate Professor in the Strategic Management Department at the Wroclaw University of Economics and Business. Since 2023, she has been Head of Sustainable Development Office at WUEB. She is a member of Technical Committee for Social Responsibility in Polish Committee for Standardization and editorial assistant of Research Papers of the Wroclaw University of Economics, EBEN Poland, PTPS (Polish Society for Social Policy). She is the author, reviewer and editor of numerous publications on the issue of corporate social responsibility. She is the winner of the "People who change the business" award, which is the only one about the distinction of people, not companies that deserved for the development of responsible business in Poland.

**Magdalena Stefańska**, PhD, is an Associate Professor and Head of Strategic Management Department in the Institute of Management at the Poznań University of Economics and Business (PUEB), Poland. Her areas of interest are corporate social responsibility, sustainability and sustainable development. She is an author and co-author and co-editor of books dedicated to CSR, Sustainability and Sustainable Development – e-book prepared in CENETSIE project. She reviews articles for many journals. She was a visiting scholar at the University of Zagreb, the University of Texas at Dallas and Czech University of Life Sciences Prague. She is also a member of the Social Responsibility Rector's Committee at PUEB and Committee of Ethical Science Research conducted with participation of humans at PUEB.

**Justyna Szumniak-Samolej**, PhD, is an Assistant Professor at the Department of Management Theory, Warsaw School of Economics (SGH), Poland. She works as a researcher, trainer, lecturer and conference speaker. Her key research areas are management in the new economy, corporate social responsibility, social media and innovative business models. Her academic publications include books, refereed journal articles and book chapters. She is a member of Rector's Commission on Social Responsibility of Warsaw School of Economics and a member of experts committee of "Philanthropist of The Year" competition organized by Academy for the Development of Philanthropy in Poland. She was a mentor in "Sustainable Development Ambassador Programme", UN Association Poland and expert in Climate Leadership Programme, UN Environment Programme. She was also a member of the Working Group on Education and Popularization of CSR in the Ministry of Economic Development of the Republic of Poland. She was a visiting scholar at the University of Technology Sydney and conducted lectures at ESSCA School of Management, Estice International Business School and Nottingham Business School.

# Contributors

**Maria Aluchna**, PhD, is a Professor of Management, Head of the Department of Management Theory at Warsaw School of Economics and Chair of the Management Faculty Board Warsaw School of Economics. She specializes in corporate governance, ESG reporting and strategic management. She is the author of academic articles and monographs. She teaches at MBA, PhD, MA, and BA studies.

**Bolesław Rok**, PhD, is a Professor of Sustainability Management and the Head of Positive Impact Entrepreneurship Research Lab, Kozminski University, Warsaw, Poland. He specializes in impact startups development and regenerative economy. He is Co-creator of the Climate Leadership program powered by UN Environment and Member of The Academy of Business in Society Board of Directors in Brussels.

**Agnieszka Sokołowska-Durkalec**, PhD, DSc, works as a Professor and the head of the Department of Enterprise Studies at the Faculty of Business and Management at Wroclaw University of Economics and Business (Poland). Her major scientific and research interests focus on broadly understood problems of intangible assets (corporate social responsibility, corporate social irresponsibility, intellectual capital management, human resource management, small business, organizational culture, etc.). Her achievements include more than 120 scientific publications (monographs, chapters in monographs, articles), management and participation in several research projects, active participation in over 100 national and international conferences, seminars and scientific symposia. The professor was also awarded many times with national and university awards for research and teaching.

**Dominika Hadro**, PhD, is an Associate Professor at the Department of Finance (Wroclaw University of Economics and Business), where she is also a member of the Strategic Management Committee, Advisor at the Sustainability Office and Editor-in-Chief of the *Financial Sciences Journal*. She is currently also a Visiting Professor at the University of Turin and a visiting researcher at the University of Bologna. Her research fields link together finance, sustainability and corporate communication, with a special interest in textual analysis tools and measures.

**Karolina Daszyńska-Żygadło, PhD,** holds the position of Assistant Professor in the Department of Corporate Finance and Public Finance at Wroclaw University of Economics and Business in Poland. Her research fields are business valuation, financial planning and corporate sustainability. In 2015, her book on scenarios approach in business valuation was published in Poland. Along with academic carrier, she works as a business coach and mentor with early-stage businesses and startups in the system thinking and systems.

**Justyna Fijałkowska, PhD**, is an Associate Professor and the director of the Institute of Finance and the vice-rector for International Cooperation at the University of Social Sciences in Poland, research and lecturer at the Institute of Finance, Faculty of Economics and Sociology, University of Lodz, Poland. She got her PhD at the Management Faculty of the University of Lodz. She has lectured at the University of Turin and the University of Bologna as a Visiting Professor. She has held research internships at the University of Perugia and the ISEG Lisbon School of Economics & Management. Her research interests include sustainability, integrated reporting, non-financial reporting, intellectual capital.

**Valerio Brescia, PhD**, is an Assistant Professor at the University of Turin, holding a PhD in Business Management from the same institution. He serves as Associate Professor at the Społeczna Akademia Nauk, University of Social Sciences, in Łódź, Poland. His specialization lies in the Consolidated Financial Statements of municipalities, accounting standards and popular reports. Additionally, his interests include technology applications in accounting and management, smart cities and citizen involvement. He is a technical advisor for the Standard Setter Board on accrual principles for the public sector for the MEF – Italian Ministry of Finance.

**Ewa Mazur-Wierzbicka, PhD**, is an Associate Professor of Szczecin University, Institute of Management. She specializes mainly in the field of corporate social responsibility (CSR) (with emphasis on diversity management, ethical and equality-related actions), sustainable development and human capital management. She is the author of more than 150 publications both in Polish and English. She is an external expert of CSR of the Responsible Business Forum. University of Szczecin's plenipotentiary to the Technical Committee no. 305 for Social Responsibility operating at the Polish Committee for Standardization, advisor of the Polish Agency for Enterprise Development in terms of CSR. Expert of the European Institute for Gender Equality (01.12.2018–30.11.2024).

**Anna Cierniak-Emerych** is a Professor and Head of the Department of Labour, Capital and Innovation, Wroclaw University of Economics and Business (Poland) and Dean for student's affairs, Faculty of Business. Anna Cierniak-Emerych is the author of more than 180 publications and co-author of the monograph *Labour Potential Management and the Satisfaction of Employee Interests* ed. Wroclaw UEW, Wroclaw 2022. Anna Cierniak-Emerych's research interests relate mainly to human and work in the company, particularly corporate social responsibility (CSR), development of tangible and intangible working conditions, employee participation, greater flexibility in employment, human resources management, satisfaction of employees, the interests of employees and employers in the enterprise and their respect.

**Agata Austen, PhD**, is an Associate Professor, employed at the University of Economics in Katowice, Poland. Her research interests include sustainable HRM, interorganizational networks and HRM effectiveness. She is the author of more than 100 scientific publications. Over her 20-year career as a researcher, she has been involved in various scientific and practice-oriented research projects focusing on HRM (such as employability and sustainable HRM), as well as public management (including interorganizational networks effectiveness and stakeholder management) and entrepreneurship (such as entrepreneurial learning from failure and real options reasoning). She is an active reviewer, collaborating with publishers like Emerald and Wiley. Additionally, she works as a business consultant specializing in HRM.

**Katarzyna Piwowar-Sulej, PhD**, is a Professor employed at Wroclaw University of Economics and Business in Poland. Her research interests are sustainable HRM, sustainable leadership, agile and sustainable project management. She is an experienced HR manager and project manager. She is the winner of two scholarship competitions financed by the European Social Fund. She is the author of more than 180 publications and participant of more than 60 conferences as a lecturer or expert, and an active reviewer (cooperation, i.a., with Elsevier, Emerald and Springer). In 2023, she was awarded by Wiley for a top downloaded article, and by Emerald for an outstanding paper and reviews.

**Dariusz Nowak, PhD**, is an Associate Professor and Head of the Department of Corporate Resources Management, business practitioner. He is a member of the Scientific Society of Organization and Management, Expert of the National Centre for Research and Development, Expert of Polish National Agency for Academic Exchange and Chairman of the Regional Committee of the Entrepreneurship Olympics. He is the author of more than 150 publications. His scientific interests include interorganizational relations, industrial cooperation and industry development, production management, enterprise resources, core competences, sustainable development and waste of resources. He cooperates with many universities from Central and Eastern Europe as Lecturer, Teacher, Coach and Instructor.

**Beata Skowron-Mielnik, PhD**, is an Associate Professor at the Poznań University of Economics and Business, Department of Corporate Resources Management. She has been teaching for 30 years in the field of management. She is the author of almost 100 publications on human resources management. Her research focuses on human resource management, work organization, job design, hybrid working, time management, competence development and interim management. She initiated and coordinated a number of business studies and projects. She is a member of program boards of scientific management conferences.

**Krzysztof Janasz, PhD**, is an Associate Professor at the University of Szczecin, Department of Corporate Management, Institute of Management. His interests include business management, innovation management, strategic management, risk management, innovation financing and macroeconomics. He is the author of over 130 publications in Polish and English and Head of doctoral studies at the Faculty of Economics and Management in 2015–2019. He worked in the banking sector for many years. He is a member of the Polish Innovation Management Association, the Institute for Innovation and Entrepreneurship Research and the Polish Economic Society.

**Joanna Bernacka, PhD**, is Student at the Doctoral School of PUEB and holds a master's degree in Commodity Science. In 2004, she also completed an executive MBA program at WSB Poznań and AUSE Helsinki. Her research interests focus on theories of organizational development and management, strategic management, enterprise resource management and HRM, particularly employee engagement and motivation. She successfully combines practical management knowledge with 25 years of managerial experience with her research interests. She has previously worked for Schlumberger, the largest oilfield service company spanning three continents, as well as in the aerospace industry (UTC) and Philips Lighting Electronics.

**Marcin Gołembski, PhD**, is an Assistant Professor at the Poznań University of Economics and Business, Faculty of Management. He conducts research in Human Development Theory, Managerial Economics and Human Resources. He is also the co-leader of the Decision Support Initiative (www.wsparciedecyzji.pl) and holds a habilitated doctorate in economic sciences. As an academic lecturer at PUEB, he has spent the past 17 years as a trainer, an expert in HR and a consultant in human resource management, HR function organization, organizational methods, management and leadership. Additionally, he co-founded and directs the elite postgraduate training program "Master of Business Training" offered at PUEB. He has co-authored training programs implemented as part of nationwide projects funded by the EU. Dr Gołembski is the author of the monograph titled "The HR Function in a Company:

Current Trends and Development Prospects," along with over 40 other publications in the field of management, published in industry journals and scientific publications both in Poland and abroad.

**Małgorzata Budzanowska-Drzewiecka, PhD**, is an Assistant Professor at the Jagiellonian University in Krakow, Poland. Her research interests center on consumer behaviors and communication on the Internet, especially in social media. In her work, she focuses on the persuasiveness of electronic word-of-mouth communication (eWOM). Her current research activity includes also individuals' pro-environmental behaviors, management diversity and quality of education. Her research has been published in a number of peer-reviewed journals and monographs.

**Paulina Jędrzejczyk, PhD**, is a Professor for Business Administration, HRM, Employer Consulting and Diversity Management at the University of Applied Labour Studies in Mannheim (Germany). She studied Business Education at the Johannes Gutenberg University in Mainz and graduated as a business teacher in 2000. She completed her doctorate in 2007 on the subject of "Multicultural Teams in Organizations"; 2013–2014 certificate course in Coaching and Mediation (Univ.) at the International Academy for Innovative Pedagogy, Psychology and Economics/Free University of Berlin; 2007–2017 Interim Professorships at different Universities of Applied Sciences in Germany.

**Justyna M. Bugaj, PhD**, is a Professor at Krakow University of Economics, Poland. Her research centers on strategic management and quality assurance in higher education institutions. She is the author of numerous articles, reports and expert opinions commissioned by Polish and foreign organizations.

**Bohdan Rożnowski, PhD**, is employed at The John Paul II Catholic University of Lublin, Institute of Psychology Work, Organization & Psychosocial Rehabilitation Psychology Chair. Bohdan is the author of many scientific monographs, articles and presentations on work and organizational psychology (stress and job analysis, work engagement, self-efficacy, job crafting), career guidance (career transitions) and organizational psychology (conflict management, motivation and attitudes) and member of international scientific teams and professional organizations European Work and Organizational Psychology, Polish Association of Organizational Psychology (PAOP), National Forum for Career Guidance, Polish Psychological Association.

**Blaženka Knežević, PhD**, is a full Professor at the Faculty of Economics and Business, University of Zagreb, Croatia. Her research interests are retail information systems, economics of electronic commerce, procurement management, supplier relationship management and sustainability in given fields. She participated in various scientific research projects and published numerous papers in conference proceedings, books and academic journals. She is a member of the editorial board in a couple of academic journals and a regular reviewer at several international scientific journals.

**Iwona Olejnik, PhD**, is an Associate Professor in Market Research and Services Department, Poznań University of Economics and Business in Poland. She is the author and co-author of about 100 articles and books. Her main area of interest is qualitative and quantitative market research, consumer behavior and pension system.

**Bogusława Drelich-Skulska, PhD**, is a full Professor at the Wroclaw University of Economics and Business, Vice-Rector for Accreditation and International Cooperation and Head of Department of International Business. She is an author and co-author of more than 130 research papers, seven handbooks and monographs in Polish and English, concerning the issues of Asian regionalism, institutional economics, international business, international accreditations and sustainable challenges in modern universities. She is Member of the following scientific associations: Polish Association for International Studies (PTSM), Polish Economic Society (PTE), European Southeast Asian Studies Association, Eurasia Business and Economics Society (EBES), as well as Asia-Pacific Research Center located in Wroclaw.

**Anna H. Jankowiak, PhD**, is a Professor of the University in the Department of International Business and Director of the International Cooperation Center at the Wroclaw University of Economics and Business; author and co-author of 50 articles and eight books in Polish and English concerning the issues of Asian regionalism, Asian economies, transnational corporation, international business, global production networks, and clusters in global economy; co-creator of the research projects funded by National Science Centre, Poland; Visiting Professor at many universities in Europe and Asia; visiting scholar at Seikei University in Tokio, Japan and St. Mary's University in Halifax, Canada.

**Pavel Kotyza, PhD**, is a member of Czech University of Life Sciences Prague's Department of Economics. He specializes in Agricultural Policy Reforms, Rural Development and Cooperative/Collaborative Farming. With a proven track record in international journal publications, he has contributed significantly to the field. Pavel is a successful recipient of the Erasmus+ Strategic Partnership in Higher Education grant, collaborating with eight international partners on the viability of small farms managed by young farmers (VISYFARM).

**Sergiusz Prokurat, PhD**, is an economist, historian and former manager in Hewlett Packard, DXC, Lingaro. He currently works for EU institutions. He has lectured at universities in Poland, and also in Spain, Italy, Central America and Asia. He is the author of couple of books, including *Work 2.0: Nowhere to Hide*.

# Introduction

In the previous publication, under our editorial supervision, we pointed out the essence of corporate social responsibility and its significance in creating value within an organization – economically, socially and environmentally (Bachnik et al., 2022). The authors who participated in its creation dedicated considerable attention to defining and identifying the essence of values created by organizations. At that time, delving into the issue of values in organizational activities, our attention was drawn to the topic of social impact, which seemed to be secondary in the actions of organizations.

Economic and environmental impact issues dominated both in literature and practice. Considering social impact, it was often limited to activities for employees or local communities, or took the form of philanthropic responsibility, such as sponsoring culture or sports. For organizations, it was important to initiate, organize, implement and communicate – often aligned with image creation. This could occasionally raise suspicions of greenwashing, whitewashing or concealing irresponsible behavior. This led to reflection and the question of whether organizations, given their influence, and considering economic and environmental impact – due to the economic approach to utilizing organizational resources and the obligation to assess environmental impact (e.g., the requirement for environmental impact assessments in investments) – measure and determine their social impact. Hence, the idea of writing a monograph on the essence and understanding of social impact in the context of corporate social responsibility emerged. Correct understanding ultimately boils down to making rational decisions, which, in turn, lead to better business and social outcomes.

The aim of this monograph is to discuss how organizations address the social impact as a core product or by product of their vision statement, decision making and operational procedures. Based on extensive literature review and benchmark analysis of competing publications of similar content or structure, we decided to aim at UN SDGs focused on social impact, taking a closer look at quality of life, education, workplace, equity, diversity and inclusion, and to keep reflections around social impact against the context of organizational operations, clearly indicating the environment at hand: internal and external stakeholders. In this monograph, we are specifically interested in identifying the sources of increase in generated social impact, in building greater understanding around building effective relationships with various stakeholder groups and in providing evidence of exercising social impact across industries and sectors.

The above-mentioned issues determined the final structure of this monograph. It consists of three fundamental parts. The first part focuses on the essence of social impact, as well as the assessment and measurement of positive and negative social influence. The second and third parts of the monograph depict the process of shaping social impact by various internal and external stakeholder groups and highlight the challenge they face in the process. Throughout the chapters, we intend to find answers to the following questions:

- Social impact: What is the state of art?
- What is the role of social impact in human resource management?
- What are the effects of social impact management on human well-being?
- What social impact generates diversity management?
- What is the university's role in shaping social impact?
- Social impact: What can be improved for future generations?

The fact that this monograph consists of three parts and 14 chapters allows for a multidimensional presentation of the theme of social impact.

In conclusion, we assert that loosely defined and aspirational discussions regarding social impact often fall short of materializing into tangible outcomes. It is imperative to meticulously redefine the parameters and implications of social impact, compelling institutions and organizations to undertake actions that not only yield societal benefits but also possess measurable metrics. We aspire for the monograph we are presenting to readers to serve as a meaningful contribution to this discourse by elucidating the outcomes of cutting-edge research on the contemporary landscape of corporate social responsibility. Furthermore, it sheds light on the evolving significance of social impact within the realm of business, particularly within the context of the challenges prevalent in the current times.

Editors

## Reference

Bachnik, K., Kaźmierczak, M., Rojek-Nowosielska, M., Stefańska, M., & Szumniak-Samolej, J. (Eds.). (2022). *Corporate Social Responsibility and Sustainability. From Values to Impact*. Routledge.

# Acknowledgments

This monograph would not have been created without the involvement of many individuals. We want to extend our special appreciation to all the authors for their dedication and eagerness to contribute their expertise. The design and preparation of this publication were made possible by their scientific curiosity, perseverance and pursuit of answers. Our sincere gratitude also goes to the reviewers of this publication, whose invaluable comments significantly enhanced all the chapters. We owe the successful publication of this work to the guidance and assistance provided by Brianna Ascher and Jessica Rech from Routledge, who skillfully navigated us through the publishing process and contributed to shaping it into the final version that we proudly present to you.

# Part 1

# Identifying social impact

# 1 Redefining social impact

*Katarzyna Bachnik, Magdalena Kaźmierczak, Magdalena Rojek-Nowosielska, Magdalena Stefańska and Justyna Szumniak-Samolej*

## Introduction

In today's world, social impact isn't just a buzzword – it's a movement. It reflects to what humanity can achieve when people come together (Sopact, 2023). Then, they possess the capacity to construct a world that is not only more sustainable but also more just. The social impact involves bringing about substantial and positive transformations to tackle urgent social issues. It is a comprehensive concept that includes enhancements at the local level as well as substantial changes on a global scale. In positive transformations on both small and large scales, various sectors, including business, government and non-profit organizations, can actively participate (MasterClass, 2022). Until now, numerous business organizations have primarily considered social impact as merely a potential addition to their overall strategy. Today, however, integrating social impact into a company's sustainability strategy has become imperative (Tiuttu, 2020). Indeed, there is no better time than the present to start planning a social impact strategy and see what benefits it will bring, not only to the organization itself but also to the world at large. According to P. Frumkin, founder of the Center for Social Impact Strategy at the University of Pennsylvania, "Social impact strategy is any effort to create public value that is systematic, sustainable and innovative. Effectively creating social impact is an essential challenge to all organisations, regardless of geography or sector" (Frumkin, 2023).

Social impact is an important aspect of corporate social responsibility (CSR). The term is sometimes used interchangeably with CSR. While the two concepts are certainly related, they are distinct in meaning. CSR represents a company's efforts to address social and environmental issues, often going beyond legal requirements. It includes the integration of responsible practices into core business activities, such as ethical sourcing, employee welfare and environmental sustainability. Social impact specifically highlights the intentional and measurable results a company achieves in creating positive social change through business activities and investments (Koval, 2023).

DOI: 10.4324/9781003480952-2

The term 'social impact' was first used in 1969 in a Yale University research paper on the ethical responsibilities of investors. The following year, a significant development was the enactment of the US National Environmental Policy Act (NEPA), which defined a set of practices and procedures known as Social Impact Assessment (SIA). In the years that followed, the ideology of SIA was made famous by the American social entrepreneur Bill Drayton. He is an ardent believer that everyone is capable of making a change and therefore we are all 'changemakers' (Ricee, 2021). In 1993, the first Principles and Guidelines for Social Impact Assessment were developed to assist government agencies and private entities in fulfilling their responsibilities under the NEPA statutes and the Council on Environmental Quality (Klingler-Vidra, 2020).

> Democratized in the 90s, the concept of social impact emanates from the intersection of different cultures and professional practices: the rise of the evaluation of public action, the implementation of international development programs, the development of corporate social responsibility strategies, the influence of philanthropy on the measurement of social returns, etc.
>
> (IMPACTDOTS, 2023)

Social impact was also taken into account in later years, more specifically in the concept of creating shared value (CSV) proposed by M. Porter and M. Kramer in the Harvard Business Review (2006). The idea of CSV was closely linked to social impact ('doing well by doing good') in order to create shared value and contribute to positive change in the environment. By the beginning of the 21st century, social impact was already being mapped and reported by a wide range of organizations, well beyond the NEPA reporting requirements for land use in the US (Klingler-Vidra, 2020).

Today, more and more companies, NGOs and public institutions are making a conscious effort to achieve ever greater social impact. This study is an attempt to present the ways of defining and classifying social impact. A review of the literature and discussion on the subject is a starting point for further considerations on the nature of social impact.

## Materials and methods

In pursuit of the purpose of the study presented at the beginning of this chapter, the authors have attempted to organize the resources of knowledge on social impact. Through their research, the authors aim to answer the following research questions:

- Social impact: What is the state of the art?
- What does social impact actually mean?
- What are the basic types of social impact?
- Are there any common features in the definitions of social impact?

To this end, the authors conducted an integrative review of the literature. The literature review covered the basic concepts related to the topic of social impact.

It allowed the presentation of views and research in the field analyzed. The authors focused on the review of available publications in the most cited database: Scopus. The aim of the review was to find relevant documents that could be used to find commonalities in the quoted definitions of social impact and to examine the concept from different perspectives. The basic search term was "social impact". Without applying any additional filters, a rather large pool of publications was obtained, with as many as 20,267 documents. Only after applying the right filters and AND/OR connectors did the platform allow a more thorough analysis of the data. Social impact was also associated with additional terms such as "definition", "concept" and "classification". Additional detailed filters were also applied to the Scopus database to reduce the number of documents available and create a shortlist for more in-depth review:

- Year – from 2003 to 2022. Author Frank Vanclay (2003) provides many insights into the definition of social impact in his publication titled "International Principles for Social Impact Assessment". He is also repeatedly referred to and referenced in later publications. Furthermore, in the shortlist for review, he is also the author with the greatest publishing output (11);
- Subject area – given the authors' research interests, three areas were selected for review: social sciences; business, management and accounting; economics, econometrics and finance;
- Document Type – article, book chapter, review;
- Publication stage – final;
- Source type – journals and books;
- Language – English.

Ultimately, 914 papers were found as a result of the above steps, which were designed to maximize the likelihood of finding papers that met the final purpose (Figure 1.1).

The chart above shows that the number of publications increased progressively from year to year, peaking in 2021. Most of these were: research papers (720 in total), chapters in research books (120) or reviews (74). The largest number of publications was found in the following research fields and disciplines: social sciences (178 publications); business, management and accounting (285); economics, econometrics and finance (153). The social sciences in particular are concerned with the nature of society, its structure, how it operates, the relationships between individuals and the underlying trends, and are therefore most relevant to the definition of social impact. Some publications are cross-disciplinary, which is why their total number was higher than the number of publications in the final list.

Most of the publications referring to the concept of social impact came from the following journals: *Sustainability Switzerland* (65 publications), *Journal of*

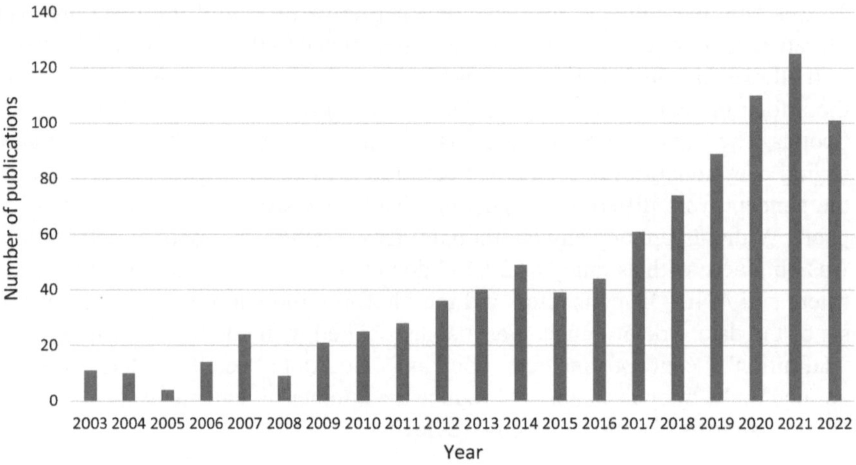


*Figure 1.1* Number of publications on "social impact" by year

*Source:* Own elaboration based on Scopus (2022).

*Cleaner Production* (18), *Impact Assessment and Project Appraisal* (15), *Environmental Impact Assessment Review* (12) and *Social Science and Medicine* (10). The most common keywords in the reviewed publications were social impacts, sustainability, social impact assessment, social change and economic and social effects.

In terms of the origin of the individual papers, the largest number of publications came from developed countries such as the USA (191), the UK (143), Australia (91), Italy (59) and Spain (56). Papers from less developed countries, such as Pakistan (4), Bangladesh (2) and Nigeria (2), were also included in the analysis due to the greater social inequalities present and the significant need for social impact.

The literature review also shows that there is still a limited number of studies that capture the essence of social impact. Therefore, an attempt has been made to take a comprehensive approach to the topic of defining social impact and demonstrating its role in a dynamically changing environment.

## Results

Defining social impact is difficult, as there are many definitions and perspectives. "There is currently a lack of consensus on the meaning of social impact, which results in the lack of a single and commonly accepted definition of social impact and the lack of one universal measurement method" (Perrini et al., 2021, p. 238). Indeed, there are no hard and fast rules for defining social impact (Lynes, 2021). At the same time, it should be noted that the concept of social impact is constantly being redefined in different ways, which makes both theoretical and practical work in the field much more difficult (Maas & Liket, 2011). Furthermore, social impact has been studied in different areas such as education, healthcare, environmental sustainability and poverty, which can be difficult to compare (Rawhouser, Cummings & Newbert, 2019). Selected definitions of social impact are presented in Table 1.1.

The lack of consensus on the definition of social impact has led to confusion and hindered the ability to study the phenomenon (Maas & Liket, 2011). Most

*Table 1.1* Selected definitions of social impact

| *Term* | *Definition* |
|---|---|
| Social Impact Assessment (Vanclay, 2003) | Social Impact Assessment includes the processes of analyzing, monitoring and managing the intended and unintended social consequences, both positive and negative, of planned interventions (policies, programs, plans, projects) and any social change processes invoked by those interventions. Its primary purpose is to bring about a more sustainable and equitable biophysical and human environment. |
| Social Impact (Clark et al., 2004) | Social Impact – the portion of the total outcome that happened as a result of the activity of the venture, above and beyond what would have happened anyway. |
| Social Impact (Kolodinsky et al., 2006) | Social Impact can be identified as value obtained by the beneficiaries and other recipients of the intervention undertaken. |
| Social Impact (IMPACT, 2011) | Social Impact – a much wider range of activities that includes any change to social, economic and/ or environmental welfare. |
| Social Impact (Perrini & Vurro, 2013) | Social Impact – the ability of socially entrepreneurial ventures to change the status quo within a given area of intervention. |
| Social impact (Stephan et al., 2016) | Social Impact – beneficial outcomes resulting from prosocial behavior that are enjoyed by the intended targets of that behavior and/or by the broader community of individuals, organizations and/ or environments. |
| Social impact (Dufour, 2019) | Social impacts include all social and cultural consequences to human populations of any public or private actions that alter the ways in which people live, work, play, relate to one another, organize to meet their needs and generally cope as members of society. |
| OCM Solution (2023) | Social impact meaning encompasses the broader outcomes and consequences of actions, policies, programs or projects beyond purely economic considerations, focusing on the improvement of social well-being and the resolution of social challenges. |

*Source:* Own elaboration based on Clark et al. (2004); Dufour (2019); IMPACT, (2011); International Association for Impact Assessment (1994); Kolodinsky et al. (2006); OCM Solution (2023); Perrini & Vurro (2013); Stephan et al. (2016); The International Association for Impact Assessment, (2022); Vanclay (2003).

glaring is the difference between entrepreneurs' and social scientists' definitions of the terms "impact", "output", "outcome" and "social return" (Clark et al., 2004, p. 6). According to J. Głowacki (2018), in order to fully grasp the concept of social impact, it is necessary to move from a process perspective, which focuses primarily on the implementation of specific measures, to an outcome perspective, which emphasizes the effects of these measures. Therefore, the definition of social impact developed by Clark et al. (2004) is based on the impact value chain: Inputs – Activities – Outputs – Outcomes (= Impact) – Goal Alignment. Outputs are the results that a company, non-profit organization or project manager can directly measure or evaluate. Outcomes are the ultimate changes you are trying to make in the world. Social impact consists of all the consequences (developments, changes and disruptions) of an organization's activities for direct or indirect external stakeholders (beneficiaries, users and clients) in its field, for people within the organization (employees, volunteers) and for society in general (French Council for the Social and Solidarity Economy, 2017). Furthermore, the outcomes produced as a result of a given action can be direct (easier to measure) or indirect (more difficult to measure). Burdge (2003) therefore argues for the need for a more holistic definition of social impact, taking into account both individuals and the communities in which programs are implemented. Based on the above considerations, the authors have therefore adopted the following definition of social impact for the purposes of this monograph, as developed by the Interorganizational Committee on Guidelines and Principles for Social Impact Assessment (1994):

> Social impacts – the consequences to human populations of any public or private actions -that alter the ways in which people live, work, play, relate to one another, organize to meet their needs and generally cope as members of society. The term also includes cultural impacts involving changes to the norms, values, and beliefs that guide and rationalize their cognition of themselves and their society.

Many studies address not only the positive but also the negative social impact of various phenomena or activities. In addition, the literature on the subject distinguishes between indirect and direct social impact (Table 1.2).

Vague and aspirational conversations about social impact do not translate into much real impact. There is a need to clearly redefine what social impact is/entails/covers, and to effectively push institutions and organizations to take actions that not only generate social impact but are also able to measure it.

## Discussion and conclusion

The difficulty of developing measurement methods and then applying them in practice is compounded by the myriad of definitions of social impact and the lack of a clear indication of the core meaning of the concept. The overview

*Table 1.2* Types of social impact

| *Type of social impact* | *Description* |
|---|---|
| Direct impact | Organizations and businesses use their products or services to create direct impacts. You can quantify and measure direct impacts since they outline how an organization's interactions generate results. |
| Indirect impact | Partnerships are the main form of indirect impact. When a company or organization connects with community partners to create social change, their collaborative results are a form of indirect impact. |
| Negative impact | As the opposite of positive impact, negative impact describes any change that detrimentally impacts a community or the environment. An example of a negative environmental impact is an increase in pollution. |
| Positive impact | Any beneficial improvement an organization initiates is a form of positive impact. From a business standpoint, positive impacts include improving gender equality in the workplace and implementing well-being workshops. |

*Source:* Own elaboration based on Alla et al. (2017); MasterClass (2022).

in Table 1.1 shows that this concept has been defined as: social consequences (Vanclay, 2003), total outcome (Clark et al., 2004), value obtained (Kolodinsky et al., 2006), outcomes (Stephan et al., 2016), among others. Some authors have also used the terms social impact and social value interchangeably (Grieco et al., 2015). Social impact is therefore a category that defies explicit and precise definition. Its scope is further clarified to meet specific needs, such as research or the fulfillment of specific public policy tasks (Grabowska & Wójcik, 2021, p. 28). However, there are some common features in the above definitions that may be constituents of the core meaning of social impact:

- The outcome of a project, program, policy or activity, any change in social, economic and/or environmental welfare;
- Direct or indirect social impacts, both positive and negative;
- Stakeholder involvement;
- Social impact assessment (analysis, monitoring and management of the social consequences of development).

The literature review leads to conclusion. In most of the papers, the authors stress the need for a better definition of social impact. It is very difficult to find articles that discuss this concept in a general sense, most of them refer to specific sectors/contexts. Some papers dealt with only one of the three dimensions of sustainability, and it was often the area of social impact that was most neglected. In summary, there is an ongoing debate about the nature and conceptualization of the notion of 'social impact' (Martino, 2019).

The lack of consensus on a clear definition of social impact may, in turn, lead to difficulties in developing consistent classifications of methods for measuring social impact. This includes the dilemma of whether social impact will include both positive and negative, intended and unintended outcomes of actions taken, or whether it will be narrowed down to intended positive outcomes (Boyne, 2002; Sawyerr & Ebrahimi, 2022). Another difficulty in developing methods to measure social impact may stem from the intangibility of the concept and its qualitative framing, such as the reference to value, outcomes and social consequences mentioned above. In addition, both positive and negative impacts of a given company can lead to changes in, for example, the economic, social or environmental dimensions (Maas & Liket, 2011). Furthermore, these changes may be considered in the short and/or long term. Finally, it may be very difficult (especially in the long term) to determine which of the actions taken caused a particular change in the social, environmental and economic dimensions, and whether other variables may have influenced a particular outcome. The multitude of definitions of social impact has also led to a diverse approach to the assessment and measurement of social impact and, ultimately, multiple measurement methods. An evident outcome of this is reflected in the diverse array of methods for measuring social impact as documented in the literature, arising from a comprehensive critical review on the subject. For example, Dufour (2015) points to 86 methods, Grieco (Grieco et al., 2015) to 76, and Maas and Liket (2011) to 30. The wide variety of suggested social impact measurement methods can be seen as an advantage, as it offers freedom of choice depending on the varying requirements and different objectives to be met. At the same time, it can also pose a major challenge, as difficulties may arise in determining the best method to measure the full extent of impact (Hlady-Rispal & Servantie, 2018). Additionally, comparability of impact outcomes both between companies and within a given entity may be compromised if different measurement methods are used in different years.

When deciding on a measurement method, there are a number of questions that should guide the decision-maker towards the best choice. For example, the perspective from which the measurement is carried out – i.e. whether the analysis is carried out from the micro (individual), meso (the enterprise concerned) or macro (socio-economic) level – implies a different set of indicators, and thus, a different measurement will be made and a different impact will be indicated. Some methodologies allow the assessment of actions taken and completed (retrospective timeframe), while others add an assessment of expected impacts in the future (prospective timeframe). Such information can help to make investment decisions or to modify previously planned activities in terms of expected social impact. Equally important is the approach used to measure impact. In certain contexts, process-based methods are possible, which examine the cost-effectiveness and efficiency of the processes involved, although they do not as such provide an absolute measure of social "gains". Monetisation methods quantify social and environmental indicators which can then be expressed in a specific currency and compared with the company's other financial indicators. Further analysis can reveal the dynamics and structure of change. From a management process perspective, this information can facilitate decision-making and planning about the scope and direction of change. There are also methods that measure the result of actions taken (operational outputs), i.e. the incremental outcome that would not have been possible without the initiatives taken beforehand. These methods, called impact methods, are actually the core of social impact measurement, but in Maas and Liket's (2011) classification of different measurement methods, only 8 of the 30 methods analyzed were classified as actually measuring impact.

Measuring social impact, although it involves a great deal of financial, organizational and resource effort in a broad sense, can bring benefits not only to the social impact maker itself but also to its beneficiaries. These benefits can be of strategic importance. For example, the results of the measurement may lead to future changes and improvements in the operation of the company (as a whole or in specific areas of the company), as well as improvements in the initiatives undertaken so far (Grieco et al., 2015). This may be due to the fact that the awareness of social impact derived from the measurement carried out had to be preceded by an in-depth analysis of the manner, scope and purpose of resource allocation, in order to consequently obtain the best results. Decisions taken in this way also lead to improvements in accounting and reporting practices, which in turn ensure the clarity and reliability of information provided to stakeholders in the area of activities undertaken and the reliability of subsequent accounting. This further influences the gaining and/or maintaining of public confidence and also shapes the image of the company accordingly.

Thus presented, the optics of the changes resulting from the social initiatives undertaken show the company's perspective. It should not be forgotten that these changes also (if not primarily) affect the beneficiaries of the company's activities. Therefore, quoting Vanclay (2003, p. 8), we can speak of changes in the following areas:

- People's way of life – that is, how they live, work, play and interact with one another on a day-to-day basis;
- Their culture – that is, their shared beliefs, customs, values and language or dialect;
- Their community – its cohesion, stability, character, services and facilities;
- Their political systems – the extent to which people are able to participate in decisions that affect their lives, the level of democratization that is taking place and the resources provided for this purpose;
- Their environment – the quality of the air and water people use; the availability and quality of the food they eat; the level of hazard or risk, dust and noise they are exposed to; the adequacy of sanitation, their physical safety and their access to and control over resources;
- Their health and well-being – health is a state of complete physical, mental, social and spiritual well-being and not merely the absence of disease or infirmity;

- Their personal and property rights – particularly whether people are economically affected, or experience personal disadvantage which may include a violation of their civil liberties;
- Their fears and aspirations – their perceptions about their safety, their fears about the future of their community and their aspirations for their future and the future of their children.

Given the areas of change presented, which concern the enterprises themselves on the one hand and the beneficiaries on the other, it is possible to propose a classification of the changes in terms of their focus and scale of the potential impact. Thus, the perspective of the enterprise itself and the changes that occur within the enterprise as a result of the initiatives taken can be classified as micro-scale and inward-focused. Changes on the part of the beneficiaries of the actions taken are characterized by a greater reach, so we can speak of mesoscale and outward focus. There is also the most far-reaching – the macro scale with an outward focus, which has not been discussed so far, and which concerns transformational change. As a result of the evolution of micro- and mesoscale changes, there may be further diffusion of transformations in social relations, the diffusion of knowledge or the socio-economic model. This may lead to transformations of existing paradigms, models, institutions, social structures or directions of further development. Transformational change can occur at the latest by virtue of its scope and focus, as it takes the longest time to occur. The social impact resulting from the launch of an initiative is also the most difficult to measure.

As is clear from the discussion above, defining social impact does not necessarily lead directly to a simple solution to the problem of assessing and measuring it. However, this does not mean that we should not try. After all, the power of social impact is enormous. The social impact is becoming an indispensable part of the strategy of modern organizations. Today, organizations following the path of sustainable development and implementing socially responsible activities should be aware of the impact they have on society as a whole, including economic, social and environmental aspects. The mentioned organization's social impact awareness should result in the need and willingness to change and take specific actions. Do not let laziness, lack of knowledge, lack of goodwill or avoidance of responsibility turn into the sin of omission, the consequences of which will affect current and future generations.

## References

Alla, K., Hall, W.D., Whiteford, H.A., Head, B.W., & Meurk, C.S. (2017). How do we define the policy impact of public health research? A systematic review. *Health Research Policy and Systems*, *15*(1), 1–12.

Boyne, G.A. (2002). Public and private management: What's the difference? *Journal of Management Studies*, *39*(1), 97–121. https://doi.org/10.1111/1467-6486.00284

Burdge, R.J. (2003). The practice of social impact assessment background. *Impact Assessment and Project Appraisal, 21*(2), 84–88. https://doi.org/10.3152/147154603781766356

Clark, C., Rosenzweig, W., Long, D., & Olsen, S. (2004). Double bottom line project report: Assessing social impact in double bottom line ventures. *UC Berkeley: Center for Responsible Business.* Retrieved from https://escholarship.org/uc/item/80n4f1mf

Dufour, B. (2019). Social impact measurement: What can impact investment practices and the policy evaluation paradigm learn from each other? *Research in international business and finance*, 47, 18–30. https://doi.org/10.1016/j.ribaf.2018.02.003. Elsevier. https://doi.org/10.1016/j.ribaf.2018.02.003

Dufour, B. (2015). State of the art in social impact measurement: Methods for work integration social enterprises measuring their impact in a public context. *5th EMES International Research Conference on Social Enterprise: "Building a Scientific Field to Foster the Social Enterprise Eco-System*", EMES, 1–24.

French Council for the Social and Solidarity Economy. (2017). *Handbook assessing social impact. A source of insight for those funding an activity of social utility.* Retrieved from https://www.avise.org/sites/default/files/atoms/files/20210315/mde_impact-social_uk_2021_web.pdf

Frumkin, P. (2023). *The center for social impact strategy.* Retrieved from https://csis.upenn.edu/history/

Głowacki, J. (2018). *Jak uzyskać i zmierzyć wpływ społeczny?* Retrieved from https://nowakonfederacja.pl/raport/uzyskac-zmierzyc-wplyw-spoleczny/

Grabowska, I., & Wójcik, Sz. (2021). *Oddziaływanie społeczne przedsiębiorstw społecznych w teorii i praktyce.* Wydawnictwa Uniwersytetu Warszawskiego.

Grieco, C., Michelini, L., & Iasevoli, G. (2015). Measuring value creation in social enterprises: A cluster analysis of social impact assessment models. *Nonprofit and Voluntary Sector Quarterly, 44*(6), 1173–1193. https://doi.org/10.1177/0899764014555986

Hlady-Rispal, M., & Servantie, V. (2018). Deconstructing the way in which value is created in the context of social entrepreneurship. *International Journal of Management Reviews, 20*(1), 62–80. https://doi.org/10.1111/ijmr.12113

IMPACT. (2011). *Impact measurement and performance analysis of CSR.* Retrieved from https://www.csr- impact.eu/documents/documents-detail.html?documentid=2

IMPACTDOTS. (2023). *Social impact history, definition, and dimensions.* Retrieved from https://impactdots.com/blog/social-impact-history-definition-and-dimensions/

International Association for Impact Assessment. (1994). *Guidelines and principles for social impact assessment.* NOAA Technical Memorandum NMFS-F/SPO-16. Retrieved May 31, 2019, from https://www.st.nmfs.noaa.gov/tm/spo/spo16.pdf.

Klingler-Vidra, R. (2020). *Social impact. What does it mean, and how should we measure it?* Retrieved from https://impact.economist.com/sustainability/social-sustainability/social_impact

Kolodinsky, J., Stewart, C., & Bullard, A. (2006). Measuring economic and social impacts of membership in a community development financial institution. *Journal of Family and Economic Issues, 27*(1), 27–47.

Koval, A. (2023). *ESG ≠ social impact: 3 Important differences. An emerging framework for risk management and the Stakeholder value chain.* Retrieved from https://bthechange.com/esg-social-impact-3-important-differences-ea507c39203c

Lynes, K. (2021). *What is social impact and why does it matter?* Retrieved from https://blog.upmetrics.com/social-impact

Maas, K., & Liket, K. (2011). Social impact measurement: Classification of methods. *Environmental Management Accounting and Supply Chain Management*, *27*, 171–202. https://doi.org/10.1007/978-94-007-1390-1_8

Martino, A. (2019). *Classification of social impact definitions*. Retrieved from https://www.politesi.polimi.it/bitstream/10589/151081/1/2019_12_Martino.pdf

MasterClass. (2022). *Social impact definition: How to measure social impact*. Retrieved from https://www.masterclass.com/articles/social-impact

OCM Solution. (2023). *Social Impact Assessment (SIA) guide with template and measurement samples*. Retrieved from https://www.ocmsolution.com/social-impact-measurement/

Perrini, F., Costanzo, L.A., & Karatas – Ozkan, M. (2021). Measuring impact and creating change: A comparison of the main methods for social enterprises. *Corporate Governance*, *21*(2), 237–251. https://doi.org/10.1108/CG-02-2020-0062

Perrini, F., & Vurro, C. (2013). *La Valutazione Degli Impatti Sociali: Approcci e Strumenti Applicative*. Milan, EGEA.

Porter, M.E., & Kramer, M.R. (2006). Strategy and society: The link between competitive advantage and corporate social responsibility. *Harvard Business Review*, *84*(12),78–92.

Rawhouser, H., Cummings, M., & Newbert, S.L. (2019). Social impact measurement: Current approaches and future directions for social entrepreneurship research. *Entrepreneurship Theory and Practice*, *43*(1), 82–115. https://doi.org/10.1177/1042258717727718

Ricee, S. (2021). *Diversity for social impact*. Retrieved from https://diversity.social/social-impact/

Sawyerr, O.O., & Ebrahimi, B.P. (2022). Executive environmental scanning and strategic uncertainty: The impact of institutional context. *International Studies of Management and Organization*, *52*(1), 7–24. https://doi.org/10.1080/00208825.2021.2023442

Sopact. (2023). *Social impact: Transforming communities for good*. Retrieved from https://www.sopact.com/guides/social-impact

Stephan, U., Patterson, M., Kelly, C., & Mair, J. (2016). Organizations driving positive social change a review and an integrative framework of change processes. *Journal of Management*, *42*(5), 1250–1281.

The International Association for Impact Assessment. (2022), Social Impact Assessment, Retrieved from https://www.iaia.org/wiki-details.php?ID=23

The Interorganizational Committee on Principles and Guidelines for Social Impact Assessment. (1994). *Guidelines and principles for social impact assessment*. Retrieved from https://www.iaia.org/pdf/IAIAMemberDocuments/Publications/Guidelines_Principles/SIA%20Guide.PDF

Tiuttu, T.A. (2020). *What is social impact?* Retrieved from https://4circularity.com/what-is-social-impact/

Vanclay, F. (2003). International principles for social impact assessment. *Impact Assessment and Project Appraisal*, *21*(1), 5–12. https://doi.org/10.3152/147154603781766491. https://www.tandfonline.com/doi/abs/10.3152/147154603781766491

# 2 Impact assessment. The startup perspective

*Maria Aluchna and Bolesław Rok*

## Introduction

The growing awareness of social and environmental challenges strengthened by stakeholder and regulatory pressure acts as a driver for business transition towards sustainability. Companies are formulating strategies that incorporate environmental, social, and governance (ESG) goals, increase non-financial disclosure, and introduce different technological and organizational solutions to lower their negative impact on society (Margolis & Walsh, 2003; Hiyuy et al., 2022). While both the academic literature and business practices offer evidence for sustainability actions, disclosure, and performance assessment, the concept of impact measurement, in particular social impact measurement, remains unexplored.

Paterson-Young and Hazenberg (2022) emphasize the importance of the social impact measurement since it serves as a key element for increasing transparency and disclosure, strengthening accountability of company decision-makers, and assessing the effectiveness of social investments. Credible and well-designed methodology of measuring the social impact is viewed as an essential requirement for channelling finance towards sustainable projects that allow socially responsible ventures to develop. In other words, with the substantial funds available for sustainable and impact investments, investors need a solid tool to effectively assess the potential for the social impact of a selected venture. More effective measurement methodology helps understand the value a venture contributes to its stakeholders and supports the development of sustainable projects (Pirolo & Presutti, 2010; Nguyen et al., 2015; Arnold et al., 2022). The requirement is even more critical taking into account the challenges of selective disclosure, complexity of ESG dimensions, the issue of vulnerability, and limited scaling up of sustainability projects.

Social impact is understood as outcomes related to the potential of social value creation (Lall, 2019), both of a positive and negative nature, and focuses on how certain organizational actions influence the lives of individuals, communities, and society. It emphasizes the quantification of the change and the process

DOI: 10.4324/9781003480952-3

that drives this change. Thus, the social impact measurement refers more to the process of assessing effects of given actions rather than structures in which these actions are undertaken (Hazenberg & Paterson-Young, 2022).

In this chapter, we outline the concept of assessing social impact focusing on startups that incorporate UN Sustainable Development Goals (SDGs) in their mission and strategy. While in the existing literature the main focus is given to startup activity, still little is known about the methods and tools to assess their factual performance with regard to social impact. With the intention to fill the existing gap, our goal is to propose a framework to measure social impact that we can apply for the case study analysis of eight impact startups. Our research led to the formulation of a set of metrics to assess startup outcomes with regard to the implementation of UN SDGs. The proposed methodology corresponds with investor expectations regarding a tool to compare startups performance and decide about potential investments.

## Materials and methods

### *Social impact measurement*

The literature review indicates a variety of definitions and perspectives conceptualizing social impact (Lall, 2019; Lee et al., 2021), the complexity of understanding how a company can exert its influence, as well as the number of terms used in the literature (e.g. social accounting, social value, social return). Rawhouser et al. (2019) understand social impact as "beneficial outcomes resulting from prosocial behavior that is enjoyed by the intended targets of that behavior and/or by a broader community of individuals, organizations, and/or environments". Social impact assessment represents a designed "process of analyzing, predicting, mitigating, monitoring, managing and evaluating the intended and unintended" (Taylor et al., 2021) social outcomes resulting from the undertaken interventions. According to the approach proposed by Clifford et al. (2014), the social impact reflects outcomes in a quantified form and refers to long-term as well as short-term effects. However, these outcomes should be measured taking into account the results achieved by others (alternative attribution), should control the effects that would have occurred without the given action (deadweight), should account for both positive and negative consequences (displacement), and should take into account effects declining over time (drop-off). Following the assumption that organizations intend to meet the expectations of various stakeholders, the impact measurement allows to understand and demonstrate the organizational contribution of company activities (McLoughlin et al., 2009; Hiruy et al., 2021). Since companies are expected to empower stakeholders, deliver more detailed and reliable communication about their contribution to society, and strengthen relations with their constituents, stakeholders are at the center of social impact concepts (Nguyen et al., 2015).

The social impact assessment offers a forward-looking orientation and attempts to anticipate, manage, or mitigate the effects of actions (Asselin & Parkins, 2009; Arnold et al., 2022) implemented by companies, third-sector organizations, or within different projects. Social impact assessment is also an essential element of sustainability transition, as it allows for measuring the effects of undertaken actions and implemented changes. It sets the direction for the development of new products and services that would eliminate the negative influence or even produce a positive impact on the environment, and in this way also on communities and societies. Moreover, understanding the outcomes of a given activity not only motivates decision-makers towards sustainability but also offers the possibility to quantify the effectiveness of these decisions. Similarly to the role of measuring financial performance, having reliable and informative metrics of the social impact enables a redirection of funds to ventures that create social value. The use of informative metrics on the social impact supports the implementation of a sustainable business vision (Lee et al., 2021) and increases the likelihood of acquiring funds required for its development. As a result, the social impact measurement encourages a direction of development towards sustainable and responsible business.

Prior research indicates that the social impact assessment is strongly theory-driven, includes participatory research measuring the outcomes for various stakeholders, and applies mixed methods of both qualitative and quantitative analysis (Taylor et al., 2021:451). The existing literature also offers different frameworks to design the process of impact assessment. For instance, the Social Accounting and Audit (SAA) framework, based on the use of qualitative and descriptive data, measures the present social value created by an organization (Hiruy et al., 2021). Another approach proposed by Clifford et al. (2014) is based on the theory of change and comprises five elements, including an analysis of (1) inputs (resources used in the delivery of an intervention), (2) activity (delivered by the inputs), (3) output with regard to intended beneficiaries, (4) outcome (changes in the lives of beneficiaries and others), and (5) impact understood as extents to which that change results from the intervention. An alternative framework is offered by B Impact Assessment, which is a tool that can help measure, manage, and improve positive impact performance for the environment, communities, customers, suppliers, employees, and shareholders (Bcorporation, 2022). As a quantified measure, it does not only serve as a ground for obtaining B-corp certification but also allows for comparison with other companies that conducted such an audit.

The growing body of literature reveals that social impact assessments can be effectively based on the accomplishment of UN SDGs. SDGs are a globally recognized framework of required actions that companies should meet (UN Sustainable Development Goals, 2021) addressing the main challenges of humanity. With 17 goals and 169 targets, the SDG framework challenges "existing structures of accountability, power and resource allocation" and acts "to legitimize, enable and model a different type of conversation about what matters locally" (Clifford & Barnes, 2022).

***The sample***

The startup sample used in this research was selected intentionally. Firstly, we decided to focus on the most innovative sector in the Polish startup community, i.e. impact startups. Each year, special awards are given to startups that combine sustainable impact delivering particular products or services on the market. We decided to choose startups awarded in the last three years and presented in the "Positive Impact Startups" report, i.e. 60 entities in total (Kozminski BusinessHub, 2022).

Next, we selected only startups that were established at least four years before the planned moment of the interview. The second selection criterion included startups whose founders had an explicit and central vision to implement UN SDGs, being convinced that the positive environmental/social impact was served through the same activities as economic value creation, as opposed to dependence upon public or private grants and subsidies. Known as "born sustainable firms" (BSFs), such startups were established with explicit strategic intent to operate in a sustainable manner from the outset (Osorio-Vega, 2019; Knoppen & Knight, 2022).

The process of selecting the sample of startups was in line with our research objective, according to which these enterprises should conduct economic activity for the environment and climate, with a clear focus on increasing the scale of their positive impact. These enterprises promise to be a solution to, rather than a cause of, environmental degradation. They seek to contribute directly to restoring the environment, bringing climate solutions, and driving positive changes. Studying the social impact of startups that provide solutions to environmental challenges as part of their market offer allows impact investors to better determine their overall sustainable impact. Further, we selected 15 startups delivering innovative environmental solutions to the market out of the initial sample. After sending an invitation to complete a specially prepared online survey, eight startups responded positively.

***Survey***

The survey aimed to provide information about the founder's perspective on the scope of the social impact of a given environmentally oriented-startup. Specifically, the process of self-assessment of the social impact of the conducted activity was based on the perception of the startup's contribution to the achievement of the SDG in its social areas – despite the fact that the SDGs framework reveals some shortcomings when confronted with business reality.

Most enterprises now concentrate their impact measurement efforts around three main frameworks: the SDGs, the Impact Reporting and Investment Standards (IRIS), and the Impact Management Project (IMP). These are also the most used frameworks for impact measurement and management, according to the most recent survey for those financial organizations investing in impact (Gianoncelli & Gaggiotti, 2021).

In the consultation process with selected representatives of the startup community, a preliminary set of the most important areas of social impact was proposed. Further analysis led to the formulation of 28 potential social impact categories reflecting the key targets and indicators within the SDGs. Only those activities that have a primarily social impact and are adequate to the scope of activities of sustainable startups on the Polish market were taken into account.

The above-mentioned 28 categories of social impact can be reduced to the main social objectives that should determine the overall approach to determine and assess the size of the social impact. There are some outcomes already available from the initial actions for introducing ESG indicators for reporting in the EU (European Sustainability Reporting Standards, ESRS) for the largest companies, including selected indicators in the S (social) dimension. According to the double materiality rule, not only social risks for the company but also the areas of its social impact are included in the current approach to reporting. The three social objectives suggested in international standards and previous works at the EU level refer to (1) decent work, including respect for value-chain workers; (2) adequate living standards and well-being for end-users; and (3) inclusive and sustainable communities and societies (PSF, 2022). Our approach to startups is more detailed, and we define five social objectives in the form of declared and implemented values: workplace, education, quality of life, social cohesion, diversity, and inclusion. We decided to include five or six categories from the 28 selected in each social objective.

The stakeholders who are potentially affected include employees (including co-workers), consumers, users, and business partners in the value chain, as well as communities (directly or indirectly). We argue that it is possible to assign – to a certain extent – particular social objectives to specific groups of stakeholders (Zetzsche et al., 2022). Accordingly, the workplace objectives mostly refer to employees, while the adequate quality of life standards and education objectives mainly relate to consumers and business networks. The remaining objectives – social cohesion, diversity, and inclusion – clearly focus on members of wider communities. The final framework includes five main categories:

1 Workplace

- High standards of social protection for all those in need (SDG1)
- Access to decent sanitation for all (SDG6)
- Promoting safe and secure working environments (SDG8)
- Supporting the development of responsible entrepreneurship (SDG8)
- Tackling fraud and workplace abuse in running businesses (SDG16)

2 Education

- Ensuring healthy and nutritious food practices (SDG2)
- Education for health and access to health care (SDG3)

- Promoting resource efficiency in consumption and production (SDG8)
- Protecting and safeguarding the cultural and natural heritage in cities (SDG11)
- Working with NGOs in cross-sectoral partnerships (SDG17)
- Supporting community action to achieve the Sustainable Development Goals (SDG17)

3 Quality of life

- Development of sustainable food production and distribution (SDG2)
- Promoting safety and well-being for all (SDG3)
- Supporting active lifestyle habits (SDG3)
- Access to clean and reliable energy from renewable sources (SDG7)
- Reduction of waste generation (SDG12)
- Social mobilization for climate change mitigation (SDG13, 14, 15)

4 Social cohesion

- Development of relevant professional and social skills and competencies (SDG4)
- Promoting knowledge-based culture in society (SDG4)
- Access to information and communication technologies (SDG9)
- Social innovation development (SDG9)
- Strengthening the basis for broad public participation (SDG11)
- Strengthening the societal capacity to adapt to climate change (SDG13, 14, 15)

5 Diversity and inclusion

- Ensuring equal opportunities regardless of gender (SDG5)
- Tackling energy poverty (SDG7)
- Empowering and promoting social and economic inclusion (SDG10)
- Access to basic public services for all (SDG12)
- Supporting effective and inclusive institutions for strengthening democracy (SDG16)

***Self-assessment***

For each of the categories, we asked the surveyed startup founders to choose one answer from the proposed six, the one that best suits the given startup's operations. When selecting one of the six options in a given category, different levels of impact should be taken into account: impact on employees, associates in the organization and throughout the value chain; impact on customers and consumers, potential or current; impact on citizens and communities located in the area covered by the company operations in its sphere of influence. We adopted the following approach:

- The organization contributes to the implementation of important solutions in this category (C);
- The organization generates some benefits for stakeholders in this category (B);
- The organization works to avoid harm in this category by preventing or reducing negative effects on people and society (A);
- The activities of the organization in this category may cause harm to society/the selected social group (M);
- The activities of the organization do actual harm in this category, have a negative impact (H);
- I cannot judge it/I see no relation between the activity and this impact category (N).

This proposition is based on the well-known ABC approach in impact investment, although it has been extended. Originally, the Impact Management Project (UNDP, 2021) defined differing approaches to impact through the ABC norms: "Act to avoid harm (A)", "Benefit stakeholders (B)", and "Contribute to solutions (C)". In our research, we decided to use additional points, such as "may cause harm (M)", "do actual harm (H)", and "cannot judge (N)" because of the practical value of self-assessment for the startup's founders. As a result, we can achieve two goals in our research: define the perception of priorities for particular social objectives in ecological startups – out of five proposed, as well as make a total assessment of the positive social impact of individual startups – combining ABC with MHN.

In the taxonomy framework, an important role is given to the DNSH rule (do-no-significant-harm), so it is possible that in the social taxonomy a wider perspective will be used. Mirroring the environmental taxonomy's structure, a substantial contribution to one or more social objectives can be made in three different ways, namely: (1) by enhancing the positive impact inherent in economic activities; (2) by avoiding and addressing negative impacts; and (3) through enabling activities (Zetzsche et al., 2022).

## Results

We obtained results from eight impact startups. Their names are kept anonymous – we only use the first letters of their names for the purpose of results discussion. To analyze the collected information, the following procedure was adopted: we first grouped the responses by individual startups and by five selected areas of impact, and we then assigned scores equal for each impact categories for significant solutions (3 points), benefits (2 points), harm avoidance (1 point), possibility of harm (−1 points), and real harm (−2 points). In the case of no relation of a certain category, no points were assigned. Finally, we calculated the impact of startups and within the area as a ratio between scores achieved and scores available with the maximum ratio of 1.

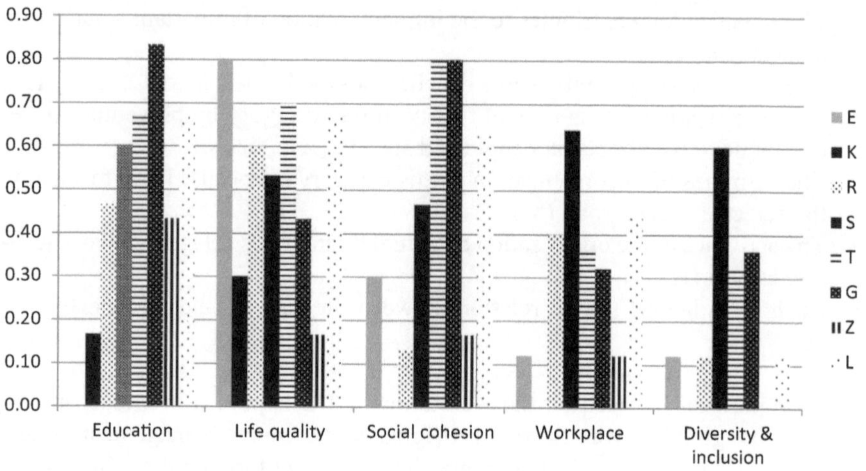


*Figure 2.1* Impact by five impact categories in sample startups

*Source:* Own elaboration.

On average, the analyzed startups had a short history of market presence, with six of them being up to two years old. Four declared to have external investors, and five had five or more products in their offers. All of them argued they had a positive social and environmental impact and declared implementation of SDGs in their business strategy.

Firstly, we discuss the results on the impact calculated for selected impact categories. The analysis reveals that the average ratios for the education category was calculated at 0.48, for life quality at 0.53, followed by social cohesion of 0.41 and workplace at 0.30. The average ratio for diversity and inclusion was estimated at 0.21. In Figure 2.1, we present the results by the analyzed categories.

As shown in Figure 2.1, the social impact in selected categories differs amongst the analyzed startups. Strikingly, startups focusing on the environment obtained the highest scores for education and life quality that can be achieved by the products they offer. This positive environmental impact made the analyzed startups appear to put less emphasis on the employee-related aspects – workplace as well as diversity and inclusion.

Next, we discuss the performance measured for each startup individually. Figure 2.2 shows the impact of the analyzed startups according to five selected areas.

As depicted in Figure 2.2, the examined startups exhibit variations in their performance levels. The average score for the analyzed startups was estimated at 0.38, ranging between 0.09 for K startups and 0.57 for S and T startups. In addition, the number of declared categories (not reported in Figure 2.2) ranged between 3 for K startups, 20 for S and T startups, and 21 for L startups (out of the

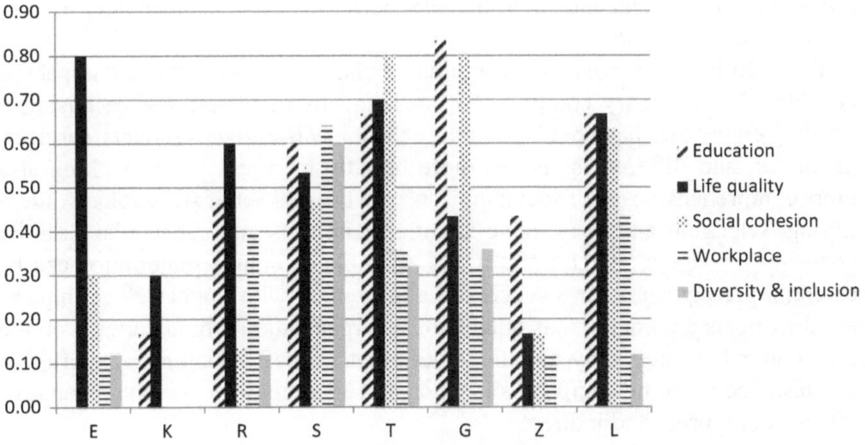


*Figure 2.2* Impact of sample startups according to five selected categories

*Source:* Own elaboration.

maximum of 28). The analyzed startups appear to have different profiles and do not cover all the selected areas of impact. We attribute these differences mostly to the size and scope of operation of the analyzed startups – for instance, K are relatively small ventures with a narrow product portfolio focused on the local market, while S, T, and L are larger startups with a wider offer, external investors, and operating on an international market. They declare greater awareness as well as possibilities for their impact.

## Discussion and conclusion

Overall, we argue that the proposed framework offers important insights on the measurement method for startup impact. Firstly, the framework remains transparent and flexibly addresses the most important aspects of SDG implementation by such a special organization as a startup. Secondly, it delivers the possibility to quantify social impact and graphically present it from different perspectives, such as the impact category and individual startup performance. Yet, other options would be available – for instance, the number of declared categories and the proportion between levels of impact (solutions, benefits, harm) could be used in further analyses. Finally, the self-assessment offers a chance for reflection for startup founders and managers, emphasizing possible areas for future development.

While our study provides an impact assessment framework that can be applied to startups, it reveals some limitations related to the sample size and the empirical data derived from the founders' response. Further analyses would be welcome, covering a larger sample of startups and using information on the startup impact based on social and environmental performance and stakeholder perceptions of these outcomes.

The creation of a positive economic, social, and environmental impact is considered a necessary condition for an innovative and responsible business. Leading companies have been examining the impacts of their products, services, processes, and different activities more broadly in recent years, looking at a more comprehensive set of social impacts on a broader set of stakeholders. Identifying, selecting, and prioritizing significant impacts and substantial risks by company managers, as required by the principle of double materiality, can be essential prerequisites for a successful engagement with impacts. The impacts are the effects a company has outside of its organizational boundaries – on the environment, the economy, and the society, that arise after a significant period or at a distance from the company's location and encompass positive and negative effects, both direct and indirect.

While measuring impact is an important issue in sustainability reporting and developing business models of corporations, the topic is gaining more importance for startups that focus on adding value by improving the quality of life in various groups, as well as the quality of the environment. Such companies are therefore not only responsible for reducing the negative impact but also – and perhaps above all – increasing the positive impact and changing the world for the better. A company with a positive social impact is an example of such an economic activity. Through innovation for sustainable development using technology and increasing the level of reliability and efficiency people acting with passion for the common good can lead to a rapid increase in the company's value, and improve the quality of life and the environment within the sphere of its social impact.

## Note

This research study was conducted in the framework of project number BPI/PST/2021/1 /00069/U/00001 financed by Polish National Agency for Academic Exchange under the Strategic Partnerships programme.

## References

Arnold, L., Hanna, K., Noble, B., Gergel, S., & Nikolais, W. (2022). Assessing the cumulative social effects of projects: Lessons from Canadian hydroelectric development. *Environmental Management, 69*(5), 1035–1048.

Asselin, J., & Parkins, J. (2009). Comparative case study as social impact assessment: Possibilities and limitations for anticipating social change in the Far North. *Social Indices Research, 94*, 483–497.

Bcorporations. (2022). *B impact assessment*. Retrieved from https://www.bcorporation.net/en-us/programs-and-tools/b-impact-assessment

Clifford, J., & Barnes, K. (2022). Why and what to measure? The justification for social impact measurement. In R. Hazenberg & C. Paterson-Young (Eds.), *Social impact measurement for a sustainable future the power of aesthetics and practical implications,* 48–70. Palgrave MacMillan, Cham.

Clifford, J., Hehenberger, L., & Fantini, M. (2014). *Proposed approaches to social impact measurement in European Commission legislation and in practice relating to: EuSEFs and the EaSI.* Eurpean Comission Report 140605. Retrieved from https://www.fi-compass.eu/publication/other-resources/proposed-approaches-social-impact-measurement-european-commission

Gianoncelli, A., & Gaggiotti, G. (2021). Managing for impact: The role of investors' networks in enhancing appropriate impact measurement and management practices. In A. Richards, J. Nicholls (Eds.), *Generation impact,* 219–233. Emerald Publishing Limited, Bingley.

Hazenberg, R., & Paterson-Young, C. (2022). The development of social impact measurement. In R. Hazenberg & C. Paterson-Young (Eds.), *Social impact measurement for a sustainable future the power of aesthetics and practical implications*, 13–26. Palgrave MacMillan, Cham.

Hiyuy, K., Elmes, A., Qian-Khoo, J., Jouce, A., & Barraket, J. (2022). Placing people at the center of social impact measurement: Current approach, challenges and future directors. In R. Hazenberg & C. Paterson-Young (Eds.), *Social impact measurement for a sustainable future the power of aesthetics and practical implications,* 27–48. Palgrave MacMillan, Cham.

Knoppen, D., & Knight, L. (2022). Pursuing sustainability advantage: The dynamic capabilities of born sustainable firms. *Business Strategy and the Environment, 31*, 1789–1813.

Kozminski BusinessHub. (2022). *The positive impact startups*. Kozminski University. Retrieved from https://kozminskihub.com/wp-content/uploads/2022/09/SPW-raport_2022-En__04.pdf

Lall, S. (2019). From legitimacy to learning: How impact measurement perceptions and practices evolve in social enterprise – social finance organization relationships. *Springer*, *30*, 562–577.

Lee, E., Lee, H., Kee, Ch., Kwan, H., & Ng, Ch. (2021). Social impact measurement in incremental social innovation. *Journal of Social Entrepreneurship*, *12*(1), 69–86.

Margolis, J.D., & Walsh, J.P. (2003). Misery loves companies: Rethinking social initiatives by business. *Administrative Science Quarterly*, *48*, 268–305.

McLoughlin, J., Kaminski, J., Sodagar, B., Khan, S., Harris, R., Arnaudo, G., & Mc Brearty, S. (2009). A strategic approach to social impact measurement of social enterprises: The SIMPLE methodology. *Social Enterprise Journal, 5*(2), 154–178.

Nguyen, L., Szkudlarek, B., & Seymour, R. (2015). Social impact measurement in social enterprises: An interdependence perspective. *Canadian Journal of Administrative Sciences, 32*, 224–237.

Osorio-Vega, P. (2019). The ethics of entrepreneurial shared value. *Journal of Business Ethics*, *157*, 981–995.

Paterson-Young, C., & Hazenberg, R. (2022). Introduction. In R. Hazenberg & C. Paterson-Young (Eds.), *Social impact measurement for a sustainable future the power of aesthetics and practical implications*, 1–10. Palgrave MacMillan, Cham.

Pirolo, L., & Presutti, M. (2010). The impact of social capital on the start-ups' performance growth. *Journal of Small Business Management*, *48*(2), 197–227.

PSF. Platform on Sustainable Finance. (2022). *Final report on social taxonomy.* Retrieved from https://ec.europa.eu/info/sites/default/files/business_economy_euro/banking_and_finance/documents/280222-sustainable-finance-platform-finance-report-social-taxonomy.pdf

Rawhouser, H., Cummings, M., & Newbert, S.L. (2019). Social impact measurement: Current approaches and future directions for social entrepreneurship research. *Entrepreneurship Theory and Practice*, *43*(1), 82–115.

Taylor, C., Mackay, M., & Perkins, H. (2021). Social impact assessment and (realist) evaluation: Meeting of the methods. *Impact Assessment and Project Appraisal*, *39*(6), 450–462.

UN. (2021). *The 17 goals*. Retrieved from https://sdgs.un.org/goals

UNDP. (2021). *Manage for impact*. Retrieved from https://sdgimpact.undp.org/

Zetzsche, D.A., Bodellini, M., & Consiglio, R. (2022). Towards a European social taxonomy: A scorecard approach. *Available at SSRN 4218874*.

# 3 Measurement of the negative social impact of a small enterprise

*Agnieszka Sokołowska-Durkalec*

## Introduction

The social impact of various organizations is frequently discussed in academic discourse (Husted & Salazar, 2006; Kent & Dacin, 2013; Rawhouser et al., 2019). The SME sector is also a significant subject of exploration regarding this impact. Social impact is indeed an important element in the analysis of the social entrepreneurship phenomenon (Lumpkin et al., 2013; Dacin et al., 2017). From this perspective, it can also be considered in the context of implementing the CSR concept.

A critical literature review on corporate social responsibility authorizes the conclusion that one of its current research areas is the effects of socially responsible corporate activities, encompassing negative effects (Carroll & Brown, 2018) and their associated consequences. Thus, the importance of systematic and multidimensional internal and external evaluation of companies' social activity and responsibility is growing (Jankalova & Jankal, 2017). This assessment is particularly challenging because it involves a sphere that is not easily quantifiable due to the immateriality, dynamism, and complexity of the subjects and objects of assessment. The concept of social irresponsibility, as part of CSR implementation or as a separate concept, which can be supported by the assumptions of social impact and the principles of its measurement, responds indirectly to this challenge. The new category of social impact is concerned with its negative facet (i.e., the negative consequences of companies' actions).

Measuring social impact arises from different needs and benefits for researchers and practitioners. Researchers find it important to analyze multidimensional phenomena and their consequences to better understand the mechanisms leading to a particular outcome. For practitioners, on the other hand, the effectiveness and efficiency of implemented activities are crucial, and impact measurement is used to formulate recommendations for future improvements (Grabowska & Wójcik, 2021).

Despite many scientific studies and practical activities indicating the need to measure social impact, there is a lack of studies in the literature combining

DOI: 10.4324/9781003480952-4

the issue of measuring social impact, particularly negative social impact, with the concept of social irresponsibility concerning the specifics of small business operations (Jenkins, 2009; Kromjong et al., 2016; Madueño et al., 2016). Therefore, there is a need to recognize the challenges and formulate methodological assumptions for measuring the negative social impact of small businesses.

Due to a significant research gap in the subject matter,[1] it is worth considering several issues in the research areas, including:

- How can the concept of negative social impact be defined from the perspective of social irresponsibility?
- Is there specificity in measuring the negative social impact of a small enterprise?
- What selected features and elements can be identified as specific to measuring the negative social impact of a small enterprise?
- What challenges do researchers and managers encounter when measuring the negative social impact of a small enterprise?

The purpose of the conceptual chapter is to characterize the concept of negative social impact from the perspective of social irresponsibility and to identify challenges and preliminary selected methodological assumptions for measuring the negative social impact of a small enterprise.

## Methods

The chapter presents the results of the literature review, along with selected findings and conclusions from the empirical research. Through a critical, narrative review of the literature and specific results from our empirical research, we were able to develop preliminary terminological and conceptual insights regarding the concept of negative social impact from the perspective of social irresponsibility. This included specifics on measuring the negative social impact of a small enterprise and a description of the challenges, along with preliminary methodological assumptions for measuring the negative social impact of a small enterprise for researchers and managers.

The author conducted both quantitative and qualitative research between September to November 2020 (quantitative) and August 2020 to December 2021 (qualitative) on a purposively selected sample of 78 small Polish[2] enterprises, including microenterprises.[3] The purposive sampling was designed for the selection of enterprises meeting specific criteria: (1) the criterion for the number of employees was related to the employment of up to 50 people by the surveyed enterprise during the research period, including microenterprises with up to ten employees; (2) the activity criterion required active participation in business activities, both in a formal and literal sense; (3) the independence criterion pertained to the economic activity of the enterprise. Hence, capital and organizational subsidiaries, being part of larger organizations or operating in networks (subsidiaries, related and partner enterprises), were excluded from the selection process; (4) the substantive criterion focused on distinguishing specific features in the assessed enterprise, highlighting its socially responsible nature. For instance, this included enterprises presenting good practices in Responsible Business Forum reports, inclusion in the list of Fair Play companies, participation in CSR Good Practice Fairs, and identification of manifestations of social responsibility management. This criterion was applied to gauge entrepreneurs' awareness of processes related to social responsibility and, by assumption, social irresponsibility.

The research aims to identify the conditions and elements involved in the process of recognizing selected manifestations of social irresponsibility within small enterprises. Additionally, the study delves into selected manifestations of negative social impact. Various methods were employed, including extensive survey questionnaires (distributed—depending on preference—via traditional mail, email, or in person) and interview questionnaires. These interviews were conducted with owner–managers and/or managers, along with selected stakeholder groups such as employees and customers. This pilot study utilized a purposive sample selection process based on the criteria outlined above. The research included questions related to manifestations of social irresponsibility (quantitative research) and specific socially irresponsible activities (qualitative research). The inquiry explored the negative impact of the surveyed enterprises on both internal and external stakeholders, along with the consequences associated with negative social impact.

Given that social impact was not the sole focus of the research, the study refrained from using indicator analyses (e.g., ESG, GRI, B Impact Assessment, GPM P5 Standard, ISO 26000) or specific social impact measurement methodologies (SIIT, 2014; Rawhouser et al., 2019). In addressing a significant research gap, such an approach represents an endeavor seeking a distinct measurement perspective within the specific environment of a small business.

## Results and discussion

### *Negative social impact—An attempt to define the concept from the perspective of social irresponsibility*

The concept of social impact is inherently ambiguous and multidimensional, encompassing a wide spectrum of potential changes resulting from specific actions. The diversity in terminology and contexts leads to varied interpretations. According to Rawhouser et al. (2019), the literature conceptualizes social impact using multiple terms. Additionally, social impact has been a subject of study in various domains, including economics, management, education, health care, environmental sustainability, and poverty, among others (Grabowska & Wójcik, 2021).

The diversity and multidirectional considerations inherent in the interdisciplinary concept of social impact necessitate the selection of the most comprehensive definition. Building on Stephan et al. (2016), the chapter assumes that social impact refers to the beneficial outcomes resulting from prosocial behavior, experienced by the intended targets of that behavior and/or the broader community of individuals, organizations, and environments. This definition is sufficiently comprehensive to encompass the most current approaches in social impact research, acknowledging that social impact often involves different conceptual constructs, phenomena, or target groups (Grabowska & Wójcik, 2021, p. 22).

An important consideration in understanding social impact is the dual nature of the changes it brings about—both positive and negative. While in many instances, social impact is defined as a force leading to positive social change (Santos, 2012; Stephan et al., 2016), it is also acknowledged as a reducer of negative phenomena (Bartling et al., 2015). Grabowska and Wójcik (2021) note that numerous studies explore the positive and negative social impact of various phenomena or activities (Rawhouser et al., 2019). This combined analytical approach, defining social impact as a synthesis of positive and negative effects, is evident in research on social performance. The impact of human actions on a diverse range of stakeholders and the lasting effects of actions—both positive and negative—are recognized as fundamental aspects of social impact.

These features are integral to the realization of the concept of corporate social responsibility (Dillenburg et al., 2003; Rawhouser et al., 2019). This stands as one of several concepts—alongside, for example, the concepts of sustainable development, social capital, or organizational balance—focused on the issue of social impact.

An extension of the CSR concept, emphasizing the effectiveness of socially responsible activities, is the concept of corporate social performance (Wood, 2010; Carrol & Brown, 2018), which involves observing changes related to social impact. Effective study and management of an enterprise's socially responsible activities can only be completed by identifying socially irresponsible activities. For this reason, negative social impact can also be considered in conjunction with corporate social irresponsibility. It can be viewed both as an element of CSR implementation or a separate concept, which can be supported by the assumptions of social impact and the principles of its measurement.

In this chapter, social irresponsibility is understood as the lack of or insufficient economic, legal, ethical, and philanthropic commitment of the company to internal and external entities/stakeholders (Sokołowska-Durkalec, 2020). The a priori implementation by companies of negative assumptions of social irresponsibility also implies a negative impact on stakeholders, the dimensions and scope of which require exploration. The negative impact, in this sense, is a new framing of the issue and will mean the negative consequences of a company's intentional or unintentional activities in the economic, legal, ethical, and philanthropic areas for internal and external stakeholders. The specificity of the negative impact, like the specificity of socially irresponsible actions, is derived from several internal and external conditions, with the size of the company being one of the important ones. The definition and components of negative impact, negative consequences, and areas require detailed descriptions. An essential part of this description is the issue of measuring social impact.

Of paramount importance is the recognition of the relationship between negative impact and social irresponsibility. These two categories are complementary, substantively enriching each other, drawing, for example, from stakeholder theory, but they can also be disconnected, especially when describing the process and outcome of socially irresponsible actions and their associated impact. According to Clark et al. (2021), social irresponsibility entails studying the decision-making process and all stages of irresponsible action, including manifestations. Negative social impact, on the other hand, places a greater focus on the effect that negative actions bring. The fusion of these two concepts is mutually beneficial. In the concept of social irresponsibility, the stage of the result can be given more prominence, especially with the utilization of multiple concepts of social impact (e.g., social value (Moss et al., 2011; Santos, 2012), social performance (Husted & Salazar, 2006; Mair & Marti, 2006; Nicholls, 2008), social returns, and social return on investment (Emerson, 2003; Hall et al., 2015)), with a strong emphasis on measurement (e.g., social accounting (Nicholls, 2008), measurement methodologies). In the concept of social impact, in addition to incorporating elements of CSR (Jankalova & Jankal, 2017), CSP (Wood, 2010), or the impact value chain (Maas & Liket, 2011; SIIT, 2014; Dufour, 2019; Grabowska & Wójcik, 2021), it becomes imperative to enrich the consideration of the issue, for example, from the perspective of the classical view of the areas of social irresponsibility: economic, legal, ethical, philanthropic, and their impact on stakeholders.

### *Specifics for measuring the negative social impact of a small enterprise*

The measurement of social impact depends on various factors, with the size of the company being one such factor (Dacin et al., 2017), along with the associated social relationships. Methodologies for measuring social impact are generally universal (aimed at all types of organizations) and encompass non-financial reporting methodologies (including, but not limited to, social accounting, financial reporting expanded to include the social dimension, and integrated reporting), as proposed by formalized systems for managing and reporting social activities. In an integrated and comprehensive approach to social impact measurement, the process comprises four phases: planning (including setting goals, methodology, and selecting indicators), executing (collecting and checking data), measuring (conducting data analysis), and revising (reporting results and making decisions based on the data) (SIIT, 2014). Selected social measurement tools include ESG, GRI, B Impact Assessment, GPM P5 Standard, among others (Rawhouser et al., 2019).

However, the assumed universality of the synthetically presented instrumentation is not always straightforward (Lumpkin et al., 2013) because there are areas of measurement in the proposals that are not suitable for the activities of small businesses, for example, elements of corporate governance or elaborate strategic management processes.

The specificity of the negative social impact of a small enterprise is attributed to the peculiarities of the activities of this group of enterprises, as well as the consideration of the negative consequences of actions from the perspective of the social irresponsibility of the enterprise. The distinctive features of the activities of a small enterprise, stemming from its territorial, economic, social, and psychological proximity to the market, as well as its special relations with stakeholders (Udayasankar, 2008), require consideration in research and management practice regarding the negative impact and its measurement. Although a complete description of a small enterprise in this area would necessitate identifying the specifics of the social impact of large and medium-sized enterprises and its measurement, it is prudent to acknowledge that the negative impact of a small enterprise and its measurement, from the perspective of social irresponsibility, is characterized by several key features.

The decision on whether to measure negative social impact is entirely up to the entrepreneur, who assesses the associated benefits or losses. Among the small business owners surveyed by the author of the chapter, 84% associate with the term ‘social impact,’ but only 7% are familiar with ‘negative social impact.’

With systematic measurement and knowledge, the benefits and costs of measurement become apparent. Only 9% of respondents recognize the potential advantages of measuring negative impact. The most popular benefit is enhancing the communication and image capabilities of the organization (i.e., presenting measurable and objective data to the public about the impact on social reality). Respondents also highlight improvements in the quality of services provided, increased motivation of internal stakeholders, better strategic planning, more effective management, elimination of ineffective operational elements, and improved financial management. However, concerns exist about revealing inconvenient, compromising data and the impact on stakeholders’ perceptions of the company and their understanding of how to measure it.

Many small business owners are usually unfamiliar with and fearful of measuring negative social impact due to the complexity of the procedures. The chapter’s author inquired with small business owners about their practices in measuring negative social impact. If they do measure it, is it a formalized process (utilizing methodologies and metrics from, for example, ESG, GRI, B Impact Assessment, GPM P5 Standard, and ISO 26000), or is it non-formalized? According to more than 95% of respondents, they currently do not find the need to measure this dimension of their business professionally. Instead, they focus on identifying only certain selected elements, primarily manifestations of social irresponsibility, in the following areas: economic and legal, much less frequently:

ethical and philanthropic. Entrepreneurs see no justification for measuring the consequences of negative social impact.

The author also inquired with entrepreneurs about specific activities related to social influence. For instance, in what areas of the implementation of the personnel function do you sometimes influence/engage in socially irresponsible behavior? What are the consequences of these socially irresponsible actions and their negative impact on employees? Respondents most frequently pointed to compensation and employee development, demonstrating a heightened awareness of the legal and ethical consequences of such actions. Conversely, when employees were asked about areas where their employer acts socially irresponsible or negatively in the implementation of the personnel function, their responses aligned with those of their superiors. However, discrepancies arose regarding the consequences of the employer's influence on their work, primarily related to the economic dimension. Similar inquiries were made about relations with other stakeholders.

The above list of selected characteristics does not cover all possibilities in this regard and presents some key challenges in measuring negative social impact for researchers and managers of small businesses.

### *Identifying the challenges of measuring the negative social impact of a small business from a researcher's and manager's perspective*

The study of negative social impact poses numerous difficulties. The initial theoretical challenge lies in the complexity of operationalizing the social change one wishes to capture. In practice, the methodologies under development constitute a compromise between what can realistically be measured and the most accurate indicators. Often, extensive qualitative data are necessary, while, for practical reasons, only quantitative data are available. Resolving these dilemmas is crucial to ensure that measurement is more than a bureaucratic 'ticking a box on a questionnaire' but contributes to understanding how a project generates social change and how it can improve further (Grabowska & Wójcik, 2021).

Precision and consistency in understanding the concept of 'negative social impact' and related elements or concepts (e.g., social value, social return) are required. It is also essential to select the concept (e.g., corporate social responsibility, corporate social irresponsibility) through whose prism (in connection with which) social impact will be identified and evaluated.

What is needed is a methodologically sound, multi-step measurement procedure that considers the multifaceted nature of the issues and the complexity of situational contexts for the entities under study (companies, their stakeholders, the course of action, and their effects). Covin and Wales (2012) argue that researchers can choose the measurement approach that best serves their research goals, recognizing that (aggregated) versus (disaggregated) models for measuring social influence are consistent with fundamentally different conceptualizations of the construct. The study of negative social impact (as well as manifestations of social irresponsibility) can present challenges due to the reluctance of respondents (owners, managers, and other stakeholders) to disclose dysfunctions, inadequacies, difficulties, and irrational, unethical, and illegal actions.

Difficulties related to the objectification of research can be alleviated by opting for triangulation of research approaches (e.g., quantitative and qualitative), methods, and research tools. Also important is the selection of direct research methods and the design of research tools, ensuring effective communication with respondents through understandable content. It is necessary to describe complex scientific categories using explanations in understandable, accessible language. It is also important to establish a precise and detailed plan for the various stages of direct research and to agree on it with entrepreneurs (small business owners typically have limited time due to their numerous organizational roles and responsibilities).

Enriching the measurement of social influence can be achieved by examining the attitudes of entrepreneurs and managers toward social influence and its negative aspects. An important element here is the intentionality of actions as a usually unconscious phenomenon, as a realized area of business activity, and an important element of the management concept, which can have its practical dimension. This can lead to a discussion of a potential gradation of conscious and irresponsible influence on social affairs. The intentions behind specific behaviors can impose a particular direction, content, and course of events. However, good intentions will not always guarantee positive action and outcomes. Conversely, an unsuccessful outcome may not necessarily result from bad intentions. The question of subjective and objective intentions and the specific conditions strongly associated with them remains.

Another important aspect is the rule of reciprocity, which, in the face of negative social impact, can result in the loss of key stakeholders, severe disruption in the construction of relational capital, and the escalation of negative social phenomena. Including this aspect in the research serves as a valuable signal of the potential negative consequences of entrepreneurs' irresponsible actions.

In addition to conceptual and theoretical challenges, social impact measurement generates various practical challenges. Implementing an evaluation of this kind is impossible without dedicating adequate resources and integrating the measurement processes into existing organizational procedures (Grabowska & Wójcik, 2021). The measurement can pose challenges for managers. A significant problem is insufficient knowledge of social impact issues and the methods for measuring them, an area where businesses should invest in improvement.

The challenge for managers is to grapple with the key features characterizing the social impact measurement process, including immeasurability (measurement cannot be performed, e.g., due to the unavailability of data), uneconomic (the cost of measurement is inadequately high concerning the benefits obtained), incompleteness (selected indicators do not allow reproducing the overall process of change), and irrelevance—the collected data are not helpful for actual decision-making. Thus, the use of high-quality measurement methodologies/tools that consider both positive and negative social impact is required. A key challenge is to mitigate the over-economization of the social impact measurement process. This is because much of the movement is supported by investors operating primarily from an economic perspective, and entrepreneurs expect rapid results. Additional challenges include defining the desired impact, determining the data to be collected and the methodology to be employed, acquiring adequate data, verification (e.g., by comparing data from different sources), analyzing the data with respect to achieving the objectives, presenting the results to stakeholders, deciding on operational changes, considering feedback from stakeholders, etc.

## Conclusion

Based on the considerations presented in the chapter, one can cautiously conclude that there is specificity in measuring the negative social impact of a small enterprise when studying the manifestations of social irresponsibility in this group. Such a conclusion is drawn from a limited set of characteristics and a purposefully selected sample of enterprises, primarily chosen due to their awareness of the need to manage social responsibility. The maturity of measuring a small enterprise's social impact, including its negative aspects, is at a very early stage. This holds true from the perspective of researchers, who rarely address this issue in their publications, and entrepreneurs. Consequently, numerous challenges are associated with the measurement process.

Due to the limited scope of the chapter, the author presents only selected theoretical, methodological, and practical aspects related to the issue at hand. Despite the extensive multi-stage (preliminary and two-stage surveys, in actuality) and multidimensional (involving entrepreneurs and other stakeholders) research process, a significant limitation is the small sample of subjects. Consequently, the conclusions can only be generalized to this group of enterprises. Directions for future research include the need to delineate precise relationships between the negative social impact of small businesses, their manifestations and areas of social irresponsibility, and the consequences of these relationships for the measurement process, along with the need to expand the research sample.

## Notes

1 An analysis of the resources of the electronic databases Web of Science and Scopus (as well as Google Scholar—including the so-called 'grey literature') for English-language articles, books, and conference proceedings on the measurement of the social impact of small businesses (search terms: measurement of social impact SME, measurement of the social impact small business) indicates their relatively small number. From 2000 to December 2022, only 16 items were published. Moreover, they mainly referred to indirect areas of social impact (mainly CSR results) and the social irresponsibility of small businesses (corruption, unethical behaviors).

2 Small enterprises included in the research sample represented 14 out of the 16 Polish voivodships.
3 Owing to the limited scope of the chapter, a detailed description of the research sample was omitted.

## References

Bartling, B., Weber, R.A., & Yao, L. (2015). Do markets erode social responsibility? *Quarterly Journal of Economics*, *130*(1), 219–266. https://econpapers.repec.org/article/oupqjecon/v_3a130_3ay_3a2015_3ai_3a1_3ap_3a219-266.htm

Carroll, A.B., & Brown, J.A. (2018). Corporate social responsibility: A review of current concepts, research, and issues. In J. Weber & D. Wasielewski (Eds.), *Corporate social responsibility,* 39–69. Emerald Publishing Co. https:/doi.org/10.1108/S2514-175920180000002002

Clark, C.E., Riera, M., & Iborra, M. (2021). Toward a theoretical framework of corporate social irresponsibility: Clarifying the gray zones between responsibility and irresponsibility. *Business & Society*, *61*(6), 1–39. https:/doi.org/10.1177/00076503211015911

Covin, J.G., & Wales, W.J. (2012). The measurement of entrepreneurial orientation. *Entrepreneurship Theory and Practice*, *36*(4), 677–702. https:/doi.org/10.1111/j.1540-6520.2010.00432.x

Dacin, P.A., Dacin, M.T., & Matear, M. (2017). Social entrepreneurship: Why we don't need a new theory and How we move forward from here. *Academy of Management Perspectives*, *24*(3), 37–57. https:/doi.org/10.5465/amp.24.3.37

Dufour, B. (2019). Social impact measurement: What can impact investment practices and the policy evaluation paradigm learn from each other? *Research in International Business and Finance*, *47*, 18–30. https:/doi.org/10.1016/j. ribaf.2018.02.003

Dillenburg, S., Greene, T., & Erekson, H. (2003). Approaching socially responsible investment with a comprehensive ratings scheme: Total social impact. *Journal of Business Ethics*, *43*(3), 167–177. https:/doi.org/0.1023/A:1022987127960

Emerson, J. (2003). The blended value proposition: Integrating social and financial returns. *California Management Review*, *45*(4), 35–51. https:/doi.org/10.2307/41166187

Grabowska, I., & Wójcik, S. (2021). *Oddziaływanie społeczne przedsiębiorstw społecznych w teorii i praktyce*. Wydawnictwa Uniwersytetu Warszawskiego, Warszawa.

Hall, M., Millo, Y., & Barman, E. (2015). Who and what really counts? Stakeholder prioritization and accounting for social value. *Journal of Management Studies*, *52*(7), 907–934. https://doi.org/10.1111/joms.12146

Husted, B.W., & Salazar, J. (2006). Taking Friedman seriously: Maximizing profits and social performance. *Journal of Management Studies*, *43*(1), 75–91. https:/doi.org/10.1111/j.1467-6486.2006.00583.x

Jankalova, M., & Jankal, R. (2017). The assessment of corporate social responsibility: Approaches analysis. Entrepreneurship and sustainability issues. *Entrepreneurship and Sustainability Center*, *4*(4), 441–459. https:/doi.org/10.9770/jesi.2017.4.4(4)

Jenkins, H. (2009). A "business opportunity" model of corporate social responsibility for small and medium-sized enterprises. *Business Ethics: A European Review*, *18*(1), 21–36. https://doi.org/10.1111/j.1467-8608.2009.01546.x

Kent, D., & Dacin, M.T. (2013). Bankers at the gate: Microfinance and the high cost of borrowed logics. *Journal of Business Venturing*, *28*(6), 759–773. https:/doi.org/10.1016/j.jbusvent.2013.03.002

Kromjong, L., Rajpal, S., & Thorns, M. (2016). *Small business big impact-SME sustainability reporting from vision to action.* Global Reporting Initiative, Amsterdam, The Netherlands.

Lumpkin, G., Moss, T., Gras, D., Kato, S., & Amezcua, A. (2013). Entrepreneurial processes in social contexts: how are they different, if at all? *Small Business Economics, 40*(3), 761–783. https:/doi.org/10.1007/s11187-011-9399-3

Maas, K., & Liket, K. (2011). Social impact measurement: Classification of methods. In R.L. Burritt, S. Schaltegger, M. Bennett, T. Pohjola, & M. Csutora (Eds.), *Environmental management accounting and supply chain management*, 171–202. Springer, Netherlands. https:/doi.org/10.1007/978-94- 007-1390-1_8

Madueño, H., Jorge, M.L., Sancho, M.P., & Martínez-Martínez, D. (2016). Development of corporate social responsibility in small and medium-sized enterprises and its nexus with quality management. *Cogent Business & Management, 3*, 1–21. https:/doi.org/10.1080/23311975.2016.1228569

Mair, J., & Marti, I. (2006). Social entrepreneurship research: A source of explanation, prediction, and delight, *Journal of World Business, 41*, 36–44. https:/doi.org/10.1016/j.jwb.2005.09.002

Moss, T.W., Short, J.C., Payne, G.T., & Lumpkin, G.T. (2011), Dual identities in social ventures: An exploratory study. *Entrepreneurship Theory and Practice, 35*(4), 805–830. https:/doi.org/10.1111/j.1540-6520.2010.00372.x

Nicholls, A. (2008). Capturing the performance of the socially entrepreneurial organisation (SEO): An organisational legitimacy approach. In J. Robinson, J. Mair, & K. Hockerts (Eds.), *International perspectives on social entrepreneurship research*, 27–74. Palgrave Macmillan.

Rawhouser, H., Cummings, M., & Newbert, S. (2019). Social impact measurement: Current approaches and future directions for social entrepreneurship research. *Entrepreneurship Theory and Practice, 43*(1), 82–115. https:/doi.org/10.1177/1042258717727718

Santos, F. (2012). A positive theory of social entrepreneurship. *Journal of Business Ethics, 111*, 335–351.

SIIT. (2014). *Measuring impact: Subject paper of the impact measurement working group.* Social Impact Investment Taskforce. Retrieved from https://iris.thegiin.org/research/measuring-impact-subject-paper-of-the-impact-measurement-working-group/summary

Sokołowska-Durkalec, A. (2020). Identification of social irresponsibility manifestations in the social responsibility management system in a small enterprise—Importance, place and conditions. In K. Bachnik, M. Kaźmierczak, M. Rojek-Nowosielska, M. Stefańska, & J. Szumniak-Samolej (Eds.), *CSR in contemporary Poland,* 41–53. Palgrave Macmillan. https:/doi.org/10.1007/978-3-030-42277-6_4

Stephan, U., Patterson, M., Kelly, C., & Mair, J. (2016). Organizations driving positive social change a review and an integrative framework of change processes. *Journal of Management, 42*(5), 1250–1281. https:/doi.org/10.1177/0149206316633268

Udayasankar, K. (2008). Corporate social responsibility and firm size. *Journal of Business Ethics, 83*, 167–175. https:/doi.org/10.1007/s10551-007-9609-8

Wood, D.J. (2010). Measuring corporate social performance: A review. *International Journal of Management Reviews, 12*(1), 50–83. https:/doi.org/10.1111/j.1468-2370.2009.00274.x

# Part 2

# Social impact on internal stakeholders

# 4 Understanding the role of ethical leadership for social impact

*Dominika Hadro, Karolina Daszyńska-Żygadło, Justyna Fijałkowska and Valerio Brescia*

## Introduction

In today's world, organizations are being called upon to take responsibility for how their operations impact societies and the environment (Quinn & Dalton, 2009). Consequently, many strive to achieve more remarkable and better social impact. In this field, the role of a leader is crucial. Organizations' leaders influence various outcomes – including turnover, customer satisfaction, sales, revenue, productivity, and more. However, appropriate leadership also creates employee's engagement and passion, which lead to higher levels of customer loyalty, service, innovation, and ultimately profits, all together translating into a potentially positive social impact. As a subject of academic study and research, social policy has given rise to a rich interdisciplinary field of analysis with a distinctive body of theory, concepts, and methods that have underpinned timely, relevant, and valuable research (Yeates & Holden, 2022). However, the existing research largely omits the importance of leadership for its social impact. Drawing on the recent definition put forth by Stephan et al. (2016), the social impact may be defined as beneficial outcomes resulting from prosocial behavior enjoyed by the intended targets of that behavior and/or by the broader community of individuals, organizations, and/or environments. According to Rawhouser et al. (2019), most definitions conceptualize social impact as engendering "positive" social change (e.g., Santos, 2012; Stephan, Patterson, Kelly, & Mair, 2016), while others define social impact in terms of the reduction of negative impacts (Bartling et al., 2015). Social impact means any significant or positive changes that solve or at least address social injustice and challenges. Businesses or organizations achieve these goals through conscious and deliberate efforts or activities in their operations and administrations that should be governed by ethical leaders.

An ethical leader is one who aims to achieve moral good and one for whom the core values of integrity, trust, respect, fairness, transparency, honesty, and morality are central. Morals, ethics, and sustainable leadership remain increasingly challenging to organizations as they adapt to changing regulations in an

DOI: 10.4324/9781003480952-6

expanding global market (McCann & Sweet, 2014). The fundamental task of ethical leadership is to promote and establish an ethical culture within the organization (Saha et al., 2020). Ethical leadership means that individuals behave according to a set of principles and values that are recognized by the majority as a sound basis for the common good. Ethical leaders provide the optimal setting for employees by inspiring, developing, and establishing a culture of trust and respect. It entails building a culture of accountability and responsibility within its processes, systems, and people. Ethical leadership results in higher employee satisfaction, trust, commitment, and organizational citizenship behaviors (Podsakoff et al., 1996). The top management's ethical leadership significantly forecasts the ethical climate, further affecting firm-level organizational citizenship behavior and economic performance (Shin et al., 2015). The employees under ethical leadership are anticipated to identify cost-saving methods to achieve a solid triple bottom line, including people, planet, and profit (Roeck & Farooq, 2018). Additionally, firms governed by ethical leadership are expected to attain more external legitimacy and a positive brand image based on their responsible and sustainable business practices (Wang et al., 2015).

An ethical leader inspires others to behave ethically and affects change towards moral goals. Strong moral leadership is crucial for companies to shift their direct involvement to fulfill the needs of financial stakeholders as well as of different stakeholder groups by delivering goods, services, and values to local communities and the needy and poorest of society.

Recently, the concepts of ethical leadership and social responsibility of companies that translate into social impact have acquired a crucial role in the competitiveness of firms operating in both manufacturing and service industries (Khan, Ali, Olya, Zulqarnain, & Khan, 2018; Roeck & Farooq, 2018). Corporate scandals, like Enron, Lehman Brothers, and Anderson – to mention a few – have raised public awareness of ethical leadership and its social impact (Wu, Kwan, Yim, Chiu, & He, 2015). Simultaneously, the globalization of business is one force that makes companies face increased pressures on the social impact resulting from ethical behavior and ethical leadership (Mishra & Schmidt, 2018). In the increasingly globalized market competition, firms are fighting for customers (Shashi, Centobelli, Cerchione, & Singh, 2019). Companies currently face a challenging management paradigm due to the context's pressures, namely intense competition, scarcity of resources, more informed and demanding consumers, progressive technological advances, climate change, and stakeholders' pressure (Silva et al., 2021). In this regard, ethical leadership and the social engagement of companies that translate into social impact may be essential factors that can lead firms to seek a competitive edge and build a clean brand image (Schinzel, 2018).

Moreover, rational consumers do not pay attention exclusively to products/services at the purchase point, but they also think about the sustainability engagement and social impact of the companies to follow (Saha et al., 2020).

Employees want to be part of an organization that is honest, fair, and reliable (Cacioppe, Forster, & Fox, 2008). Consequently, companies need an effective combination of ethical leadership and the organization's social impact to retain customers and employees. Hence, leadership that results in a social impact leading to sustainability requires leaders of extraordinary abilities. Metcalf and Benn (2013) indicate that it calls for leaders who can read and predict through complexity, think through complex problems, engage groups in dynamic adaptive organizational change, and have the emotional intelligence to engage with their emotions associated with complex problem-solving adaptively.

Although the corporate social impact has gained considerable interest in policy, academic, and practitioner debates, it is still unclear how leadership aspects such as behavior and ethics contribute to boosting corporate activities towards improving the life quality of the society. As leaders are critical organizational actors, understanding their role in social impact is necessary for sustainable development and improvement. Therefore, in this study, we formulate three research questions that will guide our analysis to understand the role of ethical leadership in social impact conducted on the basis of a bibliometric and structured literature review:

RQ 1 What is the state of art regarding ethical leadership and social impact?

RQ 2 What are the research gaps regarding ethical leadership and social impact?

## Materials and methods

To answer all RQs, we follow the phases of a systematic literature review developed by Secinaro et al. (2020). As the first step, we define primary keywords to search in the Scopus database. Initially, we put the expression *ethical leadership* and *social impact*, but we did not receive any results. We decided to expand our research using the final keywords, leadership and social impact, and we received 254 documents as initial results. Narrowing the research to three science areas: (1) business, management, and accounting; (2) economics, econometrics, and finance; (3) decision sciences and to the English language, we were left with 193 publications. Finally, choosing only scientific articles, the final sample consists of 139 papers for further analysis.

In the second phase, we collected all available information on our sample characteristics from the Scopus database. We converted the obtained files for the descriptive bibliometric analysis and created a matrix comprising all the documents. We also prepared the corpora with each abstract as a textual document ready for machine reading to analyze the keywords. In the third phase, primary, we used the open-source statistical application R for the descriptive bibliometric analysis. To expand our investigation, we applied bibliophily to develop a conceptual map, co-citation network, and WebSty developed by CLARIN-PL for the keywords' analysis. Next, in the fourth phase, the programs allowed us to obtain data reduction by using PCA and clustering. For the keyword analysis, WebSty uses the combined agglomerative-flat clustering method, recognized as an effective method for text clustering (Piasecki et al., 2018). Finally, using visualization of the results of each step in our research, we concentrated on the data interpretation and finding answers to our RQs.

## Results

Until 2015, few articles were published yearly, with a single pick in 2011. In contrast, for the last six years, we can observe a constant increase in the number of research publications analyzing leadership and social impact, with the highest number obtained in 2021 (18 articles).

The keywords most frequently cooccur with leadership and social impact are human, sustainability, sustainable development, decision making, waste management, economic and social effect, female, innovation, and communication.

There are also changes over time in the main topics discussed in the academic literature. Firstly, the authors concentrated more on social impact than on leadership. Due to the increase in the number of publications in recent years, topics are fragmented, investigating leadership and social impact from the angle of sustainable development, decision-making process, innovation, and waste management.

Table 4.1 presents the results of keyword analysis based on the articles' abstracts. We receive five clusters that differ significantly from each other by the mean frequency of keyword occurrence. To understand the main issues in each cluster, we concentrate on the first 15 most frequently used words. Only cluster 3 and cluster 4 grouped research that investigates leadership and social impact within organizations. These two clusters are the subject of our more profound analysis to answer our RQ 2.

A total of 53% of publications (74 out of 139) in our sample belong to clusters 1, 2, and 5. In cluster 1, there are 22 papers that focus on the concept of leadership and social impact in education. Cluster 2 consists of 20 publications, where the main topics concentrate on well-being and community. Citizen, governance, and responsibility are the most frequent keywords in cluster 5, for which 34 articles were qualified.

Cluster 3 grouped 27 articles, with the most frequent keywords: briefing, thinking, organization, executive, originality, and community. It implies that the main common topic is the social impact and corporate leaders' role regarding the activities for the local communities.

There are 32 research papers in cluster 4, which makes it the second-biggest cluster in our analysis. Words that occur the most frequently are enterprise, entrepreneur, innovation, model, learning, identification, and profit, indicating that the main research topic in that cluster is looking at social impact and leadership through innovation projects that include learning in an organization and entrepreneur importance. In that cluster, the words profit, output, and outcome, associated with the evaluation of financial performance, appear.

*Table 4.1* Clusters' characteristics and Mann-Whitney U test results

| | *Cluster 1, N = 22* | | | | | | *Cluster 2, N = 20* | | | | | |
|---|---|---|---|---|---|---|---|---|---|---|---|---|
| *Feature* | *Keyword* | *p-value* | *Mean in* | *Std in* | *Mean out* | *Std out* | *Keyword* | *p-value* | *Mean in* | *Std in* | *Mean out* | *Std out* |
| 1 | Education | 0.00 | 0.45 | 0.57 | 0.03 | 0.18 | Construction | 0.00 | 0.28 | 0.57 | 0.00 | 0.04 |
| 2 | Energy | 0.00 | 0.36 | 0.82 | 0.01 | 0.11 | Well-being | 0.00 | 0.24 | 0.59 | 0.00 | 0.00 |
| 3 | Student | 0.00 | 0.54 | 0.81 | 0.06 | 0.27 | Concern | 0.00 | 0.15 | 0.24 | 0.02 | 0.11 |
| 4 | Excellence | 0.00 | 0.22 | 0.80 | 0.00 | 0.00 | Community | 0.00 | 0.44 | 0.39 | 0.09 | 0.20 |
| 5 | Narrative | 0.00 | 0.22 | 0.63 | 0.00 | 0.00 | Inequality | 0.00 | 0.18 | 0.38 | 0.01 | 0.06 |
| 6 | Mean | 0.00 | 0.11 | 0.25 | 0.00 | 0.05 | Tourism | 0.00 | 0.48 | 1.18 | 0.00 | 0.00 |
| 7 | Project | 0.00 | 0.42 | 0.65 | 0.06 | 0.23 | Resident | 0.00 | 0.12 | 0.36 | 0.02 | 0.23 |
| 8 | Balance | 0.00 | 0.06 | 0.16 | 0.00 | 0.04 | Infrastructure | 0.00 | 0.17 | 0.33 | 0.01 | 0.09 |
| 9 | Complexity | 0.00 | 0.10 | 0.29 | 0.00 | 0.05 | Cost | 0.00 | 0.20 | 0.48 | 0.01 | 0.08 |
| 10 | Curriculum | 0.00 | 0.12 | 0.31 | 0.01 | 0.08 | Population | 0.00 | 0.26 | 0.64 | 0.02 | 0.18 |
| 11 | Discipline | 0.00 | 0.09 | 0.25 | 0.01 | 0.05 | Resilience | 0.00 | 0.27 | 0.61 | 0.01 | 0.10 |
| 12 | Alumnus | 0.00 | 0.05 | 0.15 | 0.00 | 0.00 | Being | 0.00 | 0.20 | 0.55 | 0.01 | 0.06 |
| 13 | Competition | 0.00 | 0.13 | 0.40 | 0.00 | 0.00 | Waste | 0.00 | 0.40 | 1.06 | 0.00 | 0.03 |
| 14 | Moment | 0.00 | 0.04 | 0.13 | 0.00 | 0.00 | City | 0.00 | 0.28 | 0.84 | 0.01 | 0.07 |
| 15 | Workshop | 0.00 | 0.05 | 0.17 | 0.00 | 0.00 | Capacity | 0.00 | 0.14 | 0.22 | 0.03 | 0.12 |

*(Continued)*

*Table 4.1* (Continued)

| | Cluster 3, N = 27 | | | | | | Cluster 4, N = 32 | | | | | |
|---|---|---|---|---|---|---|---|---|---|---|---|---|
| *Feature* | *Keyword* | *p-value* | *Mean in* | *Std in* | *Mean out* | *Std out* | *Keyword* | *p-value* | *Mean in* | *Std in* | *Mean out* | *Std out* |
| 1 | Briefing | 0.00 | 0.35 | 0.67 | 0.00 | 0.00 | Enterprise | 0.00 | 0.41 | 0.74 | 0.00 | 0.02 |
| 2 | Thinking | 0.00 | 0.39 | 0.66 | 0.01 | 0.05 | Entrepreneur | 0.00 | 0.29 | 0.62 | 0.00 | 0.00 |
| 3 | Organization | 0.00 | 0.30 | 0.38 | 0.07 | 0.23 | Innovation | 0.00 | 0.59 | 0.83 | 0.03 | 0.13 |
| 4 | Executive | 0.00 | 0.17 | 0.37 | 0.00 | 0.00 | Model | 0.00 | 0.27 | 0.50 | 0.04 | 0.15 |
| 5 | Writer | 0.00 | 0.17 | 0.37 | 0.00 | 0.00 | Learning | 0.00 | 0.18 | 0.51 | 0.03 | 0.19 |
| 6 | Peer | 0.00 | 0.38 | 0.88 | 0.00 | 0.00 | Identification | 0.00 | 0.05 | 0.16 | 0.00 | 0.00 |
| 7 | Originality | 0.00 | 0.17 | 0.25 | 0.02 | 0.09 | Profit | 0.00 | 0.10 | 0.31 | 0.00 | 0.00 |
| 8 | Community | 0.00 | 0.00 | 0.00 | 0.18 | 0.29 | Donor | 0.00 | 0.11 | 0.35 | 0.00 | 0.00 |
| 9 | Status | 0.00 | 0.17 | 0.35 | 0.01 | 0.09 | Founder | 0.00 | 0.07 | 0.21 | 0.00 | 0.00 |
| 10 | Digest | 0.00 | 0.16 | 0.39 | 0.00 | 0.00 | Fund | 0.00 | 0.08 | 0.29 | 0.00 | 0.00 |
| 11 | Edge | 0.00 | 0.16 | 0.39 | 0.00 | 0.00 | Output | 0.00 | 0.09 | 0.34 | 0.00 | 0.00 |
| 12 | Globe | 0.00 | 0.16 | 0.39 | 0.00 | 0.00 | Outcome | 0.00 | 0.16 | 0.29 | 0.04 | 0.17 |
| 13 | Employee | 0.00 | 0.23 | 0.50 | 0.03 | 0.23 | Venture | 0.00 | 0.12 | 0.32 | 0.00 | 0.03 |
| 14 | Comment | 0.00 | 0.16 | 0.35 | 0.01 | 0.10 | Alignment | 0.00 | 0.08 | 0.22 | 0.00 | 0.05 |
| 15 | Design | 0.00 | 0.24 | 0.33 | 0.05 | 0.15 | Ecosystem | 0.00 | 0.27 | 0.79 | 0.02 | 0.23 |

| | | *Cluster 5, N = 34* | | | | |
|---|---|---|---|---|---|---|
| *Feature* | *keyword* | *p-value* | *mean in* | *std in* | *mean out* | *std out* |
| 1 | Citizen | 0.00 | 0.20 | 0.57 | 0.00 | 0.00 |
| 2 | Governance | 0.00 | 0.20 | 0.58 | 0.00 | 0.00 |
| 3 | Responsibility | 0.00 | 0.22 | 0.46 | 0.02 | 0.10 |
| 4 | Observation | 0.00 | 0.07 | 0.18 | 0.01 | 0.05 |
| 5 | Integration | 0.00 | 0.11 | 0.29 | 0.01 | 0.10 |
| 6 | Government | 0.00 | 0.23 | 0.45 | 0.05 | 0.16 |
| 7 | Report | 0.00 | 0.06 | 0.19 | 0.00 | 0.00 |
| 8 | Journal | 0.00 | 0.20 | 0.76 | 0.00 | 0.00 |
| 9 | Culture | 0.00 | 0.15 | 0.48 | 0.01 | 0.08 |
| 10 | Care | 0.00 | 0.16 | 0.59 | 0.00 | 0.05 |
| 11 | Review | 0.01 | 0.15 | 0.41 | 0.02 | 0.14 |
| 12 | Issue | 0.01 | 0.13 | 0.21 | 0.05 | 0.18 |
| 13 | Sustainability | 0.01 | 0.36 | 0.66 | 0.07 | 0.21 |
| 14 | Fairness | 0.01 | 0.06 | 0.25 | 0.00 | 0.00 |
| 15 | Feedback | 0.01 | 0.03 | 0.12 | 0.00 | 0.00 |

*Source:* Own elaboration.

Further investigation of Cluster 3 and Cluster 4 shows that of 59 articles, only three of them measure social impact: in Pasricha and Rao (2018), social impact is limited to the social innovation tendency among employees measured using eight items tool proposed by Bulut et al. (2013), two articles (Álvarez García et al., 2014; Calvo-Mora et al., 2018) use EFQM Excellence Model. Also, leader(ship) style and leaders' characteristics (features) are rarely evaluated. In one paper to evaluate features of ethical leadership, authors implement the Ethical Leadership Scale developed by Brown et al. (2005), which is a 10-item instrument based on the psychometric concept. In contrast, Al-Mansoori and Koç (2019) developed their own tool for verifying transformational leadership styles. Moreover, there is a very limited number of investigations linking leadership, social impact, and financial performance. The authors of three articles analyze: impact investing and social impact (Mogapi et al., 2019), social entrepreneurship leadership style and financial performance (Kelly et al., 2022), leadership practices and financial sustainability (Nguyen et al., 2021).

In the majority of publications, qualitative methods are used, with the majority consisting of case studies (13 articles), literature reviews (12 articles), and interviews (9 articles). Among quantitative methods, authors most often use questionnaires (5 articles) and structural equation modeling (3 articles).

## Discussion

The social impact of business refers to everyone in many ways. When businesses and organizations consciously choose sustainable ways to operate, there is a chance to improve the world on Earth. A positive societal impact must be a central component of corporate strategy rather than a by-product of success. Business organizations are uniquely positioned to tackle global issues, which can bring powerful advantages for the whole society. With social impact in mind, companies can now choose greener ways to operate and create less damage to society and the environment. The focus on social impact requires a good leader with an ethical mindset. Leadership is important because it inspires, motivates, and sets an example for people to accomplish positive changes in the company and the world. While running their business, leaders should seek to tackle our world's most complex challenges to create a positive social impact.

Our bibliometric and structured literature review shows a lack of papers investigating the role of ethical leadership in social impact. In recent years, we can observe an increase in publications exploring leadership roles and social impact, which confirms the understanding of that topic's importance among scholars. However, until today, the early stage of research development is present, resulting in numerous works using qualitative methods, characteristic of explorative studies.

Using cluster analysis of abstracts and their careful reading, we identify the main research gaps: role of ethical leadership for social impact, development of ethical leadership evaluation measures, development of leadership role in social impact evaluation measures, development of social impact evaluation measures, the link between ethical leadership, social impact, and financial performance. There is also an absence of quantitative research, comparative study, and long-run analysis. We believe that growing awareness of companies' role in enhancing activities in the social area and EU regulation changes pushing European economies towards sustainability will result in a significant growth of research binding ethical leadership and social impact together.

## References

Al-Mansoori, R.S., & Koç, M. (2019). Transformational leadership, systems, and intrinsic motivation impacts on innovation in higher education institutes: Faculty perspectives in engineering colleges. *Sustainability*, *11*(15), 2–26. https://doi.org/10.3390/su11154072

Álvarez García, J., Cruz Del Río Rama, M. de la, Vila Alonso, M., & Fraiz Brea, J.A. (2014). Dependence relationship between the critical quality factors and social impact. *Revista de Administração de Empresas*, *54*, 692–705. https://doi.org/10.1590/S0034-759020140609

Bartling, B., Weber, R.A., & Yao, L. (2015). Do markets erode social responsibility? *Quarterly Journal of Economics*, *130*(1), 219–266.

Brown, M.E., Treviño, L.K., & Harrison, D.A. (2005). Ethical leadership: A social learning perspective for construct development and testing. *Organizational Behavior and Human Decision Processes*, *97*(2), 117–134. https://doi.org/10.1016/j.obhdp.2005.03.002

Bulut, C., Eren, H., & Halac, D.S. (2013). Social innovation and psychometric analysis. *Procedia - Social and Behavioral Sciences*, *82*, 122–130. https://doi.org/10.1016/j.sbspro.2013.06.235

Cacioppe, R., Forster, N., & Fox, M. (2008). A survey of managers' perceptions of corporate ethics and social responsibility and actions that may affect companies' success. *Journal of Business Ethics*, *82*, 681–700. https://doi.org/10.1007/s10551-007-9586-y

Calvo-Mora, A., Domínguez-CC, M., & Criado, F. (2018). Assessment and improvement of organizational social impact through the EFQM excellence model. *Total Quality Management & Business Excellence*, *29*(11–12), 1259–1278. https://doi.org/10.1080/14783363.2016.1253465

Kelly, L., Perkins, V., Zuraik, A., & Luse, W. (2022). Social impact: The role of authentic leadership, compassion and grit in social entrepreneurship. *The Journal of Entrepreneurship*, *31*(2), 298–329.

Khan, H.U.R., Ali, M., Olya, H.G.T., Zulqarnain, M., & Khan, Z.R. (2018). Transformational leadership, corporate social responsibility, organizational innovation, and organizational performance: Symmetrical and asymmetrical analytical approaches. *Corporate Social Responsibility and Environmental Management*, *25*(6), 1270–1283. https://doi.org/10.1002/csr.1637

Metcalf, L., & Benn, S. (2013). Leadership for sustainability: An evolution of leadership ability. *Journal of Business Ethics*, *112*(3), 369–384.

Mishra, P., & Schmidt, G.B. (2018). How can leaders of multinational organizations be ethical by contributing to corporate social responsibility initiatives? Guidelines and pitfalls for leaders trying to do good. *Business Horizons*, *61*(6), 833–843. https://doi.org/10.1016/j.bushor.2018.07.011

Mogapi, E.M., Sutherland, M.M., & Wilson-Prangley, A. (2019). Impact investing in South Africa: Managing tensions between financial returns and social impact. *European Business Review*, *31*(3), 397–419. https://doi.org/10.1108/EBR-11-2017-0212

McCann, J., & Sweet, M. (2014). The perceptions of ethical and sustainable leadership. *Journal of Business Ethics*, *121*, 373–383.

Nguyen, M.H.T., Hodgetts, D.J., & Carr, S.C. (2021). Fitting social enterprise for sustainable development in Vietnam. *Sustainability*, *13*(19), 2–16. https://doi.org/10.3390/su131910630

Pasricha, P., & Rao, M.K. (2018). The effect of ethical leadership on employee social innovation tendency in social enterprises: Mediating role of perceived social capital. *Creativity and Innovation Management*, *27*(3), 270–280. https://doi.org/10.1111/caim.12287

Piasecki, M., Walkowiak, T., & Eder, M. (2018). Open stylometric system WebSty: Integrated language processing, analysis and visualisation. *Computational Methods in Science and Technology*, *24*(1), 43–58. https://doi.org/10.12921/CMST.2018.0000007

Podsakoff, P.M., MacKenzie, S.B., & Bommer, W.H. (1996). Transformational leader behaviors and substitutes for leadership as determinants of employee satisfaction, commitment, trust, and organizational citizenship behaviors. *Journal of Management*, *22*(2), 259–298.

Quinn, L., & Dalton, M. (2009). Leading for sustainability: Implementing the tasks of leadership. *Corporate Governance: The International Journal of Business in Society*, *9*(1), 21–38.

Rawhouser, H., Cummings, M., & Newbert, S.L. (2019). Social impact measurement: Current approaches and future directions for social entrepreneurship research. *Entrepreneurship Theory and Practice*, *43*(1), 82–115.

Roeck, K.D., & Farooq, O. (2018). Corporate social responsibility and ethical leadership: Investigating their interactive effect on employees' socially responsible behaviors. *Journal of Business Ethics*, *151*, 923–939. https://doi.org/10.1007/s10551-017-3656-6

Saha, R., Cerchione, R., Singh, R., & Dahiya, R. (2020). Effect of ethical leadership and corporate social responsibility on firm performance: A systematic review. *Corporate Social Responsibility and Environmental Management*, *27*(2), 409–429.

Santos, F. (2012). A positive theory of social entrepreneurship. *Journal of Business Ethics*, *111*, 335–351.

Secinaro, S., Brescia, V., Calandra, D., & Biancone, P. (2020). Employing bibliometric analysis to identify suitable business models for electric cars. *Journal of Cleaner Production*, *264*, 121503. https://doi.org/10.1016/j.jclepro.2020.121503

Saha, R., Shashi, Cerchione, R., Singh, R., & Dahiya, R. (2020). Effect of ethical leadership and corporate social responsibility on firm performance: A systematic review. *Corporate Social Responsibility and Environmental Management*, *27*(2), 409-429.

Schinzel, U. (2018). Responsible leadership and corporate social responsibility (CSR) in Luxembourg. *International Journal of organizational analysis*, *26*(3), 415–431.

Shin, Y., Sung, S.Y., Choi, J.N., & Kim, M.S. (2015). Top management ethical leadership and firm performance: Mediating role of ethical and procedural justice climate. *Journal of Business Ethics*, *129*(1), 43–57. https://doi.org/10.1007/s10551-014-2144-5

Silva, C.S., Magano, J., Matos, A., & Nogueira, T. (2021). Sustainable quality management systems in the current paradigm: The role of leadership. *Sustainability*, *13*(4), 2056.

Stephan, U., Patterson, M., Kelly, C., & Mair, J. (2016). Organizations driving positive social change a review and an integrative framework of change processes. *Journal of Management*, *42*(5), 1250–1281.

Wang, D.H., Chen, P., Yu, T.H., & Hsio, C. (2015). The effects of corporate social responsibility on brand equity and firm performance. *Journal of Business Research*, *68*, 2232–2236. https://doi.org/10.1016/j.jbusres.2015.06.003

Wu, L., Kwan, H.K., Yim, F.H., Chiu, R.K., & He, X. (2015). CEO ethical leadership and corporate social responsibility: A moderated mediation model. *Journal of Business Ethics*, *130*, 819–831. https://doi.org/10.1007/s10551-014-2108-9

Yeates, N., & Holden, C. (2022). Introducing global socia policy. In N. Yeates & C. Holden (Eds.), *Understanding global social policy*, 1–24. The Policy Press.

# 5 Social impact of respecting employee interests in the process of modelling employment relationships in a company

*Ewa Mazur-Wierzbicka and*
*Anna Cierniak-Emerych*

## Introduction

Until recently, many organizations still had approached the subject matter of social responsibility as an opportunity to better the image of the organization both within and outside of it. Today, it often becomes one of the elements of companies' strategy, it allows for companies to be transformed into organizations that have a positive social impact – not only globally, but on a local scale too, also by accommodating employee expectations.

The above implies a focus on the issue of social impact and on the subject (the organization and its external stakeholders).

The literature does not present a uniform front when it comes to social impact (Levine & Hogg, 2010; Choi & Majumdar, 2014; Stephan et al., 2016). This term is often identified with other concepts, such as social value (Moss et al., 2011; Santos, 2012), social return on investment (Hall et al., 2015), or social performance (Husted & Salazar, 2006; Nicholls, 2008).

In generalized terms, social impact may be considered to be the influence which the organization exerts on people and communities by its activity, policy, initiatives (or failure to undertake them) and actions. The main focus here is on the effects of actions taken up by organizations. The discussion presented in this study adopts such an understanding of social impact, based on Latané's definition (1981). By default, we concentrate on the positive impact of an organization, on the fact that it focuses on implementing significant and positive changes which are a response to various challenges, also social ones, that concern the organization's internal stakeholders, on involving them and on cooperation with them for solving existing problems.

In the context of this study, it is important to focus on the work on impact, which is the management's specific way of thinking. The work on impact is indirectly linked to the social impact analysis, that is specifying whether actions taken bring expected results and identifying those actions which are fundamental.

DOI: 10.4324/9781003480952-7

Employees are key stakeholders of an organization in the aspect of social responsibility (Stuart, 2002). The achievement of intended results associated with the company's activity is linked with recognition and execution of individual interests.

Employee interests are most often described as an expression of specific expectations associated with the performance of work. At the same time, it is reserved that employees, since they have their own expectations, will strive to achieve them. Every stakeholder is bound by the company by certain stakes which point to the kind and degree of his expectations and risk (Gableta & Cierniak-Emerych, 2008). An employee, by attempting to cooperate with a given company, most often resigns from other offers of employment in the hope that this company will satisfy his interests. If companies fail to meet such interests, workers may look for jobs at other employers (Hafij, 2016).

Employee interests are a function of many variables, such as personality, experience, culture or peer influence, (Baker, 1996; Oginni et al., 2018). On top of that, they differ due to a number of factors, such as the situation on the labor market or cultural and demographic determinants, including the so-called generational changes, etc.

Employee interests concern a wide array of matters. It is worth noting that individual authors create "employee interest lists", mainly for the need of research they carry out (Strong & Campbell, 1969; Prince, 1998; Katz et al., 1999). When it comes to results of empirical research, there have been attempts in the literature to point out the most important interests for employees associated with the performance of work. Authors mainly identify the following (Gableta, 2012; Wachowiak, 2013; Paliwoda-Matiolańska, 2014):

- Satisfactory remuneration and/or remuneration adequate to responsibilities;
- Sense of security of employment;
- Safe and healthy working conditions;
- Clear criteria for assessment of task completion;
- Access to reliable information about the company and its standing;
- Friendly work atmosphere;
- Possibility for development and career progression.

These interests are associated with specific components of managing human potential (employment, working conditions or remuneration) which potentially outline the scope of issues that make up the subject matter of employment relationships.

The question of employee interests associated with these elements is mainly taken up in labor law literature by invoking the "employee rights" category. Respecting these interests is, therefore, expressed in particular in the set of guidelines concerning people and their work, formulated under labor law. The

International Labour Organization, the Council of Europe or the European Community to name just a few play a specific role in this regard. What we mean here is ensuring decent remuneration, specifying a 24h or weekly work schedule, ensuring that these guidelines are observed or creating safe and healthy working conditions. Moreover, employee interests also concern questions not regulated by laws, such as ensuring a friendly work atmosphere. It is worth highlighting here that in essence we often deal with conflicting interests which surface mainly in the relations between the employer (chief management) and employees. Therefore, the management process should involve agreeing employer's rights with employees to achieve a settlement and a compromise, that is formulating employment relationships, understood as relations and interactions between employers and employees in a company. Such interrelations are materialized during, e.g., negotiations, participation or making arrangements, and also through respecting specific employee interests (Cierniak-Emerych & Gableta, 2022). The latter is what we are interested in here.

Employees expect in particular that the organization will satisfy their material and professional aspirations. Beneficial results that flow from such social behaviors, that is the social impact related to respecting employee interests, will then be expressed in ensuring mental comfort to employees in the workplace, their sense of satisfaction and also broadly understood work security. The latter should be understood in the context of guaranteeing safe and healthy working conditions and also in the context of the comfort of having a job and earning a decent pay. The company's social impact resulting from respecting employee interests is, on top of that, expressed in preventing employee exclusion and in their sense of belonging to a community of the company and its stakeholders.

Therefore, given the rank of employees in creating the company and its lasting operation, it is particularly important to monitor the degree of employee identification with changes in the company identity while at the same time caring for the satisfaction of their needs (Stuart, 2002). This requires knowledge of their interests and at the same time treating employees the way they wish to be treated. As concluded by M. Gableta (2012), employers, being usually guided by the principle of minimizing costs, have difficulty in building a motivational system that would truly satisfy employee interests; they assume relatively often that what is good for the company is also what employees wish for. This turns into a lack of trust from the staff.

The solutions presented above allow a conclusion that employee interests are a very sensitive subject matter that requires constant monitoring, and which is a permanently valid and at the same time important plane for conducting research (Cierniak-Emerych & Gableta, 2022).

The main aim of this chapter is that employee interests, which are a basis for designing the architecture of the subject matter of employment relationships, should be examined in the context of the company's social impact on the company's environment. This study aims to fill the lacunae in research on employee interests by specifying expressions of the social impact on the organization's environment that results from recognizing and respecting these interests. The following research questions have been formulated to achieve this goal:

- What interests relating to elements of the subject matter of employment relationships were especially important for employees?
- What interests relating to elements of the subject matter of employment relationships were in the opinion of employers especially important for employees?
- Were employee interests related to matters of employment relationships respected by employers?
- What benefits for the company's environment come from the company's social behaviors related to respecting employee interests?

Empirical research questions and an analysis of literature were used to achieve the goal of this study and to answer the research questions asked.

## Materials and methods

In an attempt to find answers to the research questions asked in this study, we referred to results of empirical research carried out under two projects:

1 In 2018–2020,[1] empirical research was carried out among employees and employers;
2 In 2020–2020,[2] empirical research was carried out among employees who come from Ukraine and who work in Poland.

A survey questionnaire was used to conduct the research in 2018–2020 on employee interests and on how they are respected. The PAPI technique (*Paper and Pencil Interview*) was used.[3] Statistical instruments were employed additionally, including a sample statistical parameter – standard deviation. The investigators used the cafeteria of interests used for research conducted on employee interests in the years that preceded the year of the start of the research (Cierniak-Emerych & Gableta, 2022). However, considering the changeability within interests under different circumstances, the final form of the survey questionnaire was designed using the existing cafeteria and the cafeteria drawn up by other researchers and practitioners (Hai-Dong & Yu-Jun 2006; Silverman, 2014; Hafij, 2016; Zhong et al., 2017). This was verified in reference to the Polish management conditions. Twenty-one interests were ultimately included in the questionnaire. Respondents marked their answers on the scale from 1 to 5, where 1 meant an interest not important to them and 5 meant a very important interest.

A randomly selected sample of employees who worked in companies registered in the territory of the Lower Silesian province was used in the study. The data from EURES (European Employment Services) shows that the population of persons employed (in the Lower Silesia province, in the companies' sector) in 2018 was 484,100. This province boasts a relatively low unemployment rate in the ranking of provinces.

A random sample with n = 274 was selected from the finite population of workers employed in companies registered in the Lower Silesia province for the needs of this research. Assuming the 6% error of estimation, the significance level alpha = 0.05 and the estimated fraction 0.5 for the finite population N = 484,100, the minimum sample size is n = 267. The sample was randomized by using a sampling frame in the form of a base of workers employed in companies registered in the territory of the Lower Silesian province who are part of the employee population defined for the needs of this study (Cierniak-Emerych & Gableta, 2022).

The investigated group was composed of persons who had been working in their current company for less than a year – 14% of cases, and persons who had worked in their companies for more than 15 years – 19% of cases. Polish respondents accounted for 97.1% of the entire group (Cierniak-Emerych & Gableta, 2022), which is important from the perspective of the second research quoted.

The research covered both employees and employers. One hundred sole traders or persons in senior and chief management positions took part in the study. Ninety-nine percent of this group were Polish.

The investigation carried out in 2020–2022 thought it important to look at employee interests through the prism of workers from Ukraine and at the approach to respecting and implementing them. It is worth adding that citizens of some 160 countries work in Poland, of which close to 79% are citizens of Ukraine (Rzemek, 2022; ZUS, 2022). Therefore, the investigators believed it important to cover this group of respondents in the research from the point of view of investigating interests of employees who perform work in Poland given the great share of Ukrainian staff in the employment structure in this country. At the same time, the analysis of available research results allowed the investigators to point out that the literature still lacks such studies. Results of such research are thus treated here as a certain supplementation, completion of results of research conducted under the first project talked about here, that is the project carried out in 2018–2020 that focused on interests of employees working in Poland. Lower Silesia province is considered a geographically significant region of economic migration from Ukraine – more than 80% of foreigners in Lower Silesia are aliens from Ukraine. The branches in which they work mainly include industry, transport, construction, services and trading. In Lower Silesia, citizens of Ukraine have set up close to 600 companies. It is worth noting there that Ukrainian citizens actually work in most large industrial enterprises located in the territory of Lower Silesia. It is confirmed by data from Statistics Poland and the Social Insurance Institution. The fact of employing so many employees from Ukraine, in a great number of companies in the territory of Lower Silesia, has become a basis to conclude that the survey carried out among Polish employees in 2018–2022 must be supplemented with research carried out among employees from Ukraine. As has been shown above, it was carried out in 2020–2022. This investigation also used the survey questionnaire drawn up for the needs of the research carried out in 2018–2020. The PAPI technique (*Paper and Pencil Interview*) was used.[4] Statistical instruments were used additionally, including a sample statistical parameter – standard deviation.

The research covered a representative sample of immigrants from Ukraine who worked in Poland legally in companies located in the territory of the Lower Silesia province. The research uses a random stratified sample from the population of companies from Lower Silesia. The total of 391 respondents took part in the study. Fifty-four percent of respondents worked in Poland for two to ten years. It is worth adding that 64.7% of respondents did not use job agencies in their employment. A total of 38.4% were employed in production, 37.1% in services and 24.6% in trade. At the same time, 91.6% of respondents claimed they were employed in non-managerial positions.

We must add here that an in-depth interview was also used in this research in both periods. It involved carrying out free interviews, choosing among those respondents who expressed their consent in both periods.

## Results

In a search for answers to the questions posed in here, we use results of the research described in part 2 of this chapter.

An analysis of employee interests for significance for themselves showed that they thought it most important to be ensured safe and healthy working conditions, immediately followed by getting a pay adequate to responsibilities. More than 90% of respondents also named a good work atmosphere and clear criteria for assessment of task completion (Table 5.1).

The responses presented in Table 5.1 confirm results of statistical parameters of the sample. In answer to the question about the importance of safe and healthy working conditions, the mean was 4.54 with standard deviation of 0.593. Five was the dominant answer to this question, that is the highest value in the measurement scale. On the other hand, the value of the coefficient of asymmetry at −1.095 means a strong left-skewed asymmetry. This means that the majority of responses were given at the above-average level.

The results of the research also prove that respondents-employees, by attributing priority to safe and healthy working conditions, in essence also accommodate under this category their sense of safety at work in organizations they are employed in. Respondents-employees were asked what the concept of work safety means to them. A total of 42.7% of respondents associated it with safe and healthy working conditions (machines, devices, lighting, etc.), while 48.2% of respondents associated work safety jointly with health and safety at work and security associated with having a job.

*Table 5.1* Interests that employee considered important or very important

| *Interests* | *% Total responses* | *Mean* | *Median* | *Dominant* | *Standard deviation* |
|---|---|---|---|---|---|
| Safe and healthy working conditions | 96.3 | 4.5 | 5 | 5 | 0.59 |
| Pay adequate to responsibilities | 92.0 | 4.5 | 5 | 5 | 0.65 |
| Good work atmosphere | 92.0 | 4.4 | 5 | 5 | 0.65 |
| Clear criteria for assessment of task completion | 91.2 | 4.4 | 5 | 5 | 0.66 |
| Appropriate information flow | 88.7 | 4.3 | 4 | 4 | 0.67 |
| Help from superiors and co-workers | 88.7 | 4.3 | 4 | 4 | 0.69 |
| Opportunity for professional development | 85.8 | 4.1 | 4 | 4 | 0.80 |
| Influence on selecting remuneration components | 85.4 | 4.2 | 4 | 4 | 0.76 |
| Clear rules of promotion | 85.0 | 4.1 | 4 | 4 | 0.85 |
| Permanent employment | 85.0 | 4.2 | 4 | 4 | 0.87 |
| Employment protection (protection against being made redundant) | 83.9 | 4.1 | 4 | 4 | 0.78 |
| Training paid by employer | 81.7 | 4.1 | 4 | 4 | 0.82 |
| Impact on organization of work time | 81.0 | 4.0 | 4 | 4 | 0.870 |
| Impact on selection of co-workers | 80.0 | 4.0 | 4 | 4 | 0.86 |
| Health care services paid by employer | 80.0 | 4.1 | 4 | 4 | 0.89 |
| Protection of social benefits | 75.6 | 4.0 | 4 | 4 | 0.89 |
| Formal procedures for expressing opinion | 74.5 | 3.9 | 4 | 4 | 0.88 |
| Assistance in lay-offs | 68.7 | 3.8 | 4 | 4 | 1.04 |
| Participation in management (consultation) | 67.5 | 3.8 | 4 | 4 | 1.05 |
| Help from unions/employee councils | 64.9 | 3.6 | 4 | 4 | 1.19 |
| Participation in management (co-decision making) | 62.8 | 3.7 | 4 | 4 | 1.15 |

*Source:* Own elaboration based on Cierniak-Emerych & Gableta, 2002.

Knowing what interests are essential to the employees, it was crucial to investigate whether they were respected in their workplace. As seen in research results, almost all respondents were guaranteed healthy and safe working conditions in their jobs – 96.7% (Figure 5.1). A good work atmosphere came second in the count of responses and help from superiors and co-workers ranked third. These elements were identified by 88.1% and 80.1% of respondents, respectively. It is worth nothing that the respondents did not mention all elements listed in Table 5.1.

The employees investigated believed that the management takes their interest into account, mainly due to having to care for reputation – 71.5% of positive responses. A fear of conflict with employees ranked second – 59.5% of responses. On the other hand, 59.1% of respondents claimed that such behaviors result from the company's organizational culture.

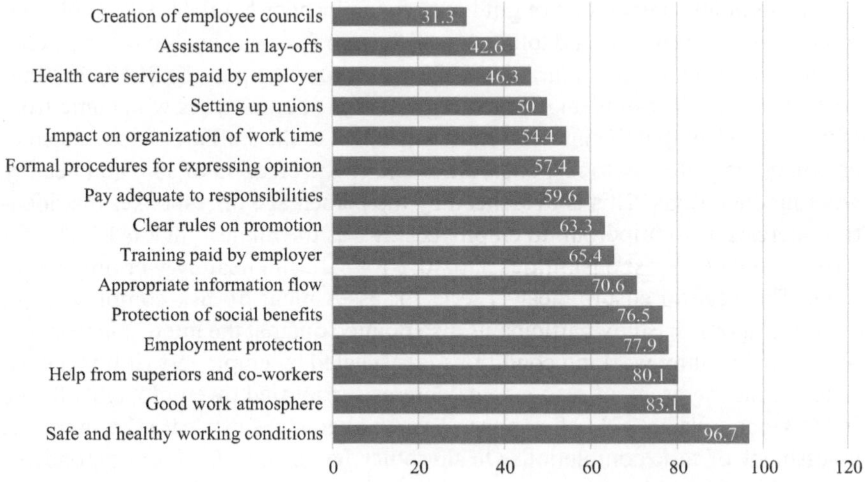


*Figure 5.1* Respecting employee interests in a company – employee perspective (%)
*Source:* Own elaboration.

Statements from respondents-employers come to the fore here. Interestingly, referring to the second research question, employees believed that the greatest interest that they expect to be ensured are clear criteria for assessment of task completion, while the second most important one was pay adequate to responsibilities. Safe and healthy working conditions took the tenths place among interests important to employees. This study shows that all employers surveyed ensured safe and healthy working conditions to their employees.

Respondents-employers also presented their opinions on why management in their companies take employee interests into consideration. Most study participants pointed to maintaining the company's good reputation in employees' opinion. Slightly fewer respondents believed that this results from the company's organizational culture. A fear of losing employees came third among reasons. These responses are partially similar to those given by employees.

The in-depth research demonstrated that ensuring a safer workplace and pay adequate to responsibilities has a positive impact on external environment-oriented activities taken up by employees employed in the enterprises investigated. This is demonstrated in socially responsible projects directed to local communities (voluntary work, educational actions, pro-social actions, pro-environmental actions, or sporting events). One company has set up its own running team. Its members are employees, who, trained by a professional coach, participate in numerous runs, especially those organized to promote a healthy lifestyle among residents of Lower Silesia. Moreover, the same company organized a charity event to collect board games for children from a Wrocław children's home. They also organized a charity project involving preparation of gift boxes for a few poor families. The employees brought in food products and toiletries which were then packed into those boxes.

The research conducted in 2020–2022 was a follow-up to the 2018–2020 investigation. Their results on recognizing interests of employees who come from Ukraine confirm that the interests most important to the staff are those related to ensuring adequate pay to responsibilities and to the creation of safe and healthy working conditions. This is evidenced by the percentage of responses that identify interests most important to employees. It was the highest, that is 86.4%, for a pay adequate to responsibilities and 80% for safe and healthy working conditions. The need to ensure clear criteria for assessment of task completion got 78% of responses. Study participants also pointed out that the interest in the form of safe and healthy working conditions is respected by employers (it was named as top in the hierarchy of respondents' interests respected by employers – 81%). In the second place (77% of responses) came guarantees of clear criteria for the assessment of task completion. On the other hand, only 61% of respondents declared that pay adequate to responsibilities, considered as the most important in the hierarchy of interests of Ukrainian workers, as we point out above, is respected by employers.

The in-depth research showed that employees from Ukraine, despite having safe working conditions ensured, do not show involvement in socially responsible actions.

## Discussion

The starting point to specify the social impact of organizations on employees, and also as a consequence of their closest environment, was to select an aspect that would be important to the employees. An analysis of relevant literature shows that interests (expectations) of employees provide such a springboard. Stages of the discussion are presented in Figure 5.2.

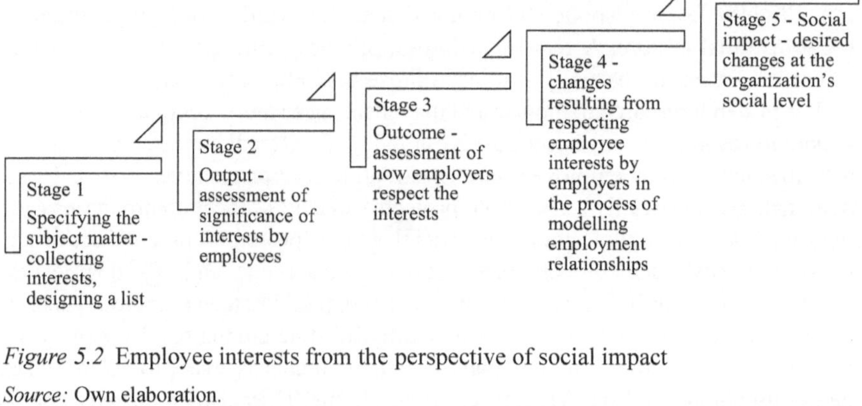


*Figure 5.2* Employee interests from the perspective of social impact

*Source:* Own elaboration.

This research shows that the management do take into consideration employee interests. This is mainly down to (more than 50% of responses): the need to care for reputation, the fear of likelihood of an outbreak of a conflict with employees or the company's organizational culture.

The most important employee interests include those associated with elements of the subject matter of employment relationships. Guaranteeing safe and healthy working conditions was considered most important by study participants. Other responses included: pay adequate to responsibilities, good atmosphere and ensuring clear criteria for assessment of task completion. Essentially, by attributing priority to safe and healthy working conditions, employees also identify their sense of safety at work in organizations they are employed in with this category. In turn, safety at work is most often associated with health and safety at work and security associated with having a job.

Employers are of the opinion that they ensure safe and healthy working conditions to their employees. As they are aware of this, employers marked safe and healthy working conditions only on the 10th position when assessing what they thought employees expected. They held the following as of highest importance: clear criteria for assessment of task completion and pay adequate to responsibilities.

Recognizing an interest in the form of safe and healthy working conditions as very important both by employees and employers seems fully reasonable in the context of the discussion conducted in here. Many studies emphasize that people can work in any conditions, but to work efficiently and at the same time to maintain good health, this work must only be performed in conditions that do not threaten health or life. The subject matter of creating a safe and healthy work set-up is also considered one of the fundamental areas and at the same time manifestations of socially responsible behaviors in a company, and more broadly – the CSR concept (Piwowar-Sulej & Bąk-Grabowska, 2021; Cierniak-Emerych & Mazur-Wierzbicka, 2022).

Ukrainian workers, in turn, believed that interests related to pay adequate to responsibilities and creation of safe and healthy working conditions were the most important. Recognizing pay adequate to responsibilities as the most crucial interest of this employee group seems rather obvious. According to data from Gorshenin Institute, more than 40% of Ukrainians active on the labor market aged between 18 and 29 were ready to leave Ukraine to get a more profitable job and career perspectives (Ukhova, 2018). It is worth adding here that pay adequate to responsibilities is an important interest for employees of Polish origin too. In contemporary changeable world, often referred to as VUCA, we cannot avoid pointing to aspects associated with remunerating persons who provide work, also with the application of methods, forms and components of remuneration that are favorable to them (Bennett & Lemoine, 2014). Analogically, recognizing the interest involving safe and healthy work environment as important seems fully justified. It is worth reserving at that, that we often deal with greater difficulties concerning training on health and safety at work in the host country due to poor language skills (Rechel et al., 2013). Some studies say that migrant workers reported greater exposure to bad, largely material, elements of working conditions (Ronda et al., 2012; Takala et al., 2014; ILO, 2015).

What is important from the perspective of the social impact, respondents (Polish and Ukrainian workers alike) pointed out that the important interest in the form of safe and healthy working conditions is one that is indeed respected by employers – 96.7% of responses.

However, a question arises in such a context of whether the actions taken up in companies that focus on respecting employee interests result from principles adopted in these companies which concern implementation of socially responsible management of labor potential. It seems that such actions do not result directly from an attempt to consciously direct such activities towards socially responsible aspects. Still though, it seems that the discussion presented here allows a conclusion that when it comes to the group of respondents investigated, we may talk about specific manifestations of the social impact on employees that results from recognizing and respecting their interests.

If we look at manifestations of this impact, that is positive outcomes that result from social behaviors that are expressed in respect for employee interests, it seems reasonable to point to improvement of security of the work of those employees, increased satisfaction from the work performed, increased involvement and also greater trust towards the employer. Respecting employee interests should also result in improved work efficiency of persons who provide such work. Generally, we may conclude that it translates into employees' better mental and social well-being. It is especially important since, as presented in the Deloitte report (2018), employees' well-being was considered one of the most important trends in HR in Poland as early as in 2018 already. Employee support programs (also those focusing on OSH) were considered the best investment. We do notice social impact in this sphere, as confirmed in actions taken up by companies, which are directed towards protection of employees' health and ensuring their sense of security. Such an impact brings about loyalty of employees who are already working in the company and their attachment to the work place. Looking from the perspective of social impact on the company's environment, a good opinion on the job market – as a company that looks after their employees, respects their interest and satisfies their expectations (primarily those that are most important for the employee) – that is helpful in acquiring new employees and talents, which today is very important. Additionally, also an opinion about the company as an entity that exercises manifestations of CSR towards the environment. It is worth examining the social impact, for example, in connection with CSR (Serafeimm, 2020).

By looking at the social impact on companies' environment, which is particularly important for us in this study, the discussion presented here allows a conclusion that when it comes to the group of respondents investigated, we may talk about specific manifestations of the social impact on the company's environment that results from recognizing and respecting the interest of employees. This is evidenced by actions pointed out by respondents, mostly of Polish origin, such as setting up a running team or organizing charity events. The same is not accentuated by employees from Ukraine. Perhaps their situation in Poland, associated with the war in Ukraine, understandably, means that they focus on getting a sense of security for themselves and using the resources earned to support family members and other persons that are staying in Ukraine.

## Notes

1 The research results presented are part of results of a broader investigation on employee interests and on how they are respected, conducted by A. Cierniak-Emerych – co-author of this article and presented in a broader context in a monograph (Cierniak-Emerych & Gableta, 2022).

2 The research is conducted under two external grants co-financed by the Wroclaw University of Economics. However, both these grants make up one research project. A. Cierniak-Emerych is the principal investigator in both these grants while E. Mazur-Wierzbicka is a member of the research team. The first of these projects, that is Employee participation in Poland – situation of immigrants from Ukraine covered 2020–2021, while the second one, that is Interests of migrant workers from Ukraine, covers the period between December 2021 and December 2022. The presented research results refer to February 2022. Given the acts of war in Ukraine since February 2022, the situation of persons with Ukrainian origin who are employed in Poland has changed. This has caused difficulties in continuing the research, but there are attempts to continue it.

3 The investigators cooperated with Instytut Badawczy IPC Sp. z o.o. at this stage of the investigation.

4 The investigators cooperated with Instytut Badawczy IPC Sp. z o.o. at this stage of the investigation.

## References

Baker, H.G. (1996). The psychological contract between employer and employee. *Psychology, 33*(3), 16–30.

Bennett, N., & Lemoine, J. (2014). What a difference a word makes: Understanding threats to performance in a VUCA world. *Business Horizons, 57*(3), 311–317. https://doi.org/10.1016/j.bushor.2014.01.001

Choi, N., & Majumdar, S. (2014). Social entrepreneurship as an essentially contested concept: Opening a new avenue for systematic future research. *Journal of Business Venturing, 29*(3), 363–376. https://doi.org/10.1016/j.jbusvent.2013.05.001

Cierniak-Emerych, A., & Gableta, M. (2022). *Gospodarowanie potencjałem pracy zorientowane na interesy pracobiorców*. Wydawnictwo UE we Wrocławiu.

Cierniak-Emerych, A., & Mazur-Wierzbicka, E. (2022). Safety and health at work as an important interest of employees from the perspective of corporate social responsibility. In K. Bachnik, M. Kaźmierczak, M. Rojek-Nowosielska, M. Stefańska, & J. Szumniak-Samolej (Eds.), *Corporate social responsibility and sustainability,* 130–140. Routledge. https://www.taylorfrancis.com/books/9781003270768/chapters/10.4324/9781003270768-13

Deloitte. (2018). *Trendy HR w Polsce*. Deloitte.

Hafij, A. (2016). *Employees expectations from employers in modern business*. Retrieved from https://www.linkedin.com/pulse/employees-expectations-from-employers-modern-business-hafij-ali

Gableta, M. (Ed.) (2012). *Interesy pracowników oraz warunki ich respektowania w przedsiębiorstwach*. Wydawnictwo Uniwersytetu Ekonomicznego we Wrocławiu.

Gableta, M., & Cierniak-Emerych, A. (2008). *Zarządzanie ludźmi w organizacjach funkcjonujących w Europie*. Wydawnictwo I-BiS.

Hai-Dong, Z., & Yu-jun, S. (2006). Relationship between employees' interests and business performance in state-owned enterprises: Evidence from Shenzhen, China. *International Conference on Management Science and Engineering*, 1307–1311. https://doi.org/10.1109/ICMSE.2006.314233

Hall, M., Millo, Y., & Barman, E. (2015). Who and what really counts? Stakeholder prioritization and accounting for social value. *Journal of Management Studies*, *52*(7), 907–934. https://doi.org/10.1111/joms.12146

Husted, B.W., & Salazar, J. de J. (2006). Taking Friedman seriously: Maximizing profits and social performance. *Journal of Management Studies*, *43*(1), 75–91. https://doi.org/10.1111/j.1467-6486.2006.00583.x

ILO. (2015). *ILO Global estimates on migrant workers: Results and methodology*. Special Focus on Migrant Domestic Workers. ILO.

Katz, L., Joyner, J.W., & Seaman, N. (1999). Effects of joint interpretation of the strong interest inventory and the Myers-Briggs type indicator in career choice. *Journal of Career Assessment*, *7*(3), 281–298. https://doi.org/10.1177/106907279900700306

Latané, B. (1981). The psychology of social impact. *American Psychologist*, *36*(4), 343–356. https://doi.org/10.1037/0003-066X.36.4.343

Levine, J.M., & Hogg, M.A. (Eds.) (2010). *Encyclopedia of group processes & intergroup relations*. SAGE Publications, Inc. https://doi.org/10.4135/9781412972017.n248

Moss, T.W., Short, J.C., Payne, G.T., & Lumpkin, G.T. (2011). Dual identities in social ventures: An exploratory study. *Entrepreneurship Theory and Practice*, *35*(4), 805–830. https://doi.org/10.1111/j.1540-6520.2010.0037

Nicholls, A. (2008). Capturing the performance of the socially entrepreneurial organisation (SEO): An organisational legitimacy approach. In J. Robinson, J. Mair, & K. Hockerts (Eds.), *International perspectives on social entrepreneurship research*, 27–74. Palgrave Macmillan.

Oginni, B.O., Dunmade, E.O., & Ogunwole, A.C. (2018). The role of employee's work expectations in job satisfaction and labour turnover in the service industry: A case of selected organisations in Lagos, Ogun and Oyo States Nigeria. *World Journal of Business and Management*, *4*(1), 1–17. https://doi.org/10.5296/wjbm.v4i1.12924

Paliwoda-Matiolańska, A. (2014). *Odpowiedzialność społeczna w procesie zarządzania przedsiębiorstwem*. Wydawnictwo C. H. Beck.

Piwowar-Sulej, K., & Bąk-Grabowska, D. (2021). The impact of mandate contract and self-employment on workers' health -evidence from Poland. *International Journal of Environmental Research and Public Health*, *18*(6), 3138. https://doi.org/10.3390/ijerph18063138

Prince, J.R. (1998). Interpreting the strong interest inventory: A case study. *The Career Development Quarterly*, *46*(4), 339–334.

Rechel, B., Mladovsky, P., Ingleby, D., Mackenbach, J.P., & McKee, M. (2013). Migration and health in an increasingly diverse Europe. *Lancet, 381*(9873), 1235–1245. https://doi.org/10.1016/S0140-6736(12)62086-8

Ronda, E.P., Benavides, F.G., Levecque, K., Love, J.G., Felt, E., & Van Rossem, R. (2012). Differences in working conditions and employment arrangements among migrant and non-migrant workers in Europe. *Ethnicity & Health*, *17*(6), 563–577. https://doi.org/10.1080/13557858.2012.730606

Santos, F. (2012). A positive theory of social entrepreneurship. *Journal of Business Ethics*, *111*, 335–351. https://doi.org/10.1007/s10551-012-1413-4

Serafeimm, G. (2020). Social-impact efforts that create real value. *Harvard Business Review*, *98*(5), 38–48.

Silverman, H. (2014). *Mastering management styles: Expert guidance for managers*. Packt Publishing.

Stephan, U., Patterson, M., Kelly, C., & Mair, J. (2016). Organizations driving positive social change a review and an integrative framework of change processes. *Journal of Management*, *42*(5), 1250–1281. https://doi.org/10.1177/0149206316633268

Strong, E.K., & Campbell, D.P. (1969). *Strong vocational interest blanks manual*. Palo Alto, CA, Stanford University Press.

Stuart, H. (2002). Employee identification with corporate identity issues and implication. *International Studies of Management & Organization*, *32*(3), 28–44. https://doi.org/10.1080/00208825.2002.11043663

Takala, J., Hämäläinen, P., Saarela, K.L., Yun, L.Y., & Manickam, K. (2014). Global estimates of the burden of injury and illness at work in 2012. *Journal of Occupational and Environmental Hygiene*, *11*(5), 326–337. https://doi.org/10.1080/15459624.2013.863131

Ukhova, A. (2018). Influence of labour migration on the economy of Ukraine. *International Scientific Journal Internauka*, *6*(46), 7–9. https://doi.org/10.25313/2520-2057-2018-6-3627

Rzemek, M. (2022). Ukraińcy na polskim rynku pracy. *Rzeczpospolita*. Retrieved April 05, 2022, from https://www.rp.pl/praca-emerytury-i-renty/art36018461-ukraincy-na-polskim-rynku-pracy-sa-najnowsze-dane

Wachowiak, P. (2013). *Wrażliwość społeczną przedsiębiorstwa. Analiza i pomiar*. Oficyna Wydawnicza SGH w Warszawie.

Zhong, N., Wang, S., & Yang, R. (2017). Does corporate governance enhance the common interests of shareholders and primary stakeholders? *Journal of Business Ethics*, *141*(2), 411–431. http://www.jstor.org/stable/44253304.

ZUS. (October 12, 2022). *Rejestr ubezpieczonych*. Retrieved from https://www.zus.pl/portal/pomoc/index.html?rejestr_ubezpieczonych.html

# 6 Impact of job (in)security on work–life balance among service sector employees

*Agata Austen and Katarzyna Piwowar-Sulej*

## Introduction

Interest in the human aspects of work has been growing for years. Some of the crucial constructs related to these aspects are work–life balance (WLB) and job security (JS). Providing both these elements for employees is one of the areas of social impact of organizations, apart from social impact that is exerted on society (Miller, Buys, & Summerville, 2007). It reflects the social impact of employers associated with beneficial outcomes for employees resulting from prosocial intended initiatives (cf. Rawhouser, Cummings, & Newbert, 2019). The authors cited emphasized that social value related to social impact can be created for employees by meeting their needs.

WLB is defined as an efficient, balanced functioning in both professional and private domains and satisfaction gained from minimizing conflicts between these domains. As Lonska et al. (2021) stated, employees' proficiency in harmoniously integrating their professional roles, family responsibilities, and personal pursuits plays a significant role in fostering a healthy environment for both their employers and their families. This balance not only enhances workplace productivity but also supports the emotional and physical well-being of their loved ones, creating a mutually beneficial situation for all parties involved. Extant literature shows that high levels of work–family conflict (WFC) are reflected in poor self-reported health among employees (Mensah & Adjei, 2020) and negatively affect their performance (Lee, Kim, Park, & Yun, 2013).

One of the factors that may positively influence WLB, thereby increasing the social impact of organizations on their employees, is JS (de Lange & Homburg, 2017), which has been described as a psychological state in which employees expect job continuity within an organization (Salas-Vallina, Alegre, & López-Cabrales, 2021). In turn, job stressors such as job insecurity (JI) that stems from the fear of losing one's present job due to unexpected and uncontrollable reasons (De Angelis, Mazzetti, & Guglielmi, 2021) negatively affect one's private life (De Cuyper et al., 2008). In his literature review, De Witte (2005) distinguished the following factors influencing JI: macro-level factors (e.g., the national

DOI: 10.4324/9781003480952-8

unemployment rate and restructuring in a company), "positional" factors (e.g., level of the position, job seniority), and individual psychological factors.

As the literature shows, the COVID-19 pandemic has decreased both the WLB and JS of many employees (Becker et al., 2022; Johnson, Willis, & Evans, 2019; Lee & Tsai, 2022; Nemteanu, Dinu, & Dabija, 2021; Obrenovic et al., 2021). The pandemic as a novel event exposed the lack of clear procedures guiding employee behavior in the workplace, which is emphasized in event system theory (Lin et al., 2021). However, a major reason why an employee experiences JI is an awareness of the reduction in staff levels by the employer (Gallie et al., 2017). Moreover, the negative relationship between JI and WLB was reported in previous research (Hu, Jiang, Probst, & Liu, 2021; Richter, Näswall, & Sverke, 2010). This relationship was also confirmed during the COVID-19 pandemic. It has been suggested that JI affects WLB because employees who fear job security may feel pressure to perform beyond explicit job requirements. JI can result in a fear of uncertain income and working hours (Yu, 2014), negatively affecting WLB.

Since previous economic crises as well as the pandemic have also increased the level of concern among employees about their professional future and financial loss (Hamouche, 2020), it is worth examining the impact of JS on WLB in pre-pandemic and post-pandemic times. Additionally, JS and WLB can change over time; however, there is a scarcity of longitudinal studies on WLB (Lee et al., 2022) and JS (Fried et al., 2003).

Moreover, the problem of JS has become a critical issue for employees working in the service sector, but little research has addressed this issue (Mani, Geetha, & Al-Khaled, 2020). There is also a call for exploring this issue in the service sector, especially during the COVID-19 pandemic (Chhabra & Pandey, 2022). As Mani et al. (2020) emphasized, the service sector is still growing, which implies that companies strive to reach high targets. The latter results in pressure on employees to work overtime. Frontline employees in the analyzed sector experience a high level of emotional labor. Moreover, temporary employment is often used in this sector, which increases JI (Shin & Hur, 2019). The consequences of the pandemic have most significantly affected the service sector, which is often based on the physical presence of customers (e.g., restaurants, gyms, tourism, and public administration). Demand for these services has decreased for two reasons. First, some consumers were afraid to use such services because the process of servicing was a potential way of being infected by the coronavirus. In turn, people who were working in the healthcare industry had to work overtime (Donthu & Gustafsson, 2020). Khan, Niazi, Nasir, Hussain, and Khan (2021) noticed that many studies identified the fear of job loss and lack of financial security as the most substantial consequences of lockdowns. However, the closure of schools and kindergartens also had a direct negative impact on WLB (Carnevale & Hatak, 2020).

In response to the calls presented above, this study aims to assess how the WLB and JS of service sector employees has changed over time, taking into consideration the following periods: before the pandemic (T0), the pandemic (T1), and after the pandemic (T2). Taking the abovementioned arguments into consideration, the authors formulated five hypotheses:

H1: JS decreased after T0 and increased after T1.
H2: WLB decreased after T0 and increased after T1.
H3: JS at an earlier point in time is related to subsequent JS.
H4: WLB at an earlier point in time is related to subsequent WLB.
H5: JS at an earlier point in time is positively related to subsequent WLB.

This study focuses on service sector employees in Poland. Since repeated observations of the same variables over time enable employers to track the behaviors and trends of WLB on a timely basis, this study applies a longitudinal research approach. Moreover, the authors used a mixed-methods approach, combining a survey method with in-depth interviews. The above constitutes the contribution of this study to the JS and WLB research fields.

## Materials and methods

In the first stage of empirical research, a survey was conducted with participants from nine Polish organizations working in different service sectors (e.g., education, information technology, and finance). Similarly to Kinnunen, Feldt, and Bloom (2019), who conducted longitudinal research on employee well-being by sampling different organizations, the authors of the current study wished to include employees from a variety of different jobs.

The survey data was collected in two waves using electronic questionnaires. First, in summer and autumn 2021 (Time 1 – T1), a total of 385 questionnaires were collected. This period reflected the so-called third wave of the COVID-19 pandemic in Poland, because it was hoped that employees had experienced some changes in WLB and JS during the first year of the pandemic. In completing the survey, respondents were also asked to assess their level of WLB and JS before the pandemic (Time zero – T0). Then, in summer 2022 (Time 2 – T2), those employees who responded in 2021 and who were still employed by the same organizations were contacted. In total, data from 235 respondents were analyzed.

Employees were asked to assess their level of JS using a five-item scale adopted from Salas-Vallina et al. (2021). The items addressed such issues as "I feel that job security is almost guaranteed to me in this job" and "If this organization were facing economic problems, employee downsizing would be the last option used". WLB was measured using a four-item questionnaire proposed by Brough et al. (2014). The sample questions were: "I currently have a good balance between the time I spend at work and the time I have available for non-work activities", and "I have difficulty balancing my work and non-work activities (R)". Items were assessed using a seven-point Likert scale. For both JS and WLB, Cronbach's alpha at all points in time was over 0.80.

The average level of variables studied was determined by means of descriptive statistics. Then, correlation analysis was conducted as a preliminary analysis to serve as a basis for the longitudinal analysis. Exogenous variables were chosen on the basis of the values of the Pearson correlation coefficient. In terms of the analysis of results, structural equation modeling (SEM) was implemented using GRETL. Two-stage least squares regression analysis (TSLS) was used to estimate the structural parameters and stochastic structure of the model. SEM is a two-stage analysis technique, where the measurement model is tested in terms of its validity and reliability in the first stage, and hypothesis testing is undertaken in the second stage.

After analyzing the quantitative data, in-depth interviews with one person from each organization were conducted to obtain explanations of the results. The interviews were recorded and lasted for approximately one hour. The focus was first and foremost on explaining the differences between the prior assumptions and empirical evidence.

## Results

The descriptive statistics enabled the authors to test the first and second research hypotheses that relate to changes in the level of JS and WLB over the periods T0, T1, and T2. Although an analysis of the mean values of JS shows the hypothesized trend, and does not confirm it for WLB, it is worth noting that there were groups of respondents who experienced an increase in the level of JS or WLB and the opposite scenario, respectively. For the majority of respondents (51.91%), JS decreased between T1 and T0, but for some of them (13.19%), there was an increase in JS. Comparing data for periods T2 and T1, we can observe an increase in the level of JS (57.7%); yet, 40% of respondents experienced a decrease in JS. Similarly, there were respondents who observed an increase in WLB (20.43% in the period T1–T0 and 49.79% in the period T2–T1). Conversely, for 42.55% of respondents, WLB decreased in the period T2–T1.

To find out whether the changes in the level of analyzed variables were significant, paired samples T-tests were used to examine the differences between T1 and T0 and T2 and T1 for JS and WLB. The values of the T-test for JS0–JS1 (MV=0.43, $p < 0.01$) and for JS1–JS2 (MV=−0.39, $p < 0.01$) make it possible to accept H1. A paired T-test revealed that differences between the mean values of analyzed variables were close to 0 and not statistically significant in the case of WLB. For this reason, H2 cannot be confirmed. The interviewees explained that they experienced lower levels of job security during the pandemic due to a lack of information about the long-term goals of their companies, as well as insufficient training. After the pandemic, the situation stabilized. In the case of WLB, they noticed the benefits of remote working, such as not having to commute to the office and the possibility of taking care of their children. For some of them, the smaller workload resulted in more time spent on private or personal matters. Supervisor support was also an important issue during the pandemic.

The results of correlation analysis are presented in Table 6.1. As supposed, there is a relationship between WLB in periods T0, T1, and T2, although relationship between WLB in periods T0 and T1 is stronger than in periods T1 and T2. For JS, there is correlation only between periods T0 and T1. There is also correlation between JS0 and WLB0, JS0 and WLB1, and between JS1 and WLB1.

For the two variables studied in the three periods, it was possible to present only one SEM model that consisted of two equations which meet the reliability and validity criteria (AIC 3097.38, *p*-value <0.01). JST1 as the dependent variable is 42% explained by JST0 (Table 6.2). Thus, hypothesis H3 can be partially supported. The next equation in the model presents JST1 and WLBT0 as determinants of WLBT1. These variables explain 48% of variance in the dependent variable (Table 6.2). Hence, hypotheses H4 and H5 can be partially confirmed as well.

The interviews enabled the researchers to draw the conclusion that in the periods T0–T1, JS was strongly dependent on employer policies. After the pandemic, employees "came out of their employer box" and noticed other employment

*Table 6.1* Pearson correlation coefficients

| | *JS0* | *JS1* | *JS2* | *WLB0* | *WLB1* |
|---|---|---|---|---|---|
| JS1 | **.672**** | | | | |
| JS2 | .034 | .001 | | | |
| WLB0 | **.272**** | **.177**** | .089 | | |
| WLB1 | **.200**** | **.306**** | .049 | **.675**** | |
| WLB2 | .90 | .75 | .96 | .142* | **.235**** |

*Source:* Own elaboration.

* $p < 05$; ** $p < .01$

*Table 6.2* Estimated model values for JST1 and WLBT1 as dependent variables

| | *Coefficient* | *Std. Error* | *t-ratio* | *p-value* | |
|---|---|---|---|---|---|
| Equation 1 – JST1 as dependent variable, *R*-squared= 0.42 | | | | | |
| const | 1.37 | 0.46 | 2.97 | 0.0033 | *** |
| WLBT1 | −0.14 | 0.13 | −1.10 | 0.2711 | |
| JST0 | 0.77 | 0.06 | 12.45 | <0.0001 | *** |
| Equation 2 – WLBT1 as dependent variable, R-squared = 0.45 | | | | | |
| const | 0.85 | 0.29 | 2.94 | 0.0036 | *** |
| JST1 | 0.17 | 0.05 | 3.37 | 0.0009 | *** |
| WLBT0 | 0.61 | 0.05 | 11.65 | <0.0001 | *** |

*Source:* Own elaboration.

opportunities on the labor market. Although WLBT1 is dependent on WLBT0 and JST1, there is no similar situation after the pandemic, when the requirements of service employees toward their employers began to emphasize flexibility rather than working conditions.

**Discussion**

This study advanced the theoretical understanding of the lagged relationships of both JS and WLB at different points in time. As shown, JS of service sector employees decreased after T0 and increased after T1. Therefore, hypothesis H1 has been supported. However, WLB did not decrease after T0 and did not increase after T1, which is evidence for the negative verification of hypothesis H2. Moreover, this study partially confirmed hypotheses H3 and H4 which assumed that JS and WLB at an earlier point in time were positively related to subsequent JS and WLB. Finally, it demonstrated that job security at an earlier point in time was partially positively related to subsequent WLB, which allows for partial confirmation of hypothesis H5.

The results of testing hypothesis H1 support previous studies which found that the pandemic contributed to job security (e.g., Lee & Tsai, 2022; Nemteanu et al., 2021). The lack of JS is not a perception solely caused by one's personality (something "in your head"). It largely results from the "objective" conditions in which people function (De Witte, 2005). In particular, the inability of employers to formulate long-term employment policy reduced the level of JS during the pandemic. Moreover, as revealed in the partially confirmed H3, one's experiences related to JS had an impact only between T0 and T1.

Although the findings related to hypothesis H2 are surprising, it is worth noting that almost 30% of respondents experienced a decrease in WLB during the pandemic. The findings presented support previous results (Becker, Belkin, Tuskey, & Conroy, 2022; Lee & Tsai, 2022), which emphasize the importance of organizational activities aimed at increasing job flexibility (Ortiz-Bonnin, Blahopoulou, García-Buades, & Montañez-Juan, 2022).

This study also reveals a possible change in factors affecting WLB in different conditions which relate to H5 and H4. Previous studies suggested that JS/JI are generally related to WLB (De Cuyper et al., 2008; de Lange & Homburg, 2017). This study confirmed that this relationship existed during a crisis period, yet not after the pandemic. Moreover, the level of WLB in T0 impacted WLB in T1, but there was no impact of WLB in T1 on WLB in T2. This may be due to a change in expectations toward the more flexible organization of their job, but also more security derived from positive changes on the external labor market.

The practical implications for the presented research enrich the area of organizations exerting social impact on their employees. To maintain a high level of JS, companies should provide intensified communication about the future of the company and employees and continue developmental HR activities. WLB depends not only on JS; therefore, employers should undertake initiatives such as providing a fit between their employees' realities and expectations of remote work (Shirmohammadi, Au, & Beigi, 2022) or offering flexible working hours (Bukowska, Tyrańska, & Wiśniewska, 2021).

The main limitation of the study is the retrospective character of the research that refers to T0. The data was collected in only one country, so the findings cannot be generalized due to possible cultural and situational differences. The other limitation stems from limited variables used in the quantitative research that may explain JS and WLB. Future research may cover other factors that are important to both JS and WLB in the new, post-pandemic environment, which has also been disturbed by the war in Ukraine.

## Note

The paper has been developed within the framework of the research project entitled "Work life balance in a (post) pandemic world" funded from the resources of the University of Economics in Katowice.

## References

Becker, W., Belkin, L., Tuskey, S., & Conroy, S. (2022). Surviving remotely: How job control and loneliness during a forced shift to remote work impacted employee work behaviors and well-being. *Human Resource Management*, *16*, 449–464. https://doi.org/10.1002/hrm.22102

Brough, P., Timms, C., O'Driscoll, M.P., Kalliath, T., Siu, O.-L., Sit, C., & Lo, D. (2014). Work–life balance: A longitudinal evaluation of a new measure across Australia and New Zealand workers. *The International Journal of Human Resource Management*, *25*(19), 2724–2744. https://doi.org/10.1080/09585192.2014.899262

Bukowska, U., Tyrańska, M., & Wiśniewska, S. (2021). The workplace and work-life balance during the COVID-19 pandemic. *Annales Universitatis Mariae Curie-Skłodowska, Sectio H – Oeconomia*, *55*(2), 19–32. https://doi.org/10.17951/h.2021.55.2.19-32

Carnevale, J.B., & Hatak, I. (2020). Employee adjustment and well-being in the era of COVID-19: Implications for human resource management. *Journal of Business Research*, *116*, 183–187. https://doi.org/10.1016/j.jbusres.2020.05.037

Chhabra, B., & Pandey, P. (2022). Job insecurity as a barrier to thriving during COVID-19 pandemic: A moderated mediation model of knowledge hiding and benevolent leadership. *Journal of Knowledge Management*, *27*(3), 632–654. https://doi.org/10.1108/JKM-05-2021-0403

De Angelis, M., Mazzetti, G., & Guglielmi, D. (2021). Job insecurity and job performance: A serial mediated relationship and the buffering effect of organizational justice. *Frontiers in Psychology*, *12*, 1–15. https://doi.org/10.3389/fpsyg.2021.694057

De Cuyper, N., de Jong, J., De Witte, H., Isaksson, K., Rigotti, T., & Schalk, R. (2008). Literature review of theory and research on the psychological impact of temporary employment: Towards a conceptual model. *International Journal of Management Reviews*, *10*(1), 25–51. https://doi.org/10.1111/j.1468-2370.2007.00221.x

de Lange, M.M., & Homburg, V.M.F. (2017). Explaining municipal civil servants' voluntary turnover intentions: Where and why do civil servants go in times of austerity? *Tékhne, 15*(1), 16–25. https://doi.org/10.1016/j.tekhne.2017.07.002

De Witte, H. (2005). Job insecurity: Review of the international literature on definitions, prevalence, antecedents and consequences. *SA Journal of Industrial Psychology, 31*(4), 1–6. https://doi.org/10.4102/sajip.v31i4.200

Donthu, N., & Gustafsson, A. (2020). Effects of COVID-19 on business and research. *Journal of Business Research, 117,* 284–289. https://doi.org/10.1016/j.jbusres.2020.06.008

Fried, Y., Slowik, L.H., Shperling, Z., Franz, C., Ben-David, H.A., Avital, N., & Yeverechyahu, U. (2003). The Moderating effect of job security on the relation between role clarity and job performance: A longitudinal field study. *Human Relations*, *56*(7), 787–805. https://doi.org/10.1177/00187267030567002

Gallie, D., Felstead, A., Green, F., & Inanc, H. (2017). The hidden face of job insecurity. *Work, Employment and Society*, *31*(1), 36–53. https://doi.org/10.1177/0950017015624399

Hamouche, S. (2020). COVID-19 and employees' mental health: Stressors, moderators and agenda for organizational actions. *Emerald Open Research*, *2*, 15. https://doi.org/10.35241/emeraldopenres.13550.1

Hu, S., Jiang, L., Probst, T.M., & Liu, M. (2021). The relationship between qualitative job insecurity and subjective well-being in Chinese employees: The role of work–family conflict and work centrality. *Economic and Industrial Democracy*, *42*(2), 203–225. https://doi.org/10.1177/0143831X18759793

Johnson, S.J., Willis, S.M., & Evans, J. (2019). An examination of stressors, strain, and resilience in academic and non-academic U.K. university job roles. *International Journal of Stress Management*, *26*(2), 162–172. https://doi.org/10.1037/str0000096

Khan, K.I., Niazi, A., Nasir, A., Hussain, M., & Khan, M.I. (2021). The effect of COVID-19 on the hospitality industry: The implication for open innovation. *Journal of Open Innovation: Technology, Market, and Complexity,* *7*(1), 30. https://doi.org/10.3390/joitmc7010030

Kinnunen, U., Feldt, T., & Bloom, J. (2019). Testing cross-lagged relationships between work-related rumination and well-being at work in a three-wave longitudinal study across 1 and 2 years. *Journal of Occupational and Organizational Psychology*, *92*(3), 645–670. https://doi.org/10.1111/joop.12256

Lee, M.-H., & Tsai, H.-Y. (2022). A study of job insecurity and life satisfaction in COVID-19: the multilevel moderating effect of perceived control and work–life balance programs. *Journal of Men's Health*, *18*(1), 21. https://doi.org/10.31083/j.jomh1801021

Lee, M.H., Lee, Y.-C., Huang, C.-H., Wu, C.-F., Hsueh, H.-W., & Wu, H.-H. (2022). A longitudinal study of nurses' work-life balance: A case of a regional teaching hospital in Taiwan. *Applied Research in Quality of Life*, *17*(1), 93–108. https://doi.org/10.1007/s11482-020-09881-8

Lee, S., Kim, S.L., Park, E.K., & Yun, S. (2013). Social support, work-family conflict, and emotional exhaustion in South Korea. *Psychological Reports*, *113*(2), 619–634. https://doi.org/10.2466/21.14.PR0.113x23z3

Lin, W., Shao, Y., Li, G., Guo, Y., & Zhan, X. (2021). The psychological implications of COVID-19 on employee job insecurity and its consequences: The mitigating role of organization adaptive practices. *Journal of Applied Psychology*, *106*(3), 317–329. https://doi.org/10.1037/apl0000896

Lonska, J., Mietule, I., Litavniece, L., Arbidane, I., Vanadzins, I., Matisane, L., & Paegle, L. (2021). Work–life balance of the employed population during the emergency situation of COVID-19 in Latvia. *Frontiers in Psychology*, *12*, 1–15. https://doi.org/10.3389/fpsyg.2021.682459

Mani, V.A., Geetha, S., & Al-Khaled, A.A.S. (2020). Factors of work life balance and its influence on job satisfaction in the service industry. *International Journal of Academic Research in Business and Social Sciences*, *10*(7), 571–589. https://doi.org/10.6007/IJARBSS/v10-i7/7472

Mensah, A., & Adjei, N.K. (2020). Work-life balance and self-reported health among working adults in Europe: a gender and welfare state regime comparative analysis. *BMC Public Health*, *20*(1), 1052. https://doi.org/10.1186/s12889-020-09139-w

Miller, E., Buys, L., & Summerville, J. (2007). Quantifying the social dimension of triple bottom line: development of a framework and indicators to assess the social impact of organisations. *International Journal of Business Governance and Ethics*, *3*(3), 223. https://doi.org/10.1504/IJBGE.2007.014314

Nemteanu, M.-S., Dinu, V., & Dabija, D.-C. (2021). Job insecurity, job instability, and job satisfaction in the context of the COVID-19 pandemic. *Journal of Competitiveness*, *13*(2), 65–82. https://doi.org/10.7441/joc.2021.02.04

Obrenovic, B., Du, J., Godinic, D., Baslom, M.M.M., & Tsoy, D. (2021). The threat of COVID-19 and job insecurity impact on depression and anxiety: An empirical study in the USA. *Frontiers in Psychology*, *12*, 1–15. https://doi.org/10.3389/fpsyg.2021.648572

Ortiz-Bonnin, S., Blahopoulou, J., García-Buades, M.E., & Montañez-Juan, M. (2022). Work-life balance satisfaction in crisis times: From luxury to necessity – The role of organization's responses during COVID-19 lockdown. *Personnel Review*, 2–18. https://doi.org/10.1108/PR-07-2021-0484

Rawhouser, H., Cummings, M., & Newbert, S.L. (2019). Social impact measurement: Current approaches and future directions for social entrepreneurship research. *Entrepreneurship Theory and Practice*, *43*(1), 82–115. https://doi.org/10.1177/1042258717727718

Richter, A., Näswall, K., & Sverke, M. (2010). Job insecurity and its relation to work—family conflict: Mediation with a longitudinal data set. *Economic and Industrial Democracy*, *31*(2), 265–280. https://doi.org/10.1177/0143831X09358370

Salas-Vallina, A., Alegre, J., & López-Cabrales, Á. (2021). The challenge of increasing employees' well-being and performance: How human resource management practices and engaging leadership work together toward reaching this goal. *Human Resource Management*, *60*(3), 333–347. https://doi.org/10.1002/hrm.22021

Shin, Y., & Hur, W.-M. (2019). When do service employees suffer more from job insecurity? The moderating role of coworker and customer incivility. *International Journal of Environmental Research and Public Health*, *16*(7), 1298. https://doi.org/10.3390/ijerph16071298

Shirmohammadi, M., Au, W.C., & Beigi, M. (2022). Remote work and work-life balance: Lessons learned from the covid-19 pandemic and suggestions for HRD practitioners. *Human Resource Development International*, *25*(2), 163–181. https://doi.org/10.1080/13678868.2022.2047380

Yu, S. (2014). Work–life balance – work intensification and job insecurity as job stressors. Labour & Industry: *A Journal of the Social and Economic Relations of Work*, *24*(3), 203–216. https://doi.org/10.1080/10301763.2014.961683

# 7 Importance of the Covid-19 pandemic experience in shaping social impact of organizations

*Dariusz Nowak, Beata Skowron-Mielnik and Krzysztof Janasz*

## Introduction

Latané's theory of social impact is a model that approaches the influence of other people as a result of social forces acting on the individual (Latané, 1981). Rawhouser et al. (2019) defined "social impact as beneficial outcomes resulting from prosocial behavior that are enjoyed by the intended targets of that behavior and/or by the broader community of individuals, organizations, and/or environments." Another definition indicates that enterprises can lead to a general social transformation by imitating prosocial organizational behavior (Bloom & Smith, 2010). However, if companies are to achieve a profound and elaborate social change, they need to find adequate strategies and mechanisms to disseminate and calibrate their social impact (Dees et al., 2004). As a result, social impact can be defined as a significant or positive change that resolves or at least addresses social injustice and other social challenges – in this case those generated by the pandemic. Social impact focuses on direct positive consequences of actions offered by companies to society and its immediate part – employees.

Actions taken in companies in the face of the rapidly spreading Covid-19 pandemic have been an example of enormous social impact in reaction to a global phenomenon and the resulting widespread restrictions. Social distancing has affected business and interpersonal relationships previously based on direct, open, and mutual contact. Given that most of the pandemic restrictions applied directly to employees, it was necessary to implement unconventional ideas, particularly in the field of human resource management. When making decisions, managers had to reconsider, first, how to influence their increasingly dispersed employees and, second, how those decisions would affect employees' families. The following aspects were highlighted as having a particularly negative effect (Awu, 2021; Elayan, 2021):

- The generally defined working conditions such as work health and safety, remuneration, autonomy, and performance evaluation;
- Disturbance of relations in the labor market;

DOI: 10.4324/9781003480952-9

- Part of the workforce working remotely;
- The need to provide employees with tools for remote work;
- Absence of employees who had to care for their children while nurseries, kindergartens, schools, and other institutions offering childcare services were closed;
- The obligation to ensure personal protective equipment for employees exposed to the virus;
- Hindered processes of recruitment, dismissal, motivation, and work assignment;
- No direct contact among employees or between employees, contractors, and other stakeholders;
- Reduced performance.

The listed limitations differed in terms of scope, force of influence, and impact on the company's operation. However, they forced organizations to implement new methods and principles, as reflected in the approach to human resources (Gołembski et al., 2022). The paradox of the new solutions was that, on the one hand, they were to have a positive impact on social resources – employees, co-workers, and their families – and, on the other hand, protect organizations against reduced productivity, which over time prompted entrepreneurs to do the opposite, e.g. force people to return to the office and increase control. As a result, a question arises about the extent of the positive and negative implications of the pandemic experience and related employee management solutions for the shaping of the working conditions also post-pandemically (Eurofound, 2022). The pandemic proved to be a test for employers verifying whether their declared social responsibility for people management was something real. It also made them aware of the importance of employees as capital. Caring for their well-being was no longer merely a way to attract new candidates. Companies' operations depended on the actual health and commitment of employees. Most employers were quick to take action to protect people's health and provide them with a sense of safety, making it their priority to care for the physical and psychological well-being of employees. Nearly 80% of companies in Poland conducted various types of actions addressed to employees during the pandemic, ranging from informing about the pandemic risks (57%) and adequate workplace preparation (54%) to social distancing (45%), remote work (40%), help with childcare (26%), psychological support (6%), and even help with shopping (Kotzian, Pancewicz & Ułamek, n.d.).

In view of the above, the aim of our study was to identify the pandemic-related actions in human resource management implemented by a selected organization and evaluate their importance in shaping the social impact of this organization. Our subject was a company operating on the maintenance and supply market. The studied period covered the time of the pandemic and related restrictions. Conducted in September 2022, a case study was adopted as a research method.

It seemed justified as an approach typically chosen for the analysis of understudied phenomena and explaining causal relationships that are too complex for a questionnaire-based survey and which cannot be explored by means of experimental analysis. The application of this method carries a significant advantage of offering an empirical description of reality, delving into emotions, behavior, and motives.

## Problems related to human resource management during the pandemic

The pandemic emerged as a challenge that requested unconventional solutions to, on the one hand, ensure the continuity of the company processes and, on the other hand, help employees survive this unprecedented situation (Dayal et al., 2021; Hamouche, 2021). Most employees experienced, either directly or indirectly, the negative effects of the pandemic and related restrictions (Collings et al., 2021). Seeking to prevent the risk, enterprises needed to demonstrate agility and flexibility to relocate resources, implement and coordinate appropriate mechanisms, and make an effective use of their potential (Liu et al., 2020).

Until 2020, human resource management was largely traditional and relied on rather rigid definitions of the workplace, rights, and responsibilities, with the performance and atmosphere of work constantly under control. This model featured a strictly defined hierarchy of relations between the respective functions, with decisions made by competent and professionally educated managers (Kambur & Yildirim, 2022). Baert et al. (2020) argue that this model can only be used in "normal times" as it does not take sudden, unexpected, and unpredictable anomalies into account, being founded on the following (Tripathi, 2002):

- Functional, process-oriented aspects, which include human resource planning, recruitment and selection, performance analysis and evaluation, motivation, remuneration, building appropriate relationships between management and employees, training, and development. In this approach, procedures, regulations, specific rules of conduct, and performance stimulation are predominant;
- Control, which includes the monitoring and supervision of employees for compliance with regulations, procedures, and designated rules of conduct. The control levels and scope are agreed upon in a compromise based on group negotiations, whereby individual preferences are not taken into account. People are directly motivated with remuneration, rewards, and fringe and other benefits as dominant tools. According to practitioners, the adoption of an appropriate employee verification and assessment model directly contributes to the achievement of strategic goals, while improving relations between the individual groups of human resources;
- Development of appropriate relationships between management and staff based on informal values and ethical norms. In practice, it is virtually

impossible to reconcile different approaches. Consequently, the task is to work out a consensus where each group's expectations are met to a satisfactory degree. The basic tool to reach agreement is through negotiations between the appointed representatives.

These general features are then accordingly modified to correspond to the profile, domain, and nature of a specific enterprise. However, practice has shown that most companies which based their actions on this traditional management model were not prepared to deal with the risks posed by a crisis situation such as the recent pandemic (Slavić et al., 2021; Wang et al., 2009). The pandemic restrictions created a new and unpredictable business environment. Many practitioners saw them as a challenge that enforced search for new objectives, ways to conduct business, and solutions allowing organizations to survive this difficult period (Hamouche, 2021).

The pandemic restrictions related to human resources were of both direct and indirect character (Bradley, 2022). The former applied to employees and aspects such as temporary layoffs, remote work, quarantine, no requirement to work when on childcare leave, etc., while the latter pertained to altered business conditions and aspects such as movement restrictions and inability to organize meetings, conferences, training courses, or direct visits to contractors' enterprises to solve problems (Carnevale & Hatak, 2020). Another important issue that forced entrepreneurs to redefine their employee management strategies was also shortages in the supply of raw materials, products, and parts, frequently causing downtime. All these factors contributed to work disorganization and reformulation of targets and tasks, leading to reduced performance. In addition, most companies were incapable of providing adequate information to their employees regarding the company strategies and operations intended to tackle the pandemic. They mostly opted for ad-hoc provisional solutions subject to constant modifications. These conditions made it relatively difficult for companies to motivate their employees, which, according to Wong et al. (2020), is crucial when dealing with a crisis.

Changes that needed to be considered and implemented concerned virtually all aspects related to employees: from performance management, training, and self-development to remuneration, recruitment, motivation, health and safety, and interpersonal relationships (Awu, 2021). Hamouche (2020) lists the provision of up-to-date, reliable, and relevant information, working conditions, staffing, performance management, training and career development, compensation management, safety and health management, and employment relationships among the particularly significant challenges of employee management in the pandemic. Moreover, given the multi-faceted character of the situation, changing one function entailed the need to modify others.

In emergency situations, companies must be in possession of reliable, adequate, and up-to-date information as the fundamental requirement for improving their ability to respond to a threat. However, because of the extremely dynamic pandemic changes, most companies had difficulty providing their employees with the right information. Enterprises either did not have direct access to it or the information available to them quickly became outdated and required modification. In many cases, the traditionally used channels of communication failed. The novel and unfamiliar nature of the threat made it necessary to develop new information systems that would enable the proper operation in line with the company's aims and objectives (Mitchell et al., 2021). Analyzing this issue, Elsafty and Ragheb (2020) indicate that problems also concerned other aspects such as insufficient information regarding the company's plans, behavior and response to the pandemic situation, behavior in the workplace, employee support systems, and financial situation. As a result, many entities withdrew from their previous commitments, leaving their business partners alone in the middle of an investment or project (Santacreu & LaBelle, 2022), which generated measurable losses.

Arguably, the Covid-19 pandemic has had the most significant impact on working conditions defined as a combination of the working environment and employment terms and conditions (Eurofound, 2022). Working conditions defined in this manner can be described by several factors such as hygiene factors, health and safety, remuneration, profit sparing, employee benefits, responsibility and accountability, workload, work schedule, occupational stress, work-life balance, commuting and business travel, autonomy, control, organizational culture, performance management, job security, and employment terms and conditions (Spacey, 2018). While the Covid-19 pandemic enforced changes in all indicated areas, the need to switch to remote work proved to be a particularly important issue from the vantage point of the company (Brynjolfsson et al., 2020; Espitia et al., 2021; Nowacki et al., 2021).

Another challenge was the necessity to reorganize the task performance schedules to prevent or significantly limit direct contact between individual workers, particularly those involved in direct production requiring physical presence at work (Koirala & Acharya, 2020). Identification of the workplaces and tasks to be carried out remotely and ensuring the necessary equipment (in particular, means of communication) for that purpose while maintaining efficiency also emerged as a considerable problem (Hamouche, 2020). The changed working mode enforced the modification of remuneration systems, affected performance, disrupted interpersonal relationships, and it had an impact on the mental health of employees (Hamouche, 2020). The pandemic-imposed solutions caused a major disruption to relationships established in the previous periods of cooperation (Claridge, 2018).

According to Cabrera and Cabrera (2005), the relational dimension of social capital emerges from the nature and quality of relationships and connections. In a stable environment, they are characterized by credibility, trust, respect for norms, and identification with other actors. During the pandemic, the basis for changes in this dimension typically involved the reorganization of work and the existing structure in the face of new tasks. The result was usually a new strategy that included reduced working time and, consequently, reduced remuneration, reduced training and qualification costs, suspension of recruitment processes, modification of responsibilities at workplaces due to an increase or reduction of tasks, etc. The latter led to employee dissatisfaction and frustration, which in extreme cases was expressed as public criticism of those whose tasks had to be taken over by other employees. Remote work, perceived by many as a benefit or distinction rather than a modified form of working, could also provide reasons for discontent.

Given the reduced business activity, the demand for workforce, including highly qualified, experienced, and skilled employees, decreased. In addition, many organizations opted for downsizing, suspension of recruitment processes, salary reduction or freeze, and incentive system modifications (Kicheva, 2021). Unpopular and controversial actions contributed to conflicts among employees, as reflected both in decreased performance and deterioration of interpersonal relations. Many employees who lost their jobs changed their profession and found employment in organizations with a completely different business profile. Another significant problem was the recruitment process – the ban on face-to-face meetings effectively hindered the recruitment of new employees. Virtual recruitment and selection methods were developed; however, they proved less effective. In parallel, unstable and unpredictable conditions were conducive to the implementation of flexible forms of work such as temporary agency work and other forms of subcontracted labor, as well as new forms of working derived from a gig economy (Spurk & Straub, 2020).

Performance management emerged as an important area of corporate decision-making associated with significant social impact (Azizi et al., 2021). Its pre-pandemic version relied on traditional tools used to reward and value employees, typically tailored to the organization, its processes, business profile, and the characteristics of individual employees (Göndöcs & Dörfler, 2021), with many organizations unprepared for the unpredictable and unprecedented threat (Mitchell et al., 2021). In the new reality, the assessment measures applied thus far often proved misleading, if not impossible to implement. For example, it was very difficult to settle remote work on an hourly basis, while the task-based approach was burdened with a variety of problems such as the lack of access to the Internet, lack of or difficulties with communication, lack of access to the necessary documentation, etc. Given the changed conditions, task performance measuring had to be limited or in many cases suspended whatsoever. Prasad and Vaidya (2020) highlight that this approach had a negative impact on employees who, forced to work remotely, felt isolated, deprived of information, and overloaded with new responsibilities and requirements. This situation inspired conflicts, generated stressors, and diminished people's commitment and trust, which consequently led to reduced performance. The previously applied tools no longer played a major role in employee performance analysis, which implied the need for their modification or suspension.

As a result of the Covid-19 pandemic, many companies that had previously invested in improving the qualifications of employees were forced to significantly reduce their training plans or rearrange them in a relatively short time, using online platforms and applications (ILO, 2021). This change in the knowledge acquisition methods puts people under a lot of pressure. The latter reflected not only in lower performance and commitment levels but also problems with mental health, well-being, and emotional approach (Bida et al., 2022). In the early days of the pandemic, remote work revealed many issues such as the lack of the technical infrastructure and skills to use communication platforms, the need to prepare digital versions of the training materials, limited access to the Internet, low motivation and commitment, and limited options for the knowledge transfer verification (Romaniuk et al., 2020). Participants of training courses found it difficult to be deprived of direct contact and thus the possibility to exchange views and experience or have a direct discussion. Applications used for the improvement of professional qualifications and career development were not always compatible, requiring the simultaneous use of several of them (Al- Rfou, 2021; Hamouche, 2021). In addition, it should be noted that training and workshops via online applications typically do not enable the acquisition of practical skills, which in many cases are the foundation of an organization's success (ILO, 2021).

Social impact on organizational decisions also included the implementation of specific procedures regarding health and safety at work (Purnima & Ravi, 2021). In particular, measures had to be taken regarding social distancing between employees, limiting the number of people in the room, covering the mouth and nose, using disinfectants, measuring body temperature, etc. The restrictions had a negative effect on both mental and physical health of many employees. On the one hand, they feared the infection and spreading the virus to the household members, but on the other, employees who worked online started feeling isolated and deprived of contact with colleagues and contractors. The basic task for managers was to raise the awareness of the staff in the use of protective measures while limiting the spread of the disease (Hamouche, 2021). In addition, it was necessary to take measures to mitigate risks related to remote work (Jeran, 2016). Among many problems that emerged in that time, the most significant ones included employees working on unsecured home devices, possible data leaks, and ensuring health and safety at work, including mental hygiene (Leśniak, 2020).

The final element that, according to Hamouche (2020), posed a challenge for managers in the face of the spreading pandemic was the relations at work. The measures intended to protect employees from Covid-19 had a negative impact on their quality of life, which deteriorated rapidly (Jennings et al., 2021). The previous work conduct based on social norms such as respect for co-workers, honesty, kindness, camaraderie, and commitment changed dramatically. Negative traits such as jealousy, envy, suspicion, and distrust came to the fore. Employees who had previously cooperated with one another started competing, withholding information and, in some cases, even acting to the detriment of others. The negative social impact of all these aspects was reflected in people's activity, with resignation, discouragement, apathy, and depression gradually taking over. The pandemic was a period of rapid increase in the number of people suffering from depression. In contrast, some researchers highlight that the popularization of remote work had a positive impact on the flexibility and performance (Beňo, 2021; Simenenko & Lentjushenkova, 2021).

While the listed issues related to human capital management concerned virtually all entrepreneurs due to the top-down character of the pandemic regulations, the methods they used also differed in the pre-pandemic times, with certain measures proving easier or more difficult to adjust to the company's specific situation and different experiences resulting from this period. Although faced with the same threat and restrictions, different actors could make different decisions and take actions of different social impacts.

## Research method and characteristics of the studied enterprise

A qualitative approach was adopted as a research method because of the need to gain a better understanding of the research problem at hand. Given that our study was motivated by the search for a deeper insight, the qualitative method was agreed as the most suitable approach. Quantitative methods may prove insufficient in research whose aim is to explore the circumstances and causes and determine the direction of relationships between the phenomena that are new to managers and relate to social aspects of organization management (Maison, 2022). The aim of qualitative research is to recognize the unique character of the studied situation, the nature of the phenomenon, its context, and interaction with other elements. Its major qualities include the researcher's participation as the main tool in data collection and analysis, and the predominance of the extensive verbal description of the phenomenon, its context, and participants. A case study is a type of qualitative research that focuses on empirical inference and exploring a contemporary phenomenon in its natural context (Barratt et al., 2011; Lucas et al., 2018; Rowley, 2002). Our research of actions implemented during the Covid-19 pandemic and their impact on human resource management as part of a company's business operations was conducted as a case study designed to answer the following research questions:

- What actions related to human resource management were implemented by the analyzed company in the first period of the pandemic marked by high levels of chaos, uncertainty, and unpredictability?

- What risks and dangers for the company's human resources were identified in terms of the social impact generated because of the pandemic?
- What actions were taken to mitigate the negative effects disrupting the long-term social and relational capital?
- How did the Covid-19 pandemic risks affect people's individual readiness to solve the emerging problems?
- Was the experience of the pandemic used to shape the positive social impact of the organization? How was it used?

A qualitative research design comprises stages such as case selection, data collection, and data analysis. Our choice of the company was dictated by two observations: (1) the company had not used remote work prior to the pandemic even though its business profile was not a counterindication for it, which suggested that the organizational solutions introduced during the pandemic would not necessarily be limited to a crisis situation and could be continued in regular operating conditions; and (2) the company's operations essentially relied on long-developed business relationships. With that in mind, our study included an analysis of the company's documentation, together with human resource management reports made during the pandemic, participatory observation, and an in-depth interview with the President of the Management Board. It was conducted in September 2022.

The company discussed in this chapter operates under the name of Biuro Handlowo-Usługowe Quay Sp. z o.o. (Quay, n.d.). It is a modern and dynamically developing organization, active both in the Polish and international markets. Its primary business domain is wholesale trade in spare parts for industry and provision of broadly defined production services, including training courses and seminars. The company operates both in the original equipment market (original equipment manufacturer, OEM) and in the spare parts market (maintenance repair and overhaul, MRO). Currently, it employs over 120 people with very high qualifications. The highly specialized business profile enforces the adoption of a two-fold organizational structure. On the one hand, it is based on the traditional functional approach with the entire enterprise managed by the president, but on the other, the flat structure dominates, with every regional manager responsible for several operational employees.

In addition to the traditional organizational units such as Accounting, Human Resources, Legal, and Marketing, the company features two dominant departments. The first is Maintenance and Supply, whose employees are in charge of the organization of deliveries of both standard, unified, and well-known parts and the highly specialized ones. The second is the Sales Department dominated by sales engineers – people with expert knowledge, experience and competencies gained through training and courses organized both by the studied company itself and international partners. Their work is of a specific character and requires direct contact with the client, typically at the client's headquarters, where documentation must be made of the equipment or device for repair or overhaul. Importantly, face-to-face meetings contributed to the development of appropriate relations based on reciprocity, kindness, acceptance, and individual diversity.

In March 2020, the analyzed entity was forced to take unconventional actions. Many manufacturers who were the company's first-tier and second-tier suppliers changed their production schedules, reduced production, or even suspended it for as long as several weeks. Similar challenges were faced by the Sales Department. The sales process became much less predictable, both in terms of activities implemented as part of the transaction cycle and their duration. Clients' interests rapidly shifted from the business-to-business model to the independent search for information about the necessary products and services. The market changes were recognized relatively quickly, which resulted in work optimization in the promotion departments, information adaptation, and extension of online communication. The pandemic also contributed to the expansion of the company's offer, particularly in the field of production services. However, as the component most affected by all these factors and formal restrictions, human resources required specific management decisions.

## Human resource management: actions and their importance during the pandemic

Based on the case study, our analysis focused on the following aspects:

- The characteristics of actions related to human resource management in the first period of the pandemic;
- Identification of risks for the company's human resources in terms of the social impact generated because of the pandemic;
- The possibilities of using the experience from the pandemic to shape the positive social impact of the organization.

Restrictions decreased value and quantity of supplies; reduced sales and disrupted interorganizational relations forced the company to make changes in human resource management. Despite a significant decrease in revenues and profit, it did not opt for redundancies (no employees lost their jobs during that period); however, no recruitment process was carried out in that time, either. The President of the Management Board emphasized that the company developed high-quality relations both between the management and the staff and among employees themselves, which proved to be of great value for the company's operations. In addition, the company's employees were people with appropriate education, competencies, and experience that take years to gain in this industry. Redundancies could lead to a significant reduction in the human capital, which could result in lower revenues and profits, as well as a market loss. This aspect of the organization's social impact proved crucial for the company's other actions and decisions because it built a positive attitude of employees in the face of organizational changes.

The actions implemented by the organization may be categorized into the following:

- Protection of employees and clients against the spread of the disease;
- Introduction of remote work;
- Securing the performance of tasks otherwise implemented by persons who during lockdowns had to focus on childcare;
- Modification of performance evaluation methods;
- Provision of appropriate competencies related to new methods and tools of work.

Because of the legal requirements related to the pandemic, the company's basic task was the development of the corresponding preventive action plan. It needed to consider multiple aspects from the legal requirements, type of work, number of employees in teams jointly responsible for a given task, the plant infrastructure, and technical solutions for the shared use of the equipment and sanitary facilities. Another important element in building relations at work during the pandemic was the possibility for employees to receive childcare allowance for children up to eight years of age. This meant that such employees could not work even for several months, and their workload had to be divided among other employees, frequently giving rise to conflicts and antagonisms (Barboukov & Nowak, 2021).

Given its nature of business, the company had a relatively complicated organizational structure that had to be updated and adapted to current events. First, in compliance with the regulations on special solutions related to the preventing, counteracting, and combating Covid-19, the decision was made to rearrange the workplaces and redistribute employees responsible for day-to-day customer service. This specifically included the installation of partitions between employees and between employees and customers, dispensers with the disinfectant, and the purchase of face masks and visors. Each employee was trained in the risks associated with the virus, also in the context of customer service and employee relations, and appropriate responses in case of infection. The organization of the working day was changed, with selected branches no longer working on Saturdays. Retail sales were significantly reduced. These measures had a positive impact on the long-term social capital. Employees' safety came first, with multiple precautions taken to protect them from the negative effects of the spreading pandemic. Most employees accepted the new rules with understanding, if not satisfaction, particularly in the light of the media coverage of the pandemic consequences in other countries.

Second, the management needed to verify the requirements and responsibilities assigned to each employee (in compliance with the regulations pursuant to which the employer could instruct the employees to perform work as instructed in the employment contract, for a specified period, outside the workplace where it is otherwise carried out). The Management Board decided relatively quickly, in March 2020, to delegate part of the staff to remote work. The main reason was the organization of sales at the company's headquarters – two customer service rooms, with a dozen or so people working in each room at the same time. The situation was similar in the Purchasing Department. Based on the analysis, it was concluded that approximately 75% of the staff could work remotely. Clear and transparent criteria of employees delegated to this type of work were adopted at the very outset. Every employee who could work remotely because of the responsibilities assigned to them in their contract was given the opportunity to do so. In parallel, the work schedule was adopted when employees worked one week from home and another at the company's headquarters. It was also agreed that 50% of the staff would work online every week. In certain cases, upon the prior consent of the business owner, work was provided in the hybrid system of three days of work from home and two in the office. This solution applied to people who had other obligations, most often private, related, for example, to providing care for children or adults. Better office space management and related savings were found to be a positive side effect of remote work.

At the same time, the introduction of remote work inspired problems and specific conflicts for a larger part of the staff as a manifestation of the negative social impact. Predicting the need to provide employees with the appropriate equipment such as efficient laptops, cameras, headphones, speakers, etc., to ensure the smooth operation of the office applications and programs, and thus communication and teamwork, the company ordered several dozen of such sets already at the beginning of the pandemic. However, the implementation of the orders was very slow, with some of them being fulfilled only a few months later. The delays in deliveries generated conflicts, resentment, and disputes over the order of the equipment allocation. Moreover, no procedures were implemented to mitigate the risks related to work from home. On the one hand, this approach was dictated by the previous experience of the highly efficient group of employees working in the field, but on the other, it was a result of the lack of knowledge about the available tools. It was established relatively soon that some employees used several devices for work which were not properly secured, for example, checking their business mail or performing minor tasks on private smartphones and tablets. As a result, the use of private devices was forbidden, while all other devices were secured against malware and data theft. In addition, dedicated applications were installed on company equipment to prevent it from being misused – primarily to prevent its use for private purposes. Many employees had a negative perception of the implemented changes, which in certain cases was expressed as irritation, exasperation and, sometimes, verbal abuse.

Interpersonal relations also deteriorated, particularly over the schedule of work, both on site and remote. Most employees preferred to work from home, with some seeing it as a reward or benefit rather than an externally imposed necessity or obligation. Conflicts and misunderstandings appeared relatively quickly, with each employee presenting specific arguments, motives, and reasons why they should be the first to be entitled to long-term remote work. The basic arguments raised by employees concerned aspects such as complicated or time-consuming commuting, caring for a child or an elderly person, fear of becoming infected, indisposition, etc. In certain cases, they took slightly caricatural forms, where people employed as cashiers, porters, warehousemen, manufacturing employees, direct sales representatives, and those for whom there was no equipment available in the initial period also applied for remote work. Cases of unethical behavior were reported where pressure was exercised on managers or attempts were made to discredit colleagues in the eyes of the management. There were also sporadic cases of denunciation and slander. This implies the negative social impact of the pandemic-driven decisions, with interpersonal relations affected by hostility, aversion, and antipathy. Seeking to counteract these negative trends, the management introduced clear criteria for remote work, which brought positive results relatively quickly and allowed the company to protect its social capital from depreciation. All employees, both those working at the headquarters and in the branches, had to familiarize themselves with the rules that clearly specified who was responsible for what tasks and on what terms and conditions.

Another problem that arose in connection with the pandemic restrictions concerned the closure of schools and other institutions providing care to children. Employees with younger children (up to eight years of age) had to focus on their safety and supervision, which forced them to take childcare leave. As a result, they could work neither on site nor remotely. This problem concerned 20% of employees in the examined company. The division and assignment of new tasks required a thorough analysis of competencies and experience of all employees, while their redistribution took several weeks. The change of responsibilities inspired a significant tension, nervousness, and even agitation among some employees, especially during the period of the analysis and reconstruction of rights and obligations. Most of them did not want to be burdened with extra work (despite the fact that due to the pandemic some of their previous responsibilities were suspended). It should be noted that some employees who opted for childcare leave were absent for several weeks or longer. After their return, they saw many of their previous functions canceled due to the company restructuring, and it was necessary to organize new jobs. Employees who had been on childcare leave were assigned new or modified tasks for which they had to be trained. Some employees were reluctant to change their position, which added to the negative social impact. Contractor service jobs proved particularly problematic, as they frequently involve the need to gain new clients. This issue was resolved spontaneously: employees who found themselves in the new reality remained in their new functions, while others were redistributed based on their previous qualifications.

Remote work settlement is extremely difficult, both from the theoretical and practical point of view. No work monitoring and, consequently, no control was carried out in the studied case. The primary responsibility of employees was to log in to the company's dedicated IT system. Company telephones were also used for control purposes. Nevertheless, in many cases, contact was hindered, employees either did not communicate or communicated with a long delay, they also did not perform the work assigned to them, giving various reasons, ranging from the technical and communication problems to the content-based issues related to, for example, the inability to understand a given task or solve a specific problem. It was pointed out that attempts to explain complicated issues through long chat posts frequently did not bring the expected results and prolonged the entire procedure. This resulted in reduced performance – in some cases, by approximately 20%. Mistakes and shortcomings occurred because of employees' simultaneous engagement in household chores during working hours, distraction, and simple forgetfulness. However, reduced performance was not a general phenomenon, and it rather concerned individual employees who had difficulty finding themselves in the new pandemic situation and for whom contact via e-mail or messenger was not as simple and obvious as a face-to-face conversation at the workplace. In principle, remote work was settled based on the number of hours declared by the employee. Everyone was obliged to log in the number of hours worked in a given period. The evaluation of performance based, for example, on the outcomes was not possible given that the company had no previous experience with such a complicated situation. Based on the assumption that the pandemic itself had a negative impact on the employees' well-being and attitude to work, it was decided that, for the sake of the company and the staff, no meticulous control of employees' activities would be conducted during remote work.

The age structure in the studied company was relatively diverse and covered practically all generations, starting from people who had just entered the labor market to those aged nearly 80. The pandemic enforced the improvement of skills necessary to use IT devices, including a variety of applications for both contractor service and direct communication. People from Generation Y and Z did not have any problems with learning new things. New knowledge was also acquired relatively quickly by those born between 1965 and 1979, i.e. Generation X. In contrast, Baby Boomers found it difficult and frequently saw the new solutions as incomprehensible and complicated. These employees tended to avoid contact with contractors and co-workers, which led to the escalation of conflicts, especially when a given task or project was to be implemented as teamwork. The lack of activity on the part of one team member or the relatively long time spent on a simple task prevented the timely performance of a given priority. As a result, the morale of some employees who, despite their great commitment, did not receive an adequate bonus dropped. The relations deteriorated, particularly between the representatives of different generations. This problem could not be solved during the lockdown. Typically, persons with extensive experience, usually representing older generations, were appointed project managers, while younger workers had to "get the job done." There were cases where the latter refused to cooperate with the former on the grounds of unequal distribution of responsibilities. These disturbances remain visible even today.

The implemented solutions contributed to the development or enhancement of certain tools used in the company's operational activities. All changes were based on a precise analysis and the implementation of creative and smart business solutions. The most important improvements were made in communication, both between the management and the employees and between the employees and contractors. People started to increasingly appreciate the lack of time and territorial constraints, the speed, direct character, and reciprocity resulting from relationships of this type. Another positive aspect of the solutions initially enforced by the pandemic was the continuation of remote work also after the pandemic, enabling flexibility in task performance. Remote work continues to be primarily carried out by people who proved their effectiveness when working from home during the pandemic and whose performance increased at that time despite the lack of control. Other positive aspects related to the impact of the pandemic on the business also include better organization and use of working time, which resulted in increased performance.

## Conclusion

> Shaping social impact consciously may include, for example, providing solutions, taking planned, measurable, and sustainable actions, supporting the community from which the company draws its goods and resources, as well as educating, engaging, and cooperating with people to solve existing problems.
> (Kotzian, Pancewicz & Ułamek, n.d.)

The pandemic and the difficulty of running a business at that time contributed to changes in organizations. While significant, their social impact could not always be predicted or controlled, and it has not always been positive. Mental health issues caused by isolation and social distancing are an example of the latter, while people's solidarity in the face of a threat can serve as a positive example (Yu et al., 2021). Equally alarming is the negative impact of the pandemic on trust, which may continue for years to come, long after the root cause ceases to exist, as the experience of the Spanish flu pandemic shows (Moglie et al., 2020). Another major challenge is the need to combine the place of working with the place of resting when working remotely. Reconciliation of work with everyday habits and family life responsibilities may cause difficulties.

Our case study shows that the Covid-19 pandemic has had a major impact on the operational and strategic actions of the studied company. The pandemic restrictions, both internal and external, disrupted virtually all areas related to human resource management in this enterprise. They affected the communication and information flow, work organization, work planning, recruitment, discipline, performance, punctuality, and all kinds of relationships, both within the organization and with external stakeholders. The decisions that were made had a particular effect on social capital that in many cases had been built for years. The impact was both positive and negative. On the one hand, the company's development was limited, but on the other, the pandemic situation stimulated people to take on new challenges and initiatives. A particularly negative effect could be seen in a shift in the approach to the performance of the assigned responsibilities – from the proactive and growth-driven to one based on minimal commitment and never seeking to exceed beyond the regular. This negative attitude was largely founded on the fear of losing a job, deterioration of working conditions, larger workload, and lower pay.

The social impact of the company's decisions made because of the pandemic has manifested itself in the following:

- Changes in the way in which work is performed – the development of hybrid work and a positive attitude of employees to remote work, also after the pandemic restrictions were lifted;
- Changes in the approach to building business relationships – it is based on IT technologies that enable faster contact, save time otherwise spent on traveling to clients, and therefore reduce the pressure resulting from the pace of work;
- Changes in the approach to performance evaluation – a greater focus on output management rather than controlling the use of the working time, which organizes the roles in the company and provides employees with a clear perspective of what they are accounted for.

All these phenomena can have a positive impact on the physical and psychological well-being of employees in the long term. In the short term, during the pandemic, these positive effects could not always be recognized – first, because of the general chaos and health risks, and second, due to the typical attitude to new solutions. The major handicap was the negative or passive attitude of some employees. In addition, work in teams was either terminated or suspended, which led to reduced performance and disruption of interpersonal relations and, eventually, longer implementation of many projects. The main reason for that was remote work, despite the clear and transparent criteria for who could or could not work from home. In many cases, remote work was perceived as a benefit, especially since it was not subject to any control while the employees' only duty was to keep records of what they did.

As a result of work disorganization, many employees experienced mood disorders and other nervous, psychoactive, and behavioral problems. Constant tension, nervousness, and stress intensified depressive moods that some employees are struggling with to this day. The implemented measures could also shape the social impact on the family life of employees who worked from home; however, given the social sensitivity of this aspect, it was not covered in this study. On the one hand, researchers highlight the time and cost savings for employees who would otherwise have to commute to work, their increased autonomy, and the particularly appreciated flexibility in the division of time for work and family life (Karunarathne, 2021). On the other hand, a sense of isolation, difficulties in combining home with workplace, loss of work-life balance, limitations regarding the family life, workaholism, depression, anxiety due to separation from the team, lower promotion opportunities, and stagnation because of losing a sense of belonging to a group are also indicated (Furmanek, 2015).

The experience from actions implemented by entrepreneurs during the Covid-19 pandemic to shape a positive social impact, both after and regardless of the pandemic, points out two key aspects: employee well-being and work performance. Both are important for employees and employers, and both suffered the most during the pandemic, with one conditioned by the other. While employee well-being is frequently emphasized in research of the pandemic period (Kotzian, Pancewicz & Ułamek, 2023), less attention seems to be paid to work performance. Some authors argue that performance management will require significant changes in the post-Covid-19 world (Wigert & Barrett, 2020; Yang, 2021), where goal setting, organization of individual meetings, feedback, and task and motivation evaluation methods should be considered as important factors affecting employee safety and work performance.

## Acknowledgments

The authors would like to thank the CEO of the company that participated in the survey and Malgorzata Sobczak (Wordlab Solutions – Translating services) for the professional translation of the chapter into English.

## References

Al- Rfou, A. (2021). Remote working environment challenges in the context of the Covid-19 pandemic. *Journal of Asian Business Strategy, 11*(2), 95–103. https://doi.org/10.18488/journal.1006.2021.112.95.103

Awu, E. (2021). The impact of Covid-19 pandemic on human resource management and the role changes of HR manager in an organization. *Academic Research International, 5*(12), 8–14. https://www.researchgate.net/publication/357476915_The_Impact_of_Covid-19_Pandemic_on_Human_Resource_Management_and_the_Role_Changes_of_HR_Manager_in_an_Organization

Azizi, M.R., Atlasi, R., Ziapour, A., Abbas, J., & Naemi, R. (2021). Innovative human resource management strategies during the Covid-19 pandemic: A systematic narrative review approach, *Heliyon, 7*(6), 1–11. https://doi.org/10.1016/j.heliyon.2021.e07233

Baert, S., Lippens, L., Moens, E., Sterkens, P., & Weytjens, J. (2020). *How do we think the Covid-19 crisis will affect our careers (if any remain)?* GLO Discussion Paper, *520*, Global Labor Organization (GLO). https://docs.iza.org/dp13164.pdf

Barboukov, A., & Nowak, D. (2021). The effect of Covid-19 on the operating activity of the enterprise - case study. In K. Kazojć (Ed.), *Zarządzanie przedsiębiorstwem w zmiennym otoczeniu: wiedza - decyzje – innowacje*, 97–106. Wydawnictwo volumina. pl Daniel Krzanowski, 161 p. ISBN 978-83-7867-826-7.

Barratt, M., Choi, T.Y., & Li, M. (2011). Qualitative case studies in operations management: Trends, research outcomes, and future research implications. *Journal of Operations Management*, *29*(4), 329–342. https://doi.org/10.1016/j.jom.2010.06.002

Beňo, M. (2021). The advantages and disadvantages of E-working: An examination using an ALDINE analysis. *Emerging Science Journal, 5,* Special Issue "Covid-19: Emerging Research", 11–20. https://doi.org/10.28991/esj-2021-SPER-02

Bida, O., Kuczaj, O., & Czyczuk, A. (2022). Wpływ pandemii Covid-19 na rozwój edukacji. *Annales Universitatis Mariae Curie-Skłodowska, XXXV*(1), 33–43. https://doi.org/10.17951/j.2022.35.1.33-43

Bloom, P.N., & Smith, B.R. (2010). Identifying the drivers of social entrepreneurial impact: Theoretical development and an exploratory empirical test of SCALERS. *Journal of Social Entrepreneurship*, *1*(1), 126–145. https://doi.org/10.1080/19420670903458042

Bradley, C. (2022). *The impact of the Covid-19 Pandemic on the human resource management practices of the American auto industry*. Honors Theses *3527*. https://scholarworks.wmich.edu/honors_theses/3527

Brynjolfsson, E., Horton, J.J., Ozimek, A., Rock, D., Sharma, G., & TuYe, H.-Y. (2020). *Covid-19 and remote work: an early look at US data.* Working Paper Series, National Bureau of Economic Research. https://www.nber.org/system/files/working_papers/w27344/w27344.pdf

Cabrera, E., & Cabrera, A. (2005). Fostering knowledge sharing through people management practices. *The International Journal of Human Resource Management, 16*(5), 720–735. https://doi.org/10.1080/09585190500083020

Carnevale, J.B., & Hatak, I. (2020). Employee adjustment and well-being in the era of Covid-19: Implications for human resource management. *Journal of Business Research, 116*, 183–187. https://doi.org/10.1016/j.jbusres.2020.05.037

Claridge, T. (2018). Dimensions of social capital - structural, cognitive, and relational. *Social Capital Research, 1,* 1–4. https://www.socialcapitalresearch.com/wp-content/uploads/2018/01/Dimensions-of-Social-Capital.pdf

Collings, D.G., McMackin, J., Nyberg, A.J., & Wright, P.M. (2021). Strategic human resource management and Covid-19: Emerging challenges and research opportunities. *Journal of Management Studies*, *58,* 1378–1382. https://doi.org/10.1111/joms.12695

Dayal, G., Thakur, D.J., & Asamoah-Appiah, W. (2021). The challenges of human resource management and opportunities for organization during (Covid-19) pandemic situation. *International Journal of Applied Research*, *7*(6), Part A, 9–12. https://doi.org/10.22271/allresearch.2021.v7.i6Sa.8601

Dees, J.G., Anderson, B.B., & Wei-Skillern, J. (2004). Scaling social impact-strategies for spreading social innovations. *Stanford Social Innovation Review*, *1*(4), 24–32.

Elayan, M.B. (2021). The impact of Covid-19 on human resource practices. In M. Alshurideh, A.E. Hassanien, & R. Masa'deh (Eds.), *The effect of coronavirus disease (Covid-19) on business intelligence.* Studies in Systems, Decision and Control, *334*, 311–321, Springer, Cham. https://doi.org/10.1007/978-3-030-67151-8_18

Elsafty, A.S., & Ragheb, M. (2020). The role of human resource management towards employees retention during Covid-19 pandemic in medical supplies sector – Egypt. *Business and Management Studies, 6*(2), 50–59. https://doi.org/10.11114/bms.v6i2.4899

Espitia, A., Mattoo, A., Rocha, N., Ruta, M., & Winkler, D. (2021). Pandemic trade: Covid-19 remote work and global value chains. *The World Economy, 45*(2), Special Issue: Covid 19, Trade and Trade Policy. https://doi.org/10.1111/twec.13117

Eurofound. (2022). *Working conditions in the time of Covid-19: Implications for the future*. European Working Conditions Telephone Survey 2021 series, Publications Office of the European Union, Luxembourg. https://www.eurofound.europa.eu/publications/report/2022/working-conditions-in-the-time-of-covid-19-implications-for-the-future

Furmanek, W. (2015). Zalety i wady telepracy. *Edukacja - Technika – Informatyka, 1*(11), 127–135. http://cejsh.icm.edu.pl/cejsh/element/bwmeta1.element.desklight-64a7d41d-2819-4f8a-89f3-e9104fdf368e

Gołembski, M., Skowron-Mielnik, B., & Wojtkowiak, G. (2022). Identification of human resource risk by managers and employees through the lens of the Covid-19 pandemic. *Scientific Papers of Silesian University of Technology – Organization and Management Series, 155*, 83–100. https://doi.org/10.29119/1641-3466.2022.155.7

Göndöcs, D., & Dörfler, V. (2021). *Post-Covid performance management the impact of remote working experience during the pandemic*. Paper presented at 12th IEEE International Conference on Cognitive Infocommunications, Győr, Hungary. https://strathprints.strath.ac.uk/78026/1/Gondocs_Dorfler_IEEE_ICCIC_2021_Post_Covid_performance_management_the_impact.pdf

Hamouche, S. (2021). Human resource management and the Covid-19 crisis: Implications, challenges, opportunities, and future organizational directions. *Journal of Management & Organization, 29*(5), 799–814. https://doi.org/10.1017/jmo.2021.15

Hamouche, S. (2020). Covid-19 and employees' mental health: Stressors, moderators and agenda for organizational actions. *Emerald Open Research, 2*(15), 1–15. https://doi.org/10.35241/emeraldopenres.13550.1

ILO. (2021). *Skills development in the time of Covid-19: Taking stock of the initial responses in technical and vocational education and training*. International Labour Organization and World Bank. https://www.ilo.org/wcmsp5/groups/public/---ed_emp/---ifp_skills/documents/publication/wcms_766557.pdf

Jennings, W., Stoker, G., Valgarðsson, V., Devine, D., & Gaskell, J. (2021). How trust, mistrust and distrust shape the governance of the Covid-19 crisis. *Journal of European Public Policy, 28*(8), 1174–1196. https://doi.org/10.1080/13501763.2021.1942151

Jeran, A. (2016). Praca zdalna jako źródło problemów realizacji funkcji pracy. *Opuscula Sociologica, 2*(16), 49–61. http://cejsh.icm.edu.pl/cejsh/element/bwmeta1.element.desklight-b9fdcab5-1f55-4768-b6f6-6f61c548e7b0

Kambur, E., & Yildirim, T. (2022). From traditional to smart human resources management. *International Journal of Manpower, 44*(3), 422–452. https://doi.org/10.1108/IJM-10-2021-0622

Karunarathne, P.D. (2021). A SWOT analysis of remote working based on review of literature. *International Journal of Business, Technology, and Organizational Behavior, 1*(4), 253–262. https://doi.org/10.52218/ijbtob.v1i4.102

Kicheva, T. (2021). Challenges for HR- practitioners during and after a pandemic. *Vanguard Scientific Instruments in Management, 17*. Retrieved from https://vsim-journal.info/index.php?journal=vsim&page=article&op=view&path[]=279

Koirala, J., & Acharya, S. (2020). *Dimensions of human resource management evolved with the outbreak of Covid-19*. Online. SSRN Scholarly Paper, 24 April 2020. Rochester, NY. 3584092. https://doi.org/10.2139/ssrn.3584092

Kotzian, J., Pancewicz, M., & Ułamek, E. (n.d.) Social impact and employee well-being. *Raport IHR*. Retrieved January 24, 2023, from https://drive.google.com/file/d/1KSUQwHNWQYg-jxti3gmY1M9y3rzc8dLY/view

Latané, B. (1981). The psychology of social impact. *American Psychologist, 36*(4), 343–356. https://doi.org/10.1037/0003-066X.36.4.343

Leśniak, J.G. (2020). *Prof. Gładoch: Praca zdalna to ryzyko pracodawcy i pracownika*. Retrieved from https://www.prawo.pl/kadry/praca-zdalna-zagrozenia-czas-pracy-efektywnosc-pracy-oszczednosci,502529.html

Liu, Y., Lee, J.M., & Lee, C. (2020). The challenges and opportunities of a global health crisis: The management and business implications of Covid-19 from an Asian perspective. *Asian Business & Management, 19*, 277–297. https://doi.org/10.1057/s41291-020-00119-x

Lucas, P., Fleming, J., & Bhosale, J. (2018). The utility of case study as a methodology for work-integrated learning research. *International Journal of Work-Integrated Learning, 19*(3), 1–8. https://files.eric.ed.gov/fulltext/EJ1196748.pdf

Maison, D. (2022). *Jakościowe metody badań społecznych. Podejście aplikacyjne*. Wydawnictwo Naukowe PWN.

Mitchell, F., Nørreklit, H., Nørreklit, L., Cinquini, L., Koeppe, F., Magnacca, F., Mauro, S.G., Jakobsen, M., Korhonen, T., Laine, T., & Liboriussen, J.M. (2021). Evaluating performance management of Covid-19 reality in three European countries: A pragmatic constructivist study. *Accounting, Auditing & Accountability Journal, 34*(6), 1345–1361. https://doi.org/10.1108/AAAJ-08-2020-4778

Moglie, M., Alfani, G., Gandolfi, F., & Aassve, A. (2020). *Pandemics and social capital: From the Spanish flu of 1918–19 to Covid-19*. CEPR. Retrieved from https://cepr.org/voxeu/columns/pandemics-and-social-capital-spanish-flu-1918-19-covid-19

Nowacki, K., Grabowska, S., & Lis, K. (2021). The impact of remote working during the Covid-19 epidemic on employee well-being. *Multidisciplinary Aspects of Production Engineering, 4*(1), 245–254. https://doi.org/10.2478/mape-2021-0022

Prasad, K., & Vaidya, R.W. (2020). Association among Covid-19 parameters, occupational stress and employee performance: An empirical study with reference to agricultural research sector in Hyderabad Metro. *Sustainable Humanosphere, 16*(2), 235–253. https://www.researchgate.net/profile/Kdv-Xxx/publication/341211360

Purnima, J.L., & Ravi, J. (2021). A conceptual study: An impact of pandemic on human resource management. *International Journal of Business and Management Invention, 10*(1), 45048. https://doi.org/10.35629/8028–1001034548

Quay. (n.d.). Retrieved November 20, 2022, from https://www.quay.pl

Rawhouser, H., Cummings, M., & Newbert, S.L. (2019). Social impact measurement: Current approaches and future directions for social entrepreneurship research. *Entrepreneurship Theory and Practice, 43*(1), 82–115. https://doi.org/10.1177/1042258717727718

Romaniuk, M.W., Łukasiewicz-Wieleba, J., & Kohut, S. (2020). Nauczyciele akademiccy wobec kryzysowej edukacji zdalnej. *E-mentor, 5*(87), 15–26. https://doi.org/10.15219/em87.1489

Rowley, J. (2002). Using case studies in research. *Management Research News*, *25*(1), 16–27. https://doi.org/10.1108/01409170210782990

Santacreu, A.M., & LaBelle, J. (2022). Global supply chain disruptions and inflation during the Covid-19 pandemic. *Federal Reserve Bank of St. Louis Review*, *104*(2), 78–91. https://doi.org/10.20955/r.104.78-91

Simenenko, O., Lentjushenkova, O. (2021). Advantages and Disadvantages of Distance Working. Paper presented at the Perspectives of Business and Entrepreneurship Development: Digital Transformation for Business Model Innovation At: Brno University of Technology, Faculty of Business and Management, Brno, Czech Republic, September 16–17. Retrieved from https://www.researchgate.net/profile/Oksana-Lentjushenkova/publication/357484444_Advantages_and_Disadvantages_of_Distance_Working/links/61d062d6e669ee0f5c7c04b3/Advantages-and-Disadvantages-of-Distance-Working.pdf

Slavić, A., Berber, N., Poór, J., & Aleksić, M. (2021). *Human resource management in the time of Covid-19 pandemic: Trends and challenges.* Conference: 26th International Scientific Conference Strategic Management and Decision Support Systems in Strategic Management. https://doi.org/10.46541/978–86–7233–397–8_124

Spacey, J. (2018). *17 types of working conditions*. Retrieved from https://simplicable.com/new/working-conditions

Spurk, D., & Straub, C. (2020). Flexible employment relationships and careers in times of the Covid-19 pandemic. *Journal of Vocational Behavior*, *119*(103435), 1–4. https://doi.org/10.1016/j.jvb.2020.103435

Tripathi, P.C. (2002). *Human resources development.* Sultan Chand & Sons.

Wang, J., Hutchins, H.M., & Garavan, T.N. (2009). Exploring the strategic role of human resource development in organizational crisis management. *Human Resource Development Review*, *8*(1), 22–53. https://doi.org/10.1177/1534484308330

Wigert, B., & Barrett, H. (2020). *Performance management must evolve*. Retrieved from https://www.gallup.com/workplace/318029/performance-management-evolve-survive-covid.aspx

Wong, E., Ho, K., Wong, S., Cheung, A., & Yeoh, E. (2020). *Workplace safety and coronavirus disease (Covid-19) pandemic: survey of employees.* World Health Organization. https://doi.org/10.2471/BLT.20.255893

Yang, K. (2021). Performance management for a Post-Covid-19 world. *Public Integrity, 23,* 636–642. https://doi.org/10.1080/10999922.2021.1971456

Yu, B., Luo, M., Liu, M., Zhou, J., Yang, S., & Jia, P. (2021). Social capital changes after COVID-19 lockdown among youths in China: COVID-19 Impact on lifestyle change survey (COINLICS). *Frontiers in Public Healrh, 16*(2021), 1–8. https://doi.org/10.3389/fpubh.2021.697068

# 8 Social impact of diversity management by inclusive organizations

*Joanna Bernacka and Marcin Gołembski*

## Introduction

The intensification of international movements, increased mobility of employees in terms of geography and occupation, and demographic changes make the work environment more and more diverse (Shore et al., 2009). Multinational corporations face formidable challenges due to growing globalization, technological change, and organizational complexity. To deal with these challenges, multinational corporations rely on innovation and renewal to achieve a sustainable, competitive advantage and to survive in the long run (Ahuja & Lampert, 2001; Blomkvist, Kappen, & Zander, 2017; Bower & Christensen, 1995; O'Reilly & Tushman, 2013). Corporate headquarters are responsible for providing the strategic leadership necessary to leverage corporate resources across regions and divisions to fully utilize the innovative capacity of the multimarket firm (Dewhurst et al., 2015; Menz, Kunisch, & Collis, 2015). In particular, the way headquarters are staffed as well as the background characteristics of top management team members are likely to have an important impact on the strategic leadership, corporate entrepreneurship initiatives, and subsequent innovation performance of multinational corporations (Heavey & Simsek, 2013; Menz et al., 2015; Talke, Salomo, & Rost, 2010). This resonates well with the claim in the upper echelon's literature that organizations are a reflection of their top managers (Hambrick & Mason, 1984). Research in this tradition has suggested that diverse backgrounds and expertise in top management help firms to address the business challenges associated with environmental uncertainty and frequent technological change (Certo, Lester, Dalton, & Dalton, 2006; Heavey & Simsek, 2013; Knight et al., 1999; Simons, Pelled, & Smith, 1999). Diversity is a fundamental value of every society, and what's more, diversity just pays off (Strzelczak, 2019), which is why it is one of the most important business topics in the world of the last two decades. Many companies introduce diversity management strategies in the hope of benefiting from an increasingly diverse workforce (Jayne & Dipboye, 2004). On the other hand, it is a controversial issue in many organizations, less examined and understood than other areas of management (Gross-Gołacka, 2018).

DOI: 10.4324/9781003480952-10

At the organizational level, the organizational culture plays a very important creative function for the atmosphere of equality, inclusion, and diversity management in general (Warwas, 2019). It is also one of the fundamental forms of corporate capital, bringing profit to both itself and its members.

***Understanding of diversity vs. inclusion***

The literature on the subject provides many established, multidimensional definitions of the concept of "diversity", whereas in relation to the concept of "inclusion", the terminological output is still in statu nascendi. Diversity focuses its optics on "who?" and "what?". Inclusion, on the other hand, refers to "how?". *Inclusion* is a specific behavior that adopts and takes into account diversity. It is about empowering an employee by respecting and appreciating what distinguishes them in terms of age, gender, ethnicity, religion, disability, sexual orientation, education, and national origin. The inclusion process engages everyone and makes people feel valued and essential to the success of the organization. While diversity can be achieved by employing different people in an organization, inclusion is a process that involves changing the way they think in an organization. Inclusion is a sort of organizational effort that is about accepting and treating people and groups with different backgrounds, appropriately and equally. These differences may be obvious, such as national origin, age, race and ethnic origin, religion, beliefs, gender, marital status, and socio-economic status, or they may be secondary and result from, e.g., education, training, professional experience, and positions held (Przytuła, 2020). The primary focus is on implementing inclusion policies at all levels.

The 2018 Gallup Report defines "Diversity" as the "full spectrum of human differences". It refers to unique characteristics in people, including gender, sexual orientations, religious beliefs, age, ethnicities, races, geographical locations, cultures, class, physical abilities, etc. "Diversity" in the workplace refers to an organization's workforce comprising people from different genders, sexual orientations, religions, races, ethnicities, ages, etc. A distinction between "employee diversity", "managing employee diversity", and managing "human resource diversity" has to be made. "Employee diversity" is a concept that originated in the 1960s in the USA, signifying the presence of differences among employees due to their individual characteristics, primarily race and gender at the time. "Diversity management" of employees emerged in the 1980s in the USA, drawing from practices and models derived from equal opportunities policies. This approach was a response to instances of discrimination in the labor market and the disadvantages experienced by certain groups of employees due to their individual characteristics. The concept of managing "human resource diversity" in an organization was developed later (1990s). This concept deals with the diversity of employees treated as the resource category of an organization and, therefore, constituting one of the management areas in an organization. Hence, it is related to the specific goals, consequences, and effects for the organization and its employees, the eventual occurrence of which is determined by many different factors. Therefore, models for the optimization of the use of this organizational resource are sought after, especially by practitioners (Rakowska, 2021).

Diversity and inclusion refer to the set of strategies, policies, and missions adopted by a company to create and encourage an inclusive workplace that attracts a diverse pool of talents from various cultural backgrounds. In addition to providing a business advantage, companies with D&I policies and practices are more creative and supportive of different voices, thereby attracting top talents in any industry. Although often used together, diversity and inclusion are two different terms (Gross- Gołacka, 2018).

World View Diversity is precisely what the term suggests: the difference and diversity in people's world views – our unique experiences, knowledge of history, beliefs, political philosophies. Inclusion in the workplace means ensuring that every employee feels included and a part of the team. An inclusive workforce will feel valued, seen, heard, and respected. Johnny C. Taylor, Jr., the CEO of the Society of Human Resource Management, mentions that many companies are now swapping the D&I label for I&D so that the primary focus is on implementing inclusion policies at all levels (O'Donnovan, 2018).

Managing people at work is deemed significant for the survival of enterprises. Most managers view the diversity of employees as an organizational resource. Therefore, just like other resources, e.g., materials or finances, it needs to be managed. Human resources within an organization, diversified based on a set of employee characteristics, are assigned specific goals and related consequences (Rakowska, 2021). It is noted that having a suitably diversified human resource within an organization is associated with both negative and positive effects (Hewstone, 2015; Wilton, 2015). Negative differentiation may concern the level of an individual, group, and the entire organization (Leslie, 2019; Nielsen, 2010). The social identity theory (Tajfel, 1982) and the related self-categorization theory (Turner et al., 1987) play an important role in understanding why an organization may experience negative and positive effects. The form of social identity becomes a function of social differentials. It is emphasized that individuals perceive groups of similar individuals as their own, and groups of individuals with different demographic characteristics as aliens. This leads to prejudices and favoritism among the members of one's own group (Cole & Salimath, 2013), which may ultimately cause conflicts (Nishii et al., 2018), which will negatively affect the integration processes (Nishii, 2013) and may influence the decision to leave from work (Peretz et al., 2015). Other related effects observed are decreasing worker morale (Tsui et al., 1992) and decreased labor productivity (Chatman et al., 1998). The lack of tools for quantifying the benefits of diversity in an organization leads companies to navigate this area intuitively. Measuring an inclusive culture, the effects of diversity management and anti-discrimination measures are often either inaccurate or arbitrary and does not allow companies to track the direction of the processes or it simply does not exist at all. There are several reasons to this: managers do not have the knowledge or belief that diversity and inclusion translate into company results, despite ample empirical research confirming such a relationship; the lack of clear definitions of basic concepts makes it difficult to determine what to measure accurately; and the use of vague indicators (Faracik, 2019). Thus, Brenman (2012) proposes several indicators for measuring inclusive culture, including: the percentage of minorities among employees at various levels of the organizational structure, the number of complaints about discrimination, the level of employee satisfaction with interpersonal relations and working conditions, the number of promotions from among minorities, the level of remuneration, position of the company/brand in the ranking of the best employers, awards for organizations from various stakeholders. There is a research gap between what practitioners need and what scientists are offering to them. The intention of this chapter, of a propaedeutic nature, is to present the importance of diversity management by multinational companies and its social impact[1]. The study also makes an attempt to find the way of measurement of the social impact, both internal and external.

## Materials and method

### *Method research paradigm*

The chapter aims to answer the one main research question: "*What are practitioners' views on and attitudes to diversity management by inclusive organizations and its social impact?*"

A research paradigm is defined as a "set of common beliefs and agreements" shared by researchers regarding "how problems should be understood and addressed" (Kuhn, 1962). Therefore, it represents a specific way of perceiving the world, a worldview that shapes the way one seeks answers to research questions. Due to the inherent nature of social science, where standardization possibilities are limited, achieving sample representativeness and data normalization for maximum depersonalization of the research process required conducting in-depth, semi-structured interviews with 17 experts. To gain insight into the experts' perspective, a set of specific questions was repeatedly asked during the semi-structured interviews, followed by open discussions to explore their understanding of the social impact of diversity management and inclusion within an international and multinational company. Qualitative research with a social constructivist ontology was employed. In-depth interviews (IDIs) and personal observations were conducted to expand on epistemology with hitherto unknown ontological facts. To understand the individual expert viewpoints, the interpretivism paradigm was utilized as a framework for the social constructivist approach. This approach posits that diversity should be inclusive (rather than purposefully managed) within corporate culture to achieve a positive social impact, both internally (among individuals within the company) and externally (in broader society).

The authors argue that enforced diversity management programs, when not genuinely integrated into the corporate culture, may have limited to no positive social impact both internally and externally. Thus, influencing the way diversity should be approached is crucial for its social impact.

#### *Data collection process*

Purposeful sampling with a minimum variation of cases was found appropriate to generate the best insights on diversity management by inclusive organizations and its social impact. Purposeful sampling is valuable in qualitative research, particularly in populations which are difficult to access, especially when combined with grounded theory approach. The sample comprises 17 experts, most of whom are at the highest executive, senior management levels, boasting extensive experience in multicultural companies or global corporations with locations worldwide. Simultaneously, and to ensure the best possible outcomes, the authors aimed for a broader participant profile, encompassing various industry sectors, generations, and genders among interviewees.

#### *Validity criteria*

To enhance the quality and trustworthiness of the research, the authors catered for interrater reliability and reflective subjectivity. Intercoder reliability was achieved through the thorough documentation of the research process and transparency of decision-making processes among the researchers, including the authors overarching research paradigm, sampling strategy, data collection through expert interviews, and description of the context of research (Gwet, 2014). Thus, the authors were able to achieve homogeneity and a degree of agreement when evaluating and interpreting their findings. Another validity criterion consisted of the authors' self-reflection during data collection and analysis. Authors' awareness of assumptions, perceptions, and communication styles contributes to the interpretation of data and helps strengthen their validity. The continuous process of self-monitoring thus led to deeper reflection and critical thinking in case concepts and themes. Self-reflection hence led to a more balanced view of subjectivity and included various types of memos, e.g., of context, own feelings, assumptions, and propositions.

#### *Data analysis*

The data has been transcribed and manually analyzed according to an integrative approach developed by Kruse (2014), mainly referring to the method of documentary interpretation and ethno-methodological conversation analysis

(Bergmann, 2010). It included five main steps: description, structuring and clustering of the results, condensation of the results, theorizing, and application of categories to other interviews. The microanalysis mainly focused on language comprising the following levels of attention: content, positioning, syntax, semantics, and interaction patterns. Following Kruse (2014), the main aim in data analysis was to elaborate on common beliefs, images, subjective patterns, themes, and views. The inductive method allowed the analysis of data during the collection process. After analyzing interview by interview, the authors developed cross-case typologies of social impact of diversity management based on the grounded classification approach of the grounded theory (Strauss & Corbin, 1998). In order to group common views and experts' comments, Atlas.ti 22 software had been used. Following the discovered logical patterns of the single cases and their characteristics, the authors formed a common meaning among the interviews.

### *Research results*

The 17 experts were selected from the group of practitioners exposed to international environment and from different organizations with the focus on the multinational companies or international companies with diversity. Over 50% of the experts either used to be employed or are still working for Schlumberger (9 out of 17). Another three experts used to be employed and one remains an employee of Pratt &Whitney Canada. To get a chance of the opposite or a different point of view, some experts are employees of other organizations, two of them hold PhD degrees. Schlumberger Limited (NYSE: SLB) is the world's largest oilfield services company. It employs over 126,000 people from over 140 countries, working in some 85 countries. The most important was to gather experts who were exposed to and are the natural practitioners of diversity management programs, no matter how the organization names it: D&I, I&D, or DEI. Therefore, it has become paramount to get the experts' perspective on the effectiveness of such programs and strategies, as well as to find out the social impact and get their insight and suggestions on how to measure it.

Most experts agreed that the diversity should be a part of the organization's values and preferably embedded in the organizational culture in the long run. One of the experts Mr. Mario Faria referred to the famous words of Peter Drucker: "*culture eats strategy for breakfast*", which exactly shows why there is a necessity to work toward creation of the diverse culture rather than create a great strategy that remains an empty statement on the wall. According to him, the diversity should be actively managed, and while it becomes more embedded in the organizational culture, it will be less managed, which exactly reflects the author's point of view further presented at Figure 8.1.

According to the above at the very start the diversity should be actively managed, and while more embedded in the organizational culture, it will be less

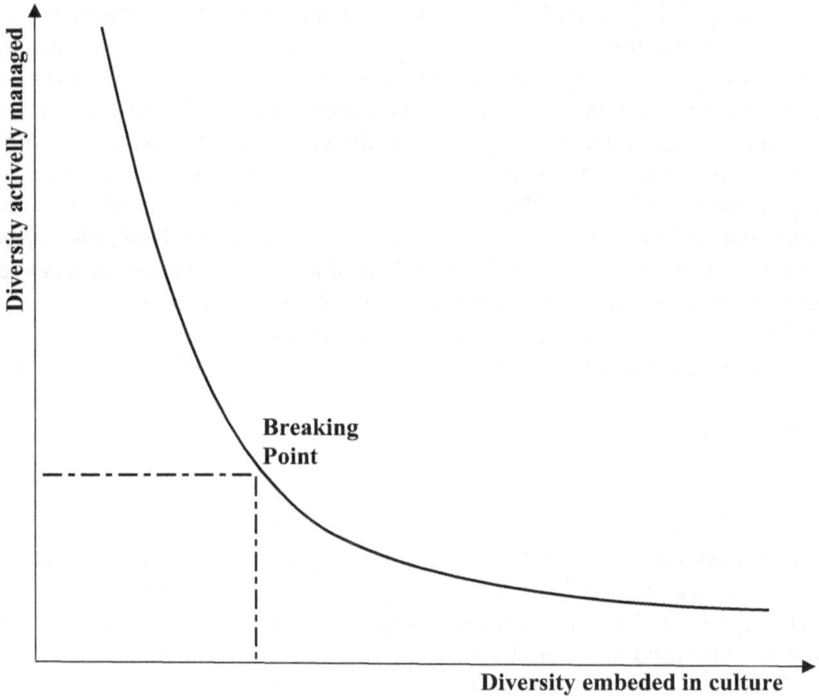


*Figure 8.1* Diversity actively managed vs. diversity embedded in the culture

*Source:* Own elaboration.

managed. The breaking point would show that there is sufficient awareness in the organization and commitment to further work on diversity inclusion toward solid embedment in the organization's culture. Regarding measurement, it became easier to find the way internally, within the organization rather than externally – outside of the organization. Some experts had really a lot of great suggestions worth considering. One of them was to measure the social impact within the organization by applying the employee net promoting score (eNPS). An eNPS survey asks one simple question: "On a scale of 0–10, how likely are you to recommend this company to your best friend?" If they answer 9–10, they are a promoter; if they answer 0–6, they are a detractor. While taking this eNPS survey into consideration, it can be a way of measuring the social impact. However, according to authors' opinion, the above question should be specifically related to diversity and inclusion, as there are many aspects beyond diversity in the company that might impact that score. Consequently, to obtain a precise view on the social impact of diversity management, it would need to be narrowed down to this aspect only.

There are some principal statements and comments gathered while interviewing the experts:

- Diversity occurs naturally, inclusion creates opportunities for diverse talents and comfort environment for the development of the unique differences of individuals;
- Diversity should be embedded in the organization's culture, at early stage managed in order to be transformed into inclusion;
- Experts agreed there are more advantages than disadvantages of diversity if properly managed;
- Having the programs for the DEI, what matters is the execution of it. Most agreed that the organization at an early stage must have such programs in place to strive for building DEI culture so that at the end there is no need of any enforcement to manage the diversity;
- All experts agreed that irrespective of the diversity management programs or any other measures, equal job opportunities must be available regardless of the diversity kind. Failure to ensure this may lead to the emergence of another minority or discrimination issues. For instance, in the case of female minority, the company might inadvertently make males feel discriminated against due to the "artificial" enforcement minority programs within the organization;
- Most experts agreed there is a social impact;
- Organizations that are truly inclusive naturally spread the positive message about diversity within its society;
- Most female experts point out that diversity needs the organization's attention and should be managed, even enforced at the beginning of the process. On the other hand, for most male experts, the organizations' core business and purpose were considered the most important;
- Some experts combined both views and they believed that the solution is the so-called *Talents' Diversity*, where it is possible to achieve the company objectives while using diverse talents.

Figure 8.2. is a graphical representation of the four quadrants of the decision-space. Each quadrant represents the level of diversity management while evaluating the maturity of diversity management and inclusion at any organization. The lower-left quadrant represents the lowest level, where an organization may have some diversities among its participants, but it is unconscious and accidental possession, with no deliberate intention to address it. While moving to the upper-left quadrant, there are organizations that recognize their diversity and begin to purposefully manage it, resulting in various outcomes, whether better or worse. The right lower quadrant represents organizations that have either become aware of their diversity or purposefully created a diverse environment within their hiring process, aiming to establish embedded DEI in their culture

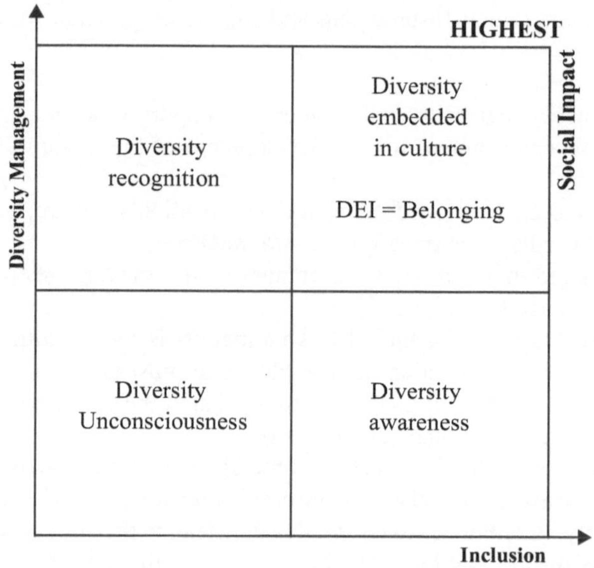


*Figure 8.2* Social impact as an outcome of diversity management and inclusion

*Source:* Own elaboration.

and move toward the upper right quadrant, symbolizing the highest level of diversity, equity, and inclusion, where every employee feels a sense of belonging. For any organization, the goal should be to strive for this level of maturity when launching DEI programs. From the perspective of a diverse employee, they would naturally prefer to be a part of an organization where, considering their own diversity, they feel equal, included, and truly belonging every aspect of the organization and its culture. The model explained to the employee could serve as a decision-making score, assessing the organization's DEI maturity level from the employee's standpoint. Both diversity management and inclusion should be deeply embedded in the company culture in the long run.

## Discussion

The recognition that employee diversity can be beneficial to an organization encourages the identification of the determinants of its positive effects. This chapter presents several approaches to managing diversity within the human resource function in an organization. On one hand, efforts have been made to emphasize the social character of the problem, while on the other, the practical nature of the discipline of management and quality studies has been taken into account. Therefore, particular emphasis has been placed on the diversity effects of workers within the context of the instrumental diversity paradigm. The analysis of the presented results shows that the effects of resource diversity management practices depend on many factors. Furthermore, the considerations undertaken by successive researchers indicate the increasingly complex nature of this issue. Despite the enormous number of publications, it is not possible to draw clear conclusions for the managers, as they remain elusive. In many cases, the opinions of the managers themselves do not coincide either. Additionally, researchers themselves point out the need to deepen the research, while the models are becoming increasingly complex, making practical implementation challenging, if not to say impossible. Thus, two parallel perspectives exist – research integrity and the pragmatic needs of the organization. An extremely important though not an easy task is to strike a reasonable balance between the needs of learning and practical applications. However, by fostering diversity and inclusion in the workplace, there are more advantages than disadvantages:

- *Higher innovation and creativity:* Diverse people come from varied backgrounds and life experiences. It enables them to present fresh ideas and creative solutions to any company's problem. John Bersin's research shows that inclusive companies are 1.7 times more likely to lead in innovation in their respective markets. New ideas lead to innovative solutions to address issues at hand.
- *Better communication:* It might be challenging at certain points due to language constraints, but the possibility of exchanging different points of view and perspectives through multicultural interactions, overall, makes communication better.
- *Higher employee retention:* Companies with a diverse and inclusive outlook have a reduced employee turnover rate and a relatively higher employee retention rate. Naturally, job seekers and employees are more likely to stay in an organization with a history of practicing diversity and inclusion at all levels. When employees feel included, they tend to last longer and give their best as well.
- *Higher employee engagement:* This benefit is absolutely a no-brainer. The more included and valued the employees feel, the higher will be their engagement in a company. Employees participate and are interested in the company culture and activities when they know that their voices matter.
- *Increased performance and efficiency:* Being a diverse and inclusive company will bring a tangible profit in the form of revenue as well. Increased employee engagement, employee retention, and higher innovation contribute to higher revenue and profits. According to McKinsey and Co.'s research, companies that push the values of diversity and inclusion in the workplace were at the top of finances and profits.
- *Better decision making/better quality of decision:* Having a diverse range of voices in your team and making them feel valued and heard will allow the privilege of having a blend of perspectives in every decision-making process.

Including a range of insights from everybody will automatically guide to make better decisions for the company. However, there are voices that sometimes better does not mean faster, some decisions have to be made under time pressure, so this is up to the company leadership when to wisely utilize diverse votes.

- *Elevates the company* reputation: Encouraging diversity and inclusion in the workplace will boost the company's brand identity as well. In the light of the current global political scenario, where representation is at the core of most discourses and narratives, it is imperative to be inclusive. Being politically aware and empathetic can do a lot to enhance the company's reputation.

It is important to emphasize in here that there are some practitioners' strong opinions, like Mr. Michał Jezioro, Managing Director at DMC Mining Service, that the diversity enforcement for the sake of having it, without prioritizing the business value proposition, is not something that he thinks "pays back" in form of the company results. Another voice of being skeptical toward the artificial enforcement of diversity in any meaning and the unsuccessful diversity management execution programs was coming from Mr Israel Losada Salvador, CEO at AutoStore™ and former Schlumberger manager, who emphasized that if during the recruitment or career orientation process, the favor is given to certain "minority" without paying full attention to the level of qualifications and competencies at first place, the person who is given the job might not be ready for the job and thus may harm the organization at the end. Referring to Figure 8.2, the proposed four quadrant model of an organization's classification in terms of DEI maturity level would pose a question of how to move to the highest level without any diversity management enforcement. This is why some voices, particularly those of female experts, argue that DEI programs should be implemented from the very early stages of their launch, gradually evolving toward becoming less controlled as DEI becomes ingrained in the organizational culture.

## Conclusions

In the world where the fight for representation, diversity, and inclusion is paramount, upholding these principles in all aspects of life should be an obvious moral and ethical choice. Furthermore, companies and organizations must recognize that their D&I/I&D/DEI policies can lead to growth, success, and a more significant business impact. Employees are the fuel and driving force of any organization. They have the right and tremendous power to hold their employers accountable and inquire about the steps to be taken to transform a diverse workplace into an inclusive one. Every employee, at every level, should feel included in this process. To truly benefit from diversity in the workplace, people must feel included. Inclusion creates a well-being environment and an open atmosphere where everyone feels important, where everyone's opinion matters. According to some experts, if one feels good surrounded by others, the rest would feel the same. Diversity and inclusion efforts are not just a feel-good corporate policy; they have a tangible economic and business impact. When properly addressed and not just treated as an unmeaningful statement on the wall, but present in the organization's vision, mission, and values, they can only have a positive social impact. Diversity without inclusion will not amount to any significant change in the company culture or employee experience. Unless and until all opinions, perspectives, and experiences count, while making decisions and policies, regardless of the differences among individuals in broad sense, there is no walk but just the talk on inclusion. According to a Harvard Business Review article, *"In the context of the workplace, diversity equals representation. Without inclusion, however, the crucial connections that attract diverse talent, encourage their participation, foster innovation, and lead to business growth won't happen".*

Diversity and inclusion are a conscious decision and not something that happens by chance. For instance, according to McKinsey, the most gender-diverse companies are 21% more likely to achieve above-average profitability. Implementing diversity hiring in the organization can result in a bigger and better talent pool, encourage different perspectives, and enhance collaboration. One of the most significant advantages of a diverse workforce is the increased creativity and innovation in the workplace. Employers should do their best to encourage employees to bring out their best creative and innovative ideas to the table. This will make employees feel seen and appreciated and usher in new avenues of business growth and success.

## Limitations and implications

Before summarizing the theoretical and practical contributions of this chapter, the study has certain acknowledged limitations that need to be taken into account when considering the results. First, the results are based upon a small sample group (17 experts) that should not be generalized to the population as they are only representants of practitioners working for multinational companies either in the past or till now. This is a major shortcoming that might be explored and addressed in future research to validate the results. Hence, to complete the overall picture, a broader survey among multinational firms by means of an extended qualitative or even a quantitative survey would be most valuable to generate more objective data. Thus, the authors acknowledge that it would be beneficial to have larger sample groups at hand. Another shortcoming of the study is that the authors only investigated the experts' point of view from just a few companies, however very diverse ones in the broad sense of this nomenclature and experts with long, practical experience of being exposed to and working with DEI.

## Note

1 Social impact as broadly defined, social impact represents "beneficial outcomes resulting from prosocial behavior that are enjoyed by the intended targets of that behavior and/or by the broader community of individuals, organizations, and/or environments" (Rawhouser, H., Cummings, M., & Newbert, S.L. (2019). Social impact measurement: Current approaches and future directions for social entrepreneurship research. *Entrepreneurship Theory and Practice*, *43*(1), 82–115.

## References

Ahuja, G., & Lampert, C.M. (2001). Entrepreneurship in the large corporation: A longitudinal study of how established firms create breakthrough inventions. *Strategic Management Journal*, *22*(6–7), 521–543.

Bergmann, J.R. (2010). *Konversationsanalyse*. In U. Flick, E. von Kardorff, & I. Steinke (Eds.), *Qualitative Forschung,* 524–537. Ein Handbuch, 8. Aufl., Rowohlt-Taschenbuch-Verlag, Reinbek and Hamburg, Hamburg.

Blomkvist, K., Kappen, P., & Zander, I. (2017). Gone are the creatures of yesteryear? On the diffusion of technological capabilities in the "modern" MNC. *Journal of World Business*, *52*(1), 1–16.

Bower, J.L., & Christensen, C.M. (1995). Disruptive technologies: Catching the wave. *Harvard Business Review*, *73*(1), 43–53.

Brenman, M. (2012) *Diversity metrics, measurement and evaluation. Workforce Diversity Network.* Retrieved from https://workforcediversitynetwork.com

Certo, S.T., Lester, R.H., Dalton, C.M., & Dalton, D.R. (2006). Top management teams, strategy and financial performance: A meta-analytic examination. *Journal of Management Studies, 43*(4), 813–839.

Chatman, J.A., Polzer, J.T., Barasade, S.G., & Neale, M.A. (1998). Being different yet filling similar: The influence of demographic composition and organizational culture on work processes and outcomes. *Administrative Science Quarterly, 43*(4), 749–780. https://doi.org/10.2307/2393615

Cole, B.M., & Salimath, M.S. (2013). Diversity identity management: An organizational perspective. *Journal of Business Ethics, 116*(1), 151–161. https://doi.org/10.1007/S10551-012-1466-4

Dewhurst, M., Harris, J., & Heywood, S. (2011). Understanding your globalization penalty. *McKinsey, Quarterly*, *3*, 12–15.

Faracik, B. (2019). *Wpływ kultury włączającej na wyniki firmy. Narzędzia, wskaźniki, dobre praktyki.* Warszawa. 2018 Gallup On-line Report. Retrieved from https://www.gallup.com/workplace/242138/requirements-diverse-inclusive-culture.aspx#:~:text=Diversity%20represents%20the%20full%20spectrum,economic%20status%20or%20physical%20disability./

Gross-Gołacka, E. (2018). *Zarządzanie* różnorodnością. Warszawa, Difin.

Gwet, K.L. (2014). *Handbook of inter-rater reliability: The definitive guide to measuring the extent of agreement among multiple raters*. Advanced Analytics, LLC, Gaithersburg.

Hambrick, D.C., & Mason, P.A. (1984). Upper echelons: The organization as a reflection of its top managers. *Academy of Management Review, 9*(2), 193–206.

Heavey, C., & Simsek, Z. (2013). Top management compositional effects on corporate entrepreneurship: The moderating role of perceived technological uncertainty. *Journal of Product Innovation Management, 30*(5), 837–855.

Hewstone, M. (2015). Consequences of diversity for social cohesion and prejudice; The missing dimension of intergroup contact. *Journal of Social Issues, 71*(2), 417–438. https://doi.org/ 10.1111/joisi.12120

Jayne, M.E.A., & Dipboye, R.L. (2004). Leveraging diversity to improve business performance: Research findings and recommendations for organizations. *Human Resource Management, 43*(4), 409–424.

Knight, D., Pearce, C.L., Smith, K.G., Olian, J.D., Sims, H.P., Smith, K.A., & Flood, P. (1999). Top management team diversity, group process, and strategic consensus. *Strategic Management Journal, 20*(5), 445–465.

Kruse, J. (2014). *Qualitative Interviewforschung. Ein integrativer Ansatz*. Beltz Juventa, Weinheim.

Kuhn, T.S. (1962). *The structure of scientific revolutions.* University of Chicago Press, Chicago, IL.

Leslie, L.M. (2019). Diversity initiative effectiveness: A typological theory of unintended consequences. *Academy of Management Review, 44*(3), 538–563. https://doi.org/10.5465/amr.2017.0087

Menz, M., Kunisch, S., & Collis, D.J. (2015). The corporate headquarters in the contemporary corporation: Advancing a multimarket firm perspective. *The Academy of Management Annals, 9*(1), 633–714.

Nielsen, S. (2010). Top management team diversity: A review of theories and methodologies. *International Journal of Management Reviews, 12*(3), 301–316. https://doi.org/10.1111/j.1468-2370.2009.00263.x

Nishii, L.H. (2013). The benefits of climate for inclusion for gender-diverse groups. *Academy of Management Journal, 56*(6), 1754–1774. https://doi.org/10.5465/amj.2009.0823

Nishii, L.H., Khattab, J., Shemla, M., & Paluch, R.M. (2018). A multi-level process model for understanding diversity practice effectiveness. *Academy of Management Annals, 12*(1), 37–82. https://doi.org/ 10.5465/annals.2016.0044

O'Donnovan, D. (2018). Diversity and inclusion in the workplace. In Editors: School of Economics and Management University of Minho, *Management and Industrial Engineering*, 73–103. Springer, Portugal.

O'Reilly, C.A., & Tushman, M.L. (2013). Organizational ambidexterity: Past, present, and future. *Academy of Management Perspectives, 27*(4), 324–338.

Peretz, H., Levi, A., & Fried, Y. (2015). Organizational diversity programs across cultures: Effects on absenteeism, turnover, performance and innovation. *The International Journal of Human Resource Management, 26*(6), 875–903. https://doi.org/10.1080/09585192.2014.991344

Przytuła, S. (2020). *Zarządzanie różnorodnością a organziacja włączająca.* Forum Odpowiedzialnego Biznesu.

Rakowska, A. (2021). *Różnorodność zasobów ludzkich w organizacji - istota, dylematy, wyzwania*. Lublin, Wydawnictwo Uniwersytetu Marii Curie-Skłodowskiej,

Shore, L., Chung-Herrera, B., Dean, M., Holcombe, K., Jung, D., Randel, A., & Singh, G. (2009). Diversity in organizations: Where are we now and where are we going? *Human Resource Management Review, 19*(2), 117–133.

Simons, T., Pelled, L.H., & Smith, K.A. (1999). Making use of difference: Diversity, debate, and decision comprehensiveness in top management teams. *Academy of Management Journal, 42*(6), 662–673.
Strauss, A.L., & Corbin, J. (1998). *Basics of qualitative research: Techniques and procedures for developing grounded theory*. Sage, Thousands Oaks, CA.
Strzelczak, M. (2019). *Rożnorodność jako szansa. Karta różnorodności wsparciem w budowaniu inkluzywnych organizacji i społeczeństw.* In I. Warwas (Ed.), *Oblicza zarządzania różnorodnością w Polsce*. NieOczywiste, Warszawa.
Tajfel, H. (1982). *Social identity and intergroup relations.* European Studies in Social Psychology. Cambridge University Press, Cambridge.
Talke, K., Salomo, S., & Rost, K. (2010). How top management team diversity affects innovativeness and performance via the strategic choice to focus on innovation fields. *Research Policy, 39*(7), 907–918.
Tsui, A.S., Egan, T.D., & O'Reilly III, C.A. (1992). Being different: Relational demography and organizational attachment. *Administrative Science Quarterly, 37*(4), 549–579.
Turner, J.C., Hogg, M.A., Oakes, P.J., Recher, S.D., & Wetherell, M.S. (1987). *Rediscovering the social group: A self-categorization theory.* Blackwell, Oxford.
Wilton, L.S. (2015). *Diversity stigma and diversity credits: The positive and negative consequences of race and gender diversity for companies and employees.* Doctoral dissertation, Rutgers University-Graduate School, New Brunwick.
Warwas, I. (2019). *Oblicza zarządzania różnorodnością w Polsce.* NieOczywiste, Warszawa.

# 9 Relevance of male perspective on gender diversity management

*Małgorzata Budzanowska-Drzewiecka, Paulina Jędrzejczyk, Justyna M. Bugaj and Bohdan Rożnowski*

## Introduction

The significance of the social impact of organizations is undeniable. Although frequently explored (e.g. Rawhouser et al., 2019; Siemieniako et al., 2021), the issue requires further study (Shepherd & Patzelt, 2022) due to the complexity and lack of conceptual clarity (Perrini et al., 2021). Social impact invariably refers to the social value that a company can create for communities outside the boundaries of the organization. It can also be broadly defined as the outcomes that benefit the intended targets (Rawhouser et al., 2019): the beneficiaries and other recipients of the intervention carried out (Hadad & Găucă, 2014; Perrini et al., 2021). It has been analyzed at different levels, on a continuum from the individual to the systemic, thus from the micro to the macro levels (Siemieniako et al., 2021).

The positive social impact of organizations can be a consequence of diversity management, as it aims to reduce inequality and improve the situation of members of minority groups, such as women. Changing the status of women in organizations leads to an improvement in their economic situation, strengthens their autonomy, and boosts empowerment. Thus, it can be considered a positive social impact of organizations on the micro level. In addition, long-term effects on the macro level can be expected as new female role models emerge and motivate young women to aspire to higher positions, influence the attitude of men toward working women in general, or induce parents to invest more resources in their daughters' education and health care (Bohnet, 2017). However, to achieve these positive effects of diversity management, especially when dealing with gender inequalities between men and women, the standpoints of both genders need to be considered. Instead, most studies on gender inequality refer to women (Stamarski & Son Hing, 2015; Dashper, 2019). By contrast, research on this topic that takes into account men's perception of gender inequality is rather rare (e.g., Flood, 2015; Essig & Soparnot, 2019), even though focusing solely on the perspectives of women can jeopardize the success of diversity management and therefore undermine the related positive social impact of organizations.

DOI: 10.4324/9781003480952-11

Focusing only on one gender can result in increased identification with one's own gender group, discrimination against the other, as well as exacerbating competition and conflicts between men and women. This can be interpreted as a negative impact on the micro level and might reinforce negative trends in societies, such as polarization or cancel culture, on the macro level. Therefore, considering men's perspectives is of critical importance.

In addition, since comparative studies on diversity management involving two or more countries are rare (Klarsfeld et al., 2016), the chapter fills this gap by comparing Generation Y men from two countries: Poland and Germany. These countries differ in the progressivity of the implementation of gender-related diversity management practices. According to the Gender Development Index (Human Development Reports, 2022), which measures gender inequalities in achieving three basic dimensions of human development, the position of women in both markets is different (GDI value: Germany 0.972; Poland 1.007). Similarly, there are differences with regard to the Gender Inequality Index (GII value: Germany 0.084; Poland 0.115) (Human Development Reports, 2022) and Gender Equality Index (GEI value: Germany 68.7; Poland 57.7) (European Institute for Gender Equality, 2022). This means that Germany is a country with lower gender inequality. In addition, our study focuses on a significant generation on the labor market, the Millennials, who exhibit greater awareness of gender inequalities and have different perceptions of discrimination compared to other generations (Baralt et al., 2020).

The objective of the study is to determine the perception of gender diversity management in the workplace by men from Generation Y in two distinct labor markets: Poland and Germany. The main research questions are as follows:

RQ1. How do Generation Y men from Poland and Germany perceive gender-related diversity management in the workplace?

RQ2: Do Generation Y men from Poland and Germany perceive threats arising from the promotion of women in their career development?

The chapter is organized as follows. First, the concept of diversity management and its relevance to social impact is explained. Next, the research procedure and the results are presented. Conclusions, implications, and limitations are formulated at the end of the chapter.

## Diversity management and the social impact of organizations

### *Gender diversity management in the workplace*

Diversity management is a management approach widely used in most industrialized countries (Köllen, 2021). It can be defined as 'a set of organizational policies and practices aimed at recruiting, retaining and managing employees of diverse backgrounds and identities and creating a culture in which everyone is equally enabled to perform and achieve organizational objectives and personal development' (Syed & Tariq, 2017). Both researchers and practitioners have strived to understand this concept and its effects on organizations and societies (Roberson, 2019; Yadav & Lenka, 2020; Garg & Sangwan, 2021). Originally introduced as a way of compensating for gender and racial discrimination, today diversity management refers to the wide range of inequalities (e.g. based on age, ethnicity, disability status, or religion). However, gender inequality is still predominant and of great importance.

Gender inequality in the workplace is a complex phenomenon (Stamarski & Son Hing, 2015). For years, organizations have made extraordinary efforts to empower women by implementing diversity management programs and practices. Numerous activities focus on the advancement of women by addressing issues that hinder female employees from realizing their potential and achieving their professional goals. Organizations introduce woman-oriented human resources practices (Stamarski & Son Hing, 2015) that focus on hiring, training, or promoting female employees (e.g. employment quotas for women). Women-only offerings, such as training, coaching, or mentoring of female employees provide women with strategies that help them to increase their confidence and assertiveness, develop their networks, and make career-related decisions more consciously (Dashper, 2019).

Gender-oriented diversity management efforts are not directed exclusively at women. Practices such as promoting an organizational culture that values differences, creating bias-free HRM systems, or using instruments that support work-life balance aim at creating supportive conditions for diversity management in general (Cox & Blake, 1991). More and more authors point out that research on diversity and diversity management has the potential to foster equality and social justice (e.g. Janssens & Zanoni, 2021). Janssens and Zanoni (2021) argue that actions taken in the context of diversity, such as establishing work standards, training employees, or raising awareness of women's rights, can bring about positive social change. Social change outcomes can be expressed in the form of recognition, respect for women's labor rights, better status and pay, social protection for women, and community formation through new types of relationships. Research also shows that gender diversity, diversity management, and organizational inclusion can be effective in predicting workplace happiness (Mousa, 2021). As gender inequality is considered a key driver of poverty (African Development Bank, 2016), diversity management helps women achieve material security and independence by supporting the growth of the careers of female employees. This could lead to substantial improvements for women around the world, as results from different countries show that women with good jobs are less likely to be victims of domestic violence (e. g. Viero et al., 2021).

In conclusion, diversity management practices improve the situation of women as members of minority groups and, more generally, redress inequalities between men and women in society. In this way, they also contribute to the positive social impact of organizations. However, these positive outcomes can be undermined or even outweighed by the negative effects of ignoring the perspective of male employees.

### *The male perspective on gender-related diversity management in the workplace*

Gender-related diversity management and developing long-term solutions for organizations require focusing on the needs of both genders, not just women. Despite this, only a few studies have examined gender inequality from the perspective of men (e.g. Essig & Soparnot, 2019; Coron, 2020). Ignoring men's perspectives can have negative effects that threaten the success of diversity management and, consequently, jeopardize the positive social impact of the organizations associated with it. This can be explained in the context of 'modern' discrimination (Cortina, 2008) that affects both genders. For example, male employees working part-time, due to occupying gender-incongruent roles, might experience less career goal-related progress, less development of their professional abilities, and a lower rate of advancement than full-time men and part-time or full-time women (van Osch & Schaveling, 2020). Furthermore, men who participate in caregiving duties are punished in the form of rejection and are seen not only as 'lesser workers' but also as 'lesser men' (Harrington, 2022).

The perception of diversity management may depend on gender. Elvi and Tunjungsari (2022) find that female employees perceive diversity management more positively than male employees. Cassino (2016) argues that men, who perceive discrimination as a zero-sum game, tend to believe that actions that support women must hurt men. From this perspective, diversity management practices appear to be threatening and discriminatory. Thus, failure to consider men's needs in diversity management can cause some problems. Firstly, if men do not perceive any advantages for themselves resulting from diversity management, either because they see it as a zero-sum game, or they experience social sanctions for making use of its measures like part-time hours, the success of diversity management can be diminished by the lack of commitment and support of men, or even torpedoed by their resistance (Jones et al., 2022). Secondly, men who feel discriminated and threatened can increasingly identify with their own gender group, seek ways to defend themselves, and even fight against women they may, in general, perceive as the group that is doing the oppressing (Cassino, 2016). The resulting conflicts cause stress, tension, and dissatisfaction for both women and men. This not only hinders women in reaching their professional goals, but also has the potential to deteriorate their position compared to the situation without diversity management.

While the phenomena described above affect social impacts at the micro level, it is important to note that there is also the danger of macro level impacts. Policies that ignore the concerns and needs of men leave great space for so-called alt-right and masculinist/antifeminist movements that use the claim that feminism devalues men and masculinity as an effective means of promoting and spreading their ideology, as well as a way to heat up the discussion in general (Nagle, 2017; de Boise, 2019). The development of such phenomena as increased identification with one's own gender groups and the escalation of intergender conflicts that increase stereotypical perceptions and discrimination tendencies can lead to the emergence of problems in society, such as the cultivation of stereotypical, hostile images of 'old white men' or cancel culture (Clark, 2020). Cancel culture can be defined as 'the withdrawal of support for individuals who have acted in a way deemed unacceptable or problematic related to social media viewership' (Mueller, 2021), which encompasses strategies to shame individuals, ranging from limiting access to public platforms, damaging reputations, or even ending careers (Norris, 2020). Critics warn that this process, which often starts with legitimate criticism, has the tendency to uncontrollable escalation, where cancel culture threatens classical liberal values and weakens the norms of open debate and toleration of differences (Norris, 2020). With open discussions lacking and the corroboration of one's views gaining the upper hand, there is a real danger of the belief polarization effect, by means of which like-minded individuals transform into more extreme versions of themselves (Talisse, 2019). Talisse (2019) points out that the belief polarization phenomenon can initiate a broader polarization dynamic that can ultimately even dissolve the democratic capacities of citizens, defined as openness to cultural otherness and to other beliefs, world views and practices, respect or tolerance of ambiguity (Council of Europe, 2018). Thus, the negative effects of ignoring the male perspective can go far beyond the boundaries of organizations. If organizations want to become a fair workplace and have a positive social impact by contributing to the development of a sustainable society, they must include the perspective of both genders in their efforts. Therefore, the following section focuses on the perspective of men.

## Materials and methods

The research was carried out among Generation Y men in two distinct labor markets: Poland and Germany*. A quantitative approach was applied. To collect data, an online survey was used. The questionnaire was prepared in German and then translated by two researchers into Polish. The equivalence of the meanings was checked within the procedure. The measures were adopted from the relevant literature. Due to the exploratory nature of the study, based on previous research (Ely et al., 2011; Vongalis-Macrow, 2014), a list of threats to professional development of men arising from the promotion of women in their career development was developed. Participants were asked to evaluate the items on a 6-point Likert scale.

Data were collected from 407 Gen Y male employees from Poland and Germany, two culturally different countries with geographical proximity that struggle with similar problems caused by changes in the environment (Bugaj et al., 2022) and differ notably in gender equality (European Institute for Gender Equality, 2022). The convenience sample was heterogeneous in terms of sociodemographic characteristics (education, having children, and seniority). Participation in the survey was voluntary and respondents received no incentives. After data reduction due to data gaps, the analysis was performed taking into account 381 correctly completed questionnaires.

All respondents were born between 1984 and 1995. Most of them have higher education (65%); more than five years of work experience (64%) and are married/ in a relationship (69%) without children (66%) (Table 9.1).

*Table 9.1* Sample characteristics

| *Variable* | *Values* | *Poland – frequency* | *Germany – frequency* | *Total frequency* |
|---|---|---|---|---|
| Year of birth | 1984 | 16 | 7 | 23 |
| | 1985 | 31 | 8 | 39 |
| | 1986 | 20 | 14 | 34 |
| | 1987 | 22 | 12 | 34 |
| | 1988 | 22 | 10 | 32 |
| | 1989 | 14 | 12 | 26 |
| | 1990 | 20 | 14 | 34 |
| | 1991 | 14 | 13 | 27 |
| | 1992 | 13 | 21 | 34 |
| | 1993 | 8 | 11 | 19 |
| | 1994 | 14 | 22 | 36 |
| | 1995 | 16 | 17 | 43 |
| Education | Elementary school | 3 | 18 | 21 |
| | Vocational training | 7 | 27 | 34 |
| | High school | 55 | 25 | 80 |
| | Bachelor | 41 | 61 | 102 |
| | Master | 91 | 36 | 127 |
| | PhD | 13 | 4 | 17 |
| Seniority in positions at work | None yet | 6 | 5 | 11 |
| | Up to one year | 0 | 11 | 11 |
| | One to two years | 9 | 15 | 24 |
| | Two to three years | 16 | 10 | 26 |
| | Three to four years | 6 | 26 | 32 |
| | Four to five years | 22 | 13 | 35 |
| | More than five years | 151 | 91 | 242 |
| Marital status | Married/in a relationship | 151 | 111 | 262 |
| | Single | 59 | 60 | 119 |
| Having children | Yes | 92 | 17 | 109 |
| | No | 118 | 134 | 252 |
| Total | | 210 | 171 | 381 |

*Source:* Own elaboration.

During the analysis, descriptive statistics and one-way ANOVA were used to present the data and determine the main effects. The analysis was performed in STATISTICA software.

## Results

### *Perception of gender-related diversity management in the workplace*

Generally, the attitude of men toward gender-related diversity in the workplace is rather ambivalent. Most of the participants perceived the organization (an employer) that emphasizes diversity management positively (287; 75%). Only 28% of Polish and 20% of German men said that an employer who emphasizes their commitment to diversity management is rather unattractive to them. However, data suggest that gender-related diversity in the workplace is not perceived by them as a relevant issue. They are neutral when it comes to the commitment of men to diversity management (m = 3.12; SD = 1.01; scale ranging from 1 to 5, unless otherwise noted). The respondents are not interested in leading (234 individuals; 61%) and participating (206 individuals; 54%) in gender-related diversity management projects aimed at men. Although 52% of German men expressed their willingness to participate in diversity management training courses, 59% of Polish men opposed it.

The respondents are divided in terms of the success of diversity management without the participation of men. Fifty-four percent believe that without men's participation, diversity management cannot succeed, and 39% declare that only when men become involved in diversity management will the issue be taken seriously in companies and other institutions. However, the Polish participants are more convinced that the participation of men is not a basis for its efficiency ($F\ (1, 379) = 4.19, p < 0.05$).

Only 26% (101 individuals) agree that companies ignore their needs in diversity practices. However, there is a clear tendency for German respondents to be more extreme in their beliefs than Poles. German men do not feel ignored ($m = 2.55$) as Polish men do ($m = 3.01$). Following their opinions, organizations take into account the needs of men in diversity management ($F(1, 379) = 17.80$, $p < 0.001$). It should be noted that only 50 participants (13%) admitted having experienced discrimination in the workplace (36 from Poland; 14 from Germany). Sixty-four percent of them (244 individuals) would like to reduce their work hours to care for their children, but 33% (127) fear a disadvantageous position that might result from it (51% of Germans and only 19% of Polish men).

Respondents from Germany and Poland have a different opinion when it comes to targeting diversity management only for women ($F(1, 379) = 4.44$, $p < 0.05$). In general, 31% (119 individuals) agree with that statement. As before, German men have a greater tendency to disagree with the statement that

'Diversity management is all about promoting women' ($m = 2.77$). Furthermore, 25% (96 individuals) believe that 'Diversity management should take more into account the needs of men'. In that case, men from Poland and Germany also have a different opinion ($F$ (1, 379) = 17.65, $p < 0.001$).

***Diversity management supporting women in the workplace: Threats perceived by men***

Most of the participants, both from Poland and Germany, have positive attitudes toward promoting women in their career development (55%; 211 individuals). However, they do not see the benefits of this practice for themselves (69%; 381 individuals). Interestingly, 20% of the respondents (77 individuals), regardless of their nationality, feel discriminated by these activities.

Men in both countries do not view the promotion of women as a threat to their career development (Table 9.2).

*Table 9.2* Threats to men's professional development arising from the promotion of women in their career development – men's opinions

| *Potential threats* | *Mean Poland* | *Mean Germany* | *Mean total* | *Mode* | *Mode – quantity* | *Standard deviation* | *F-value* |
|---|---|---|---|---|---|---|---|
| Employment quotas for women | 3.59 | 3.00 | 3.33 | 1 | 89 | 1.74 | 10.991*** |
| Changes in organizational culture resulting from the implementation of diversity management | 3.17 | 2.06 | 2.68 | 1 | 136 | 1.63 | 48.858*** |
| Women-only leadership | 2.96 | 2.30 | 2.66 | 1 | 131 | 1.60 | 16.891*** |
| Special programs to support/promote women | 2.99 | 2.15 | 2.62 | 1 | 136 | 1.58 | 28.826*** |
| Coaching only for women | 3.08 | 1.94 | 2.56 | 1 | 148 | 1.63 | 52.499*** |
| Women-only networking | 3.11 | 1.77 | 2.50 | 1 | 162 | 1.62 | 77.095*** |
| Mentoring only for women | 2.99 | 1.74 | 2.43 | 1 | 155 | 1.55 | 74.415*** |
| Flexible working-time models | 2.69 | 1.65 | 2.22 | 1 | 195 | 1.53 | 49.2945*** |

Scale: from 1 to 6; 1 – the lowest rating

***$p < 0.001$

*Source:* Own elaboration.

However, the differences in assessments depending on the country are noticeable ($F(8, 372) = 14.82$, $p < 0.001$). Polish men treat these actions as a greater threat. Among the activities that promote women's careers, women's employment quotas are the most threatening to them. This is a bigger problem for Polish men, while German men perceived it as less of a threat ($F(1, 379) = 10.99$, $p < 0.001$).

Furthermore, the men surveyed mostly do not see any danger for themselves in women being supported by organizations ($m = 2.93$; SD = 1.17). Similarly, they do not see any negative consequences for women arising from discrimination against men ($m = 2.75$; SD = 1.12). However, there is a difference in opinions depending on the country. In both cases, Poles perceived the practices as the greatest danger ($F(1, 379) = 8.26$, $p < 0.01$) and are more convinced that discrimination against men has negative consequences for women ($F(1, 379) = 49.17$, $p < 0.001$).

Beyond the country, it was verified that men's experiences of suffering discrimination in the workplace differed their attitudes. The results showed that men who experienced discrimination rated support of women given by organizations as a greater threat to themselves ($F(1, 378) = 17.28$, $p < 0.001$) and more negative consequences for women arising from discrimination against men ($F(1, 378) = 4.51$, $p < 0.05$).

Gender-related diversity management practices carried out by organizations can have a social impact on the position of men and women on the labor market. For instance, this could refer to the image of gender, in the relations between the genders in the workplace, or fairness in career paths. The results showed that the respondents are consistent in terms of the effects of gender-related diversity management on the image of women. Regardless of the country, they tend to believe that diversity management activities do not reinforce the image of women as the 'weak' gender. However, the disparities in their attitudes occur in terms of uncertainty in interactions between employees of different genders as a consequence of diversity management activities. For Germans, the problem does not exist, but Poles are not as sure ($F(1, 379) = 11.60$, $p < 0.001$). It should be noted that Poles see the threat of women's employment quotas as the main criterion for selecting the candidate instead of qualifications; however, the difference is not statistically significant ($F(1, 379) = 3.08$, $p = 0.08$).

## Conclusions

This chapter contributes to research on the social impacts of organizations. Analyzing the perspective of men, it stresses the need to take into account the expectations of both genders when planning gender-related diversity management in the workplace, in order to create higher value for broader communities and change game rule (not sum-zero game) (Jones et al., 2022).

In general, the results show that men from Generation Y are barely involved in gender-related diversity in the workplace, although this varies according to the country (Bader et al., 2022). Poles feel more threatened than their German counterparts by activities supporting women, like leadership programs for women, networking, coaching, or mentoring. In addition, men who have experienced discrimination approach practices supporting women with more caution, perceiving them as a greater threat. On the one hand, this tendency may be related to the differences in the Gender Inequality Index. On the other hand, it could be related to the psychological mechanisms underlying the responses toward increasing gender diversity. According to intergroup threat theory (Jones et al., 2022), realistic threats underlie resistance. Poles are more likely to consider gender-related diversity in the workplace as a women-only practice which will reinforce negative defensive responses from men (Flood, 2015), such as negative attitudes toward women's employment quotas. The small group of respondents posed an obstacle for gender diversity management. It calls for further research on the characteristics of that group of men and within-sex differences based on individual gender-related attitudes and beliefs (Martins & Parsons, 2007).

From a theoretical perspective, the findings of the study boost our understanding of the determinants of gender-related diversity management. Previous research was mostly women-oriented (cf. Stamarski & Son Hing, 2015; Dashper, 2019; Yadav & Lenka, 2020). The present results suggest that there are salient needs among men who have been discriminated in the workplace or feel threatened by practices solely oriented at women that should be addressed in diversity management practice. From the practical perspective, HR experts would be well advised to look for ways to make diversity management more attractive to men by communicating the advantages of diversity management and gender equality for them, such as less career pressure or greater freedom of choice, etc. It would also be promising to transfer part of the responsibility for diversity management to male employees. In this way, the chances of success can be increased, as diversity management would be perceived by male employees as a shared, mutual initiative and not as an imposed, forced instrument (Köllen, 2021).

The results of the present research in two different Polish and German markets have some limitations. The findings are subject to representative bias associated with the use of a convenience sample of one generation of male employees. Today, Generation Y is an important component of the workforce; however, the use of a more representative sample in future research, extended to other generations, would help validate the findings. The results that Poles are more threatened than German participants by activities supporting women may be a consequence of the sample used in this study. Future research should focus on an analysis of the male perspective on diversity management from different countries. Moreover, there is a further need to explore the impact of diversity management beyond the organization. The points made here on the theoretical level, regarding the relevance of diversity management in the context of the social impact of organizations, need to be examined empirically.

## Note

The study, entitled *Generation Y Men and Women in the Labor Market*, was funded under a cooperative research project implemented by the Jagiellonian University in Cracow and the University of Applied Labor Studies in Mannheim.

## References

African Development Bank. (2016). Gender inequality: A double break on poverty reduction. In *African Development Report 2015*.

Bader, A.K., Froese, F.J., Cooke, F.L., & Schuster, T. (2022). Gender diversity management in foreign subsidiaries: A comparative study in Germany and Japan. *Journal of International Management*, *28*(3), 100921. https://doi.org/10.1016/j.intman.2021.100921

Baralt, L., Carian, E.K., Johnson, A.L., Lim, S., & Yoon, S.Y. (2020). Millennials and gender in an era of growing inequality. *Sociological Perspectives*, *63*(3), 452–460. https://doi.org/10.1177/0731121420915870

Bohnet, I. (2017). *What Works. Wie das Verhaltensdesign die Gleichstellung revolutionieren kann*. C. H. Beck. https://doi.org/10.1109/MSECP.2003.1236240

Bugaj, J.M., Budzanowska-Drzewiecka, M., & Jędrzejczyk, P. (2022). Generation Y employee career engagement: Research results from Poland and Germany. *HRM* [Zarządzanie Zasobami Ludzkimi], *149*(5), 26–43. https://doi.org/10.5604/01.3001.0016.2044

Cassino, D. (2016). Why more American men feel discriminated against. *Harvard Business Review*, September. https://hbr.org/2016/09/why-more-american-men-feel-discriminated-against

Clark, M. (2020). Drag them: A brief etymology of so-called "cancel culture." *Communication and the Public*, *5*(3–4), 88–92. https://doi.org/10.1177/2057047320961562

Coron, C. (2020). What does "gender equality" mean? Social representations of gender equality in the workplace among French workers. *Equality, Diversity and Inclusion*, *39*(8), 825–847. https://doi.org/10.1108/EDI-06-2019-0185

Cortina, L.M. (2008). Unseen injustice: Incivility as modern discrimination in organizations. *Academy of Management Review*, *33*(1), 55–75. https://doi.org/10.5465/AMR.2008.27745097

Council of Europe. (2018). *Reference framework of competences* (Vol. 2).

Cox, T.H., & Blake, S. (1991). Managing cultural implications for competitiveness organizational. *The Executive (Academy of Management)*, *5*(3), 45–56.

Dashper, K. (2019). Challenging the gendered rhetoric of success? The limitations of women-only mentoring for tackling gender inequality in the workplace. *Gender, Work and Organization*, *26*(4), 541–557. https://doi.org/10.1111/gwao.12262

de Boise, S. (2019). Editorial: Is masculinity toxic? *International Journal for Masculinity Studies*, *14*(3), 147–151. https://doi.org/10.1080/18902138.2019.1654742

Elvi, E., & Tunjungsari, H.K. (2022). Gender, diversity management perceptions, workplace happiness, and organizational citizenship behavior. *Proceedings of the Tenth International Conference on Entrepreneurship and Business Management 2021 (ICEBM 2021)*, *653*(Icebm 2021), 350–355. https://doi.org/10.2991/aebmr.k.220501.053

Ely, R.J., Ibarra, H., & Kolb, D.M. (2011). Taking gender into account: Theory and design for women's leadership development programs. *Academy of Management Learning & Education*, *10*(3), 474–493. https://doi.org/10.5465/amle.2010.0046

Essig, E., & Soparnot, R. (2019). Re-thinking gender inequality in the workplace: A framework from the male perspective. *Management (France)*, *22*(3), 373–410. https://doi.org/10.3917/mana.223.0373

European Institute for Gender Equality. (2022). *Gender equality index*. Retrieved January10, 2023, from https://eige.europa.eu/gender-equality-index/2022

Flood, M.G. (2015). Men and gender equality. In M.G. Flood & R. Howson (Eds.), *Engaging men in building gender equality*, 1–31. Cambridge Scholars Publishing.

Garg, S., & Sangwan, S. (2021). Literature review on diversity and inclusion at workplace, 2010–2017. *Vision*, *25*(1), 12–22. https://doi.org/10.1177/0972262920959523

Hadad, S., & Găucă, O. (Drumea). (2014). Social impact measurement in social entrepreneurial organizations. *Management and Marketing*, *9*(2), 117–134.

Harrington, B. (2022). The new dad: The career-caregiving conundrum. In M. Grau, M. Maestro, & H.R. Bowles (Eds.), *Engaged fatherhood for men, families and gender equality,* 197–212. Springer.

Human Development Reports. (2022). *Gender development index*. Retrieved January10, 2023, from https://hdr.undp.org/data-center/thematic-composite-indices/gender-inequality-index#/indicies/GII

Janssens, M., & Zanoni, P. (2021). Making diversity research matter for social change: New conversations beyond the firm. *Organization Theory*, *2*(2), 1–21. https://doi.org/10.1177/26317877211004603

Jones, A., Turner, R.N., & Latu, I.M. (2022). Resistance towards increasing gender diversity in masculine domains: The role of intergroup threat. *Group Processes and Intergroup Relations*, *25*(3), NP24–NP53. https://doi.org/10.1177/13684302211042424

Klarsfeld, A., Ng, E.S.W., Booysen, L., Christiansen, L.C., & Kuvaas, B. (2016). Comparative equality and diversity: Main findings and research gaps. *Cross Cultural and Strategic Management*, *23*(3), 394–412. https://doi.org/10.1108/CCSM-03-2016-0083

Köllen, T. (2021). Diversity management: A critical review and agenda for the future. *Journal of Management Inquiry*, *30*(3), 259–272. https://doi.org/10.1177/1056492619868025

Martins, L.L., & Parsons, C.K. (2007). Effects of gender diversity management on perceptions of organizational attractiveness: The role of individual differences in attitudes and beliefs. *Journal of Applied Psychology*, *92*(3), 865–875. https://doi.org/10.1037/0021-9010.92.3.865

Mousa, M. (2021). Does gender diversity affect workplace happiness for academics? The role of diversity management and organizational inclusion. *Public Organization Review*, *21*(1), 119–135. https://doi.org/10.1007/s11115-020-00479-0

Mueller, T.S. (2021). Blame, then shame? Psychological predictors in cancel culture behavior. *Social Science Journal*, *00*(00), 1–14. https://doi.org/10.1080/03623319.2021.1949552

Nagle, A. (2017). *Kill all normies: Online culture Wars from 4chan and Tumblr to Trump and the Alt-right*. Zero Books.

Norris, P. (2020). *Closed minds? Is a "cancel culture" stifling academic freedom and intellectual debate in political science?* Faculty Research Working Paper Series (No. RWP20–025).

Perrini, F., Costanzo, L.A., & Karatas-Ozkan, M. (2021). Measuring impact and creating change: A comparison of the main methods for social enterprises. *Corporate Governance (Bingley)*, *21*(2), 237–251. https://doi.org/10.1108/CG-02-2020-0062

Rawhouser, H., Cummings, M., & Newbert, S.L. (2019). Social impact measurement: Current approaches and future directions for social entrepreneurship research. *Entrepreneurship: Theory and Practice*, *43*(1), 82–115. https://doi.org/10.1177/1042258717727718

Roberson, Q.M. (2019). Diversity in the workplace: A review, synthesis, and future research agenda. *Annual Review of Organizational Psychology and Organizational Behavior*, *6*(October 2018), 69–88. https://doi.org/10.1146/annurev-orgpsych-012218-015243

Shepherd, D.A., & Patzelt, H. (2022). A call for research on the scaling of organizations and the scaling of social impact. *Entrepreneurship: Theory and Practice*, *46*(2), 255–268. https://doi.org/10.1177/1042258720950599

Siemieniako, D., Kubacki, K., & Mitręga, M. (2021). Inter-organisational relationships for social impact: A systematic literature review. *Journal of Business Research*, *132*, 453–469. https://doi.org/10.1016/j.jbusres.2021.04.026

Stamarski, C.S., & Son Hing, L.S. (2015). Gender inequalities in the workplace: The effects of organizational structures, processes, practices, and decision makers' sexism. *Frontiers in Psychology*, *6*, 1–20. https://doi.org/10.3389/fpsyg.2015.01400

Syed, J., & Tariq, M. (2017). Global Diversity Management. Oxford Research Encyclopedia of Business and Management. Retrieved 2 Apr. 2024, from https://oxfordre.com/business/view/10.1093/acrefore/9780190224851.001.0001/acrefore-9780190224851-e-62.

Talisse, R.B. (2019). *Overdoing democracy: Why we must put politics in its place*. Oxford University Press. https://doi.org/10.5817/PC2022-1-96

van Osch, Y., & Schaveling, J. (2020). The effects of part-time employment and gender on organizational career growth. *Journal of Career Development*, *47*(3), 328–343. https://doi.org/10.1177/0894845317728359

Viero, A., Barbara, G., Montisci, M., Kustermann, K., & Cattaneo, C. (2021). Violence against women in the Covid-19 pandemic: A review of the literature and a call for shared strategies to tackle health and social emergencies. *Forensic Science International*, *319*, 110650. https://doi.org/10.1016/j.forsciint.2020.110650

Vongalis-Macrow, A. (2014). *Career moves. Mentoring for women advancing their career and leadership in academia*. Rotterdam: SensePublishers. https://doi.org/10.1007/978-94-6209-485-7

Yadav, S., & Lenka, U. (2020). Diversity management: A systematic review. *Equality, Diversity and Inclusion*, *39*(8), 901–929. https://doi.org/10.1108/EDI-07-2019-0197

# Part 3

# Social impact on external stakeholders

# 10 Social impact of retailers on consumers. Building sustainable consumption

*Magdalena Stefańska, Blaženka Knežević and Iwona Olejnik*

## Introduction

In the 21st century, bolstering sustainable consumption has evolved into an indispensable component of the strategic approach adopted by companies engaged in B2C markets (Scherer & Palazzo, 2011). In particular, retailers have the opportunity to play a key role in educating consumers and meeting their need to protect the environment from further degradation. Considering consumers, this phenomenon is primarily manifested through their acquisition and utilization of products that align with the principles of sustainable consumption (Kuchinka et al., 2018).

Retail enterprises undoubtedly try to integrate Sustainable Development Goals (SDGs) and sustainable consumption within marketing strategies and technologies that strengthen responsible shopping and sustainable consumer attitudes and behavior. The frequent interactions between retailers and consumers empower them to shape buying habits, that support both positive outcomes, i.e. promoting responsible attitudes, as well as negative ones, i.e. those detrimental to the environment and society such as fast fashion, or even ultra-fast fashion.

This study aims to highlight the dilemma faced by retailers, who play a crucial role in shaping parallel consumption patterns, sustainable consumption, and ntensive consumption. From one side, retailers declare effects of their social impact (RSI) on consumers' awareness, attitudes, and shopping behavior through sales and communication strategies, focused on promoting sustainability and sustainable consumption. But on the other side, they implement strategies based on intensive consumption that often leads to overconsumption, creates waste, and are harmful for the environment. The conflict occurs between profit maximization for shareholders and broadly understood social goals. While economic success is not harmful, neglecting social or environmental objectives can be disruptive. The marginalization of environmental and social goals in the implementation of economic goals leads to many violations and deterioration of the quality of life and well-being of societies.

DOI: 10.4324/9781003480952-13

The chapter on RSI focuses on dimensions identified by Vanclay (2003) and includes everyday life, health, well-being, and the environment. It begins with the description of the theoretical underpinnings of social impact (SI) and sustainable consumption. Then, it shows the role of retail organizations in shaping consumption habits and introduces a framework for RSI on fostering sustainable consumption. The empirical section presents and discusses consumer research findings on perceived RSI.

## Theoretical foundations

### *Social impact*

Social impact can be defined and manifested in various ways. Taking into account the SDGs, social impact may manifest through specific attitudes and behaviors aimed at reducing certain social phenomena, such as discrimination based on age, gender, religion, views, or social exclusion, as well as addressing issues like lack of social cohesion and social inequalities. It is often integrated with environmental goals, as investments in the protection of the natural environment are beneficial for society.

Usually, SI is defined as "the intended and unintended social consequences, both positive and negative, of planned interventions (policies, programs, plans, projects) and any social change processes invoked by those interventions" (Vanclay et al., 2015). According to Stephan et al. (2016), SI is a beneficial outcome resulting from prosocial behavior that is noticed by individuals, organizations, or the environment. In essence, SI act is any significant or positive change that solves or at least addresses social injustice and challenges. Businesses or organizations achieve these goals through conscious and deliberate efforts or activities in their operations. The SI is mutual, with local communities seeing beneficial changes throughout the project, and volunteers returning home enlightened as global citizens (Henriques, 2010).

Social impact refers to the long-term, sustainable impact that a business has on society and the environment (IIC, 2023; Vanclay, 2020). According to Latané (1981), SI encompasses "any alterations in physiological states, subjective feelings, motivations, emotions, cognitions, beliefs, values, and behaviors that manifest in an individual, human, or animal due to the actual, implied, or perceived presence or actions of other individuals." While the process of conceptualization remains ongoing, certain common elements can be identified. Primarily, it entails a transformation in the knowledge, attitudes, or behaviors of the recipient groups for whom the objectives of SI were established by any given entity. Secondly, this impact can manifest as either positive or negative. In practice, organizations often report on their SI, yet they tend to focus on specifying their actions rather than quantitatively assessing the outcomes for the target groups. This tendency is particularly noticeable when dealing with customers. However, in the case of employees, the effects are typically more readily discernible.

The retail sector serves as a notable example of an industry that encounters challenges in reporting its SI. These difficulties stem from the imperative to harmonize economic objectives while aligning with the prevailing trends toward sustainable development and consumption.

### *Sustainable consumption vs food waste*

In accordance with the findings of Webb, Mohr, and Harris (2008), a socially responsible consumer is an individual who shapes his or her acquisition, usage, and disposition of products with the intention of minimizing or eradicating any adverse impacts while maximizing the enduring positive effects on society and the environment. In the opposition to sustainable consumption, consumption and even overconsumption leads to many social problems. The surge in lifestyle-related illnesses in the 21st century is related not only to personal choices but also to the abundance of low-health-value, affordable products (e.g., fast food, fast fashion).

Responsible consumption takes various forms, including the reduction of consumption by purchasing fewer items and cultivating heightened awareness regarding the ecological repercussions of one's personal consumption habits. Moreover, the embodiment of responsible consumption extends to the integration of models like the 3R or 5R principles (reduce, reuse, recycle, repair, rot) into daily life practices (Benton, 2015; Palmeira & Musso, 2020). Additionally, forward-thinking business models actively endorse sustainable consumption, exemplified by enterprises such as secondhand stores, social supermarkets, as well as platforms facilitating the sharing and distribution of food resources (Borusiak, 2021). Another domain contributing to the advancement of sustainable consumption is a cluster of enterprises that facilitate access to products, aiming to optimize the utility of owned resources, thereby operating within the framework of a sharing economy.

Sustainable consumption holds a prominent position within the United Nations SDGs, specifically under goal 2 (Zero Hunger) and goal 12 (Responsible Consumption and Production). These SDGs arise from significant imbalances in food distribution and consumption and are formulated to establish sustainable patterns in consumption and production. Notably, developed nations grapple with the issue of food waste. Eurostat data from 2020 reveals an alarming figure of 127 kilograms of wasted food per European Union citizen. Assuming an individual consumes over 650 kilograms of food annually, and with the EU population standing at approximately 450 million inhabitants, the theoretical amount of discarded food is substantial enough to sustain millions of people for a year in accordance with European nutritional standards.

Sustainable consumption (SC) is consistent with SI. Given that households are substantial contributors to food wastage, accounting for over 55% of the total, the imperative to address consumer behavior becomes paramount. This necessitates a multifaceted approach involving the rationalization of purchasing decisions, adept management of owned goods to curtail waste, and the dissemination of educational efforts to enlighten consumers about the repercussions of excessive consumption.

### *The retail sector and its role in shaping sustainable consumption attitudes and behavior*

At the turn of the 20th and 21st centuries, the retail sector in European countries witnessed notable shifts in producer-consumer relationships and strategies aligning with consumer needs and SDGs. Globalization, together with advancements in communication technologies, led to significant quantitative and qualitative transformations in this sector. These changes involved structural modifications, such as increased concentration marked by fewer retail outlets with larger sales areas, vertical integration where retail companies became integrators within distribution channels, and horizontal integration via the establishment of large network structures. Retail companies have evolved into "gatekeepers" within distribution channels, determining which producers and brands secure shelf space. Meanwhile, the virtualization of commerce and the rise of e-marketing and e-commerce have revolutionized consumer convenience in terms of accessibility, timing, and product variety, contributing to increased consumption. Retailers' omnichannel and multichannel strategies, together with technological advancements, have empowered consumers to effortlessly fulfill their needs. Notably, the emergence of new e-commerce giants like Amazon, Samsung, Ali Express, eBay, and Shein, among others, adeptly cater to the expectations of digital consumers through effective sales strategies (Lampert, 2024).

Recognizing their dual role as providers of goods and influential shapers of consumption trends, retailers stand poised to play a pivotal role in championing and supporting sustainable consumption initiatives. Consumers now enjoy unlimited options, making purchases at their convenience, choosing payment methods, delivery locations, and pickup preferences.

Without definitively attributing the driving force behind the change to either consumers or retail companies, a thesis that highlights mutual interactions influencing consumers can be posited. These interactions prompt shifts in consumer perspectives on consumption, their attitudes toward purchased goods and services, as well as alterations in shopping behaviors and the overall decision-making process related to purchases. This influence can yield both positive outcomes, enhancing consumers' quality of life, as well as negative consequences, fostering a propensity for excessive consumption and unnecessary purchases often triggered by emotional responses to specific communication (Table 10.1).

*Table 10.1* Declared goals of social impact by retailers

| *Goals (everyday life, health and well-being, and environment)* |
| --- |
| – Building awareness of responsible purchasing<br>– Educating consumers<br>– Promoting the consumption of products from responsible companies and responsibly produced goods<br>– Limiting the presence of harmful products for consumers through quality control<br>– Reducing the purchasing costs (both time and money) for buyers<br>– Rationalizing purchases by offering diverse product sizes<br>– Implementing product recycling policies<br>– Supporting the development of less developed countries by creating job opportunities<br>– Promoting locally manufactured products to bolster local employment<br>– Enabling suppliers to sell products in multiple countries where the company operates<br>– Rehabilitating neglected areas or spaces |

*Source:* Own elaboration based on CSR and Sustainable Development reports published online by retailers.

Identifying crucial social goals for a retailer involves understanding stakeholders' needs, both as buyers and representatives of local communities frequenting the store. Vadakkepatt et al. (2021) confirmed in their research that retail initiatives, serving as a bridge between suppliers and consumers, play a role in reducing, reusing, and recycling. Retailers can utilize their position in the supply chain to endorse social issues and achieve goals at both store and corporate levels. Tailored sales strategies at the store level and comprehensive corporate strategies based on social responsibility can drive these achievements.

Within a model framework, retailers possess the capacity to shape their customers' sustainable consumption – knowledge regarding the products they buy and their associated features, their overall attitude toward the retailer and their offers, as well as their preferences and ultimate purchasing decisions (Figure 10.1). This influence takes place during each store visit, exposure to advertising, or when customers are subject to various sensory stimuli. Visiting websites also supports consumers' knowledge and has an impact on them. As a result, several inquiries naturally emerge whether retailers exert their influence across all three domains (cognitive, affective, and conative), if the degree of influence varies, and whether this influence leans toward a positive or negative direction. Nevertheless, the overarching question that lingers is the fundamental purpose behind this influence.

Therefore, a reflection arises on how the role of retailers is perceived by consumers, what they know about retailers' SI, and how their perception as well as their attitude toward sustainable consumption and purchasing behavior are influenced.

There is a lack of systematic research on the SI of retailers. In the CSR or SD reports of retailers, numerous instances of initiatives directed toward local communities or consumers can be found. However, a common deficiency lies in the

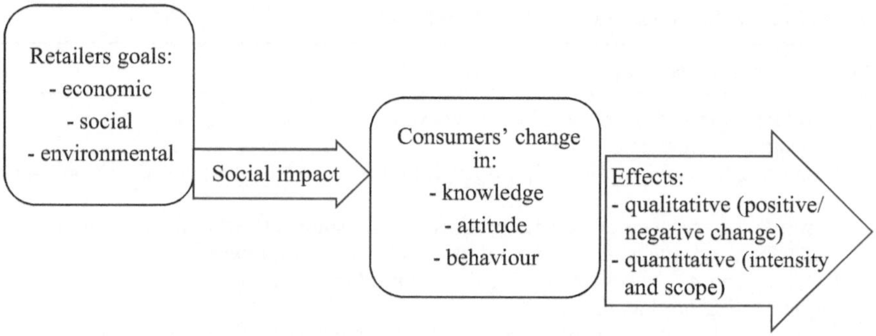


*Figure 10.1* Retailer influence on consumers – conceptual model

absence of evaluations regarding whether these actions have effectively yielded the intended quantitative outcomes (social change) if they were defined.

## Methodology of research

The aim of the research was to recognize perceived RSI through changes in consumers' awareness, attitudes, and shopping behavior – through communication strategies, focused on promoting sustainability and sustainable consumption. An online survey was conducted in 2023, on a sample of 558 students from the universities of economics in both of the studied countries, i.e. Croatia and Poland. Poland and Croatia share some economic similarities. Both countries have transitioned from centrally planned economies to market-oriented ones after the fall of communism (1989/1990), and they are now members of the European Union (Poland since 2004, Croatia since 2013). This change was especially observed in the retail sector in which several major transformations took place in both countries which increased competition and brought higher standards for consumers. In addition, consolidation of the retail market is the outcome of increased competition introduced by large international players that enter both analyzed markets. In the quest for higher market share or survival in the market, retailers have to increase their productivity per employee and enlarge their market share. As a consequence, since mid-2010-ties, the leading five companies in the retail market control more than 40% of the retail market (Knežević et al., 2014; Špička, 2016) in Poland even more. Finally, e-commerce has brought new challenges since the start of the new millennium which again leads us to discuss possible changes in consumer behavior in given markets. E-commerce brought new players to the market and new formats of sales.

The research instrument was constructed based on Alvarado-Herrera et al. (2017), designed to assess SI and measure corporate social responsibility (CSR in three key areas: social, environmental, and economic impact (Singhapakdi et al., 1996). Additionally, insights gained from in-depth interviews conducted

*Table 10.2* Characteristics of the sample

| | *Country of origin* | | | | | |
|---|---|---|---|---|---|---|
| | *Croatia* | | *Poland* | | *Total* | |
| | *frequency* | *%* | *frequency* | *%* | *frequency* | *%* |
| **Gender** | | | | | | |
| Female | 210 | 67 | 161 | 66 | 371 | 66 |
| Male | 102 | 32 | 80 | 33 | 182 | 33 |
| I don't want to answer | 2 | 1 | 3 | 1 | 5 | 1 |
| Total | 314 | 100 | 244 | 100 | 558 | 100 |
| **Monthly income** | | | | | | |
| they are enough for me, and I still manage to save a bit | 162 | 52 | 143 | 59 | 305 | 55 |
| I have enough for everything, but I can't spare anything | 105 | 33 | 78 | 32 | 183 | 33 |
| sometimes I am short of money by the end of the month | 35 | 11 | 16 | 7 | 51 | 9 |
| I often lack money by the end of the month | 12 | 4 | 7 | 3 | 19 | 3 |
| Total | 314 | 100 | 244 | 100 | 558 | 100 |

within student groups as part of the sustainable development and quality of life course were used to formulate questions aimed at gaining a deeper understanding of the influence of retailers.

Table 10.2 presents the demographic characteristics of the sample. The majority of respondents in both countries were female. Most respondents assessed their financial situation as sufficient, even allowing for savings. Furthermore, the average age of respondents was consistent in both groups, placing them within the end of Generation Y or the beginning of Generation Z. The generations are perceived as the drivers for change when considering sustainable consumption (Bentley, Fine & Neil, 2004; Fien, Neil & Bentley, 2008; Hume, 2010). While both groups rated satisfaction with their diets as 7 on a 10-point scale, Croatians exhibited a slightly higher level of satisfaction. The median score for both groups was 6 (Table 10.2).

## Results of research

### *Social impact perceived by consumers' and retailers'*

In the first stage of the analysis, the respondents' attitudes toward the perceived SI of retailers were examined. Social engagement of retailers in the fields of sports, culture, and education, as well as adherence to ethical standards and contribution to improving the quality of life of local communities, was assessed.

*Table 10.3* Perceived social impact of retailers – comparison between countries

| *Opinions* | *Croatia* | | *Poland* | | *Total* | |
|---|---|---|---|---|---|---|
| | *Mean* | *St. dev.* | *Mean* | *St. dev.* | *Mean* | *St. dev.* |
| Sponsor educational initiatives* | 3.07 | 0.89 | 2.59 | 1.00 | 2.86 | 0.97 |
| Sponsor public health protection activities (not only for employees) * | 3.19 | 0.93 | 2.64 | 1.03 | 2.95 | 1.01 |
| Implement/are highly committed to ethical principles and practices* | 3.16 | 0.93 | 2.82 | 1.00 | 3.01 | 0.98 |
| Sponsor cultural activities (concerts, events, meetings with authors, etc.) | 3.46 | 0.91 | 3.32 | 1.06 | 3.40 | 0.98 |
| Donate money/goods for social purposes | 3.32 | 1.00 | 3.41 | 1.00 | 3.36 | 1.00 |
| Help improve the quality of life of local communities (e.g. build roads, sidewalks, playgrounds, etc.) * | 2.96 | 1.13 | 2.37 | 1.10 | 2.71 | 1.16 |

*Source:* Own elaboration.
*$p < 0{,}001$

The results of the analysis are presented in Table 10.3. It can be concluded that, firstly, the overall assessment of SI is at a neutral level (close to the midpoint of the scale). Slightly higher ratings are given by respondents from Croatia, while respondents from Poland tend to be slightly more skeptical. Secondly, in most areas, respondents, regardless of their country of origin, perceive the SI differently. Only in some respects – sponsoring culture and making donations – there were no statistically significant differences observed. Furthermore, in these areas, the highest averages were obtained.

The key to identifying the impact is to determine whether there has been a change in the assessment of the messages by the recipients. Respondents may not have had knowledge about the actions of the retailer in the indicated areas, which could have been a reason for cautious judgment regarding SI. Nevertheless, responses about the consumer's perception of a change in their level of knowledge may exhibit greater decisiveness.

The findings regarding the SI, in the form of change, are outlined in Table 10.4. The respondents from Croatia exhibit a slightly stronger belief that their knowledge has expanded due to interactions with retailers. On the contrary, the respondents, especially those from Poland, tend to reject the idea of relying on retailers for guidance on their purchasing decisions, including what to buy and consume. Consequently, it can be inferred that these consumers are inclined toward autonomy and may not seek education in this domain.

Generally, consumers from both countries are not strongly convinced of the SI of retailers. The average value is close to 3.0, which reflects *neither agree nor disagree* opinion. As far as knowledge is concerned, Croatians are more convinced about the impact on their knowledge than Polish respondents. Also, Croatians

*Table 10.4* Perceived by consumers cognitive-affective-conative (CAC) results of social impact – comparison

| | *Mean* | *St. dev.* | *Mean* | *St. dev.* | *Mean* | *St. dev.* |
|---|---|---|---|---|---|---|
| **Knowledge** | | | | | | |
| I know more about many foods, thanks to additional information obtained in stores* | 2.90 | 0.97 | 2.57 | 1.09 | 2.76 | 1.03 |
| Shops do not enrich my knowledge about healthy eating.* | 3.57 | 1.00 | 3.76 | 1.17 | 3.65 | 1.08 |
| It happens that the products offered in a given network are accompanied by additional information in the store that I did not know* | 2.98 | 0.91 | 2.71 | 1.12 | 2.87 | 1.01 |
| I don't need suggestions from the store to know what I want to buy and eat* | 3.66 | 1.06 | 4.04 | 1.10 | 3.83 | 1.09 |
| I think that shops inform me about products that are beneficial for my health (e.g. about reducing the amount of salt in the product or reducing the amount of sugar) | 3.01 | 1.06 | 2.84 | 1.14 | 2.94 | 1.10 |
| **Emotions** | | | | | | |
| I feel that the activities of the stores have nothing to do with promoting healthy eating habits | 3.36 | 0.98 | 3.43 | 1.12 | 3.39 | 1.04 |
| I have a feeling that the stores shape my eating habits in a positive way* | 2.71 | 1.06 | 2.27 | 1.07 | 2.52 | 1.09 |
| I feel that the activities of the stores do not help me in making the so-called reasonable purchases* | 3.43 | 0.96 | 3.67 | 1.18 | 3.53 | 1.06 |
| I feel that I am helping someone by participating in fundraisers organized in stores | 3.30 | 1.06 | 3.35 | 1.15 | 3.32 | 1.10 |
| The fact that the store where I shop has a social campaign (charity collections) evokes positive emotions in me* | 3.30 | 1.04 | 3.48 | 1.13 | 3.38 | 1.08 |
| **Shopping Behavior** | | | | | | |
| Grocery stores – have a positive influence on me in the long term – I eat better** | 2.97 | 1.01 | 2.48 | 1.05 | 2.76 | 1.06 |
| The presence of shops with products I like influences the routes I take to and from home. ** | 3.15 | 0.99 | 3.36 | 1.25 | 3.24 | 1.11 |
| Thanks to shopping in stores, I like – I can better adjust my shopping to my daily rhythm | 3.31 | 0.94 | 3.43 | 1.09 | 3.36 | 1.01 |

(*Continued*)

*Table 10.4* (Continued)

| | *Mean* | *St. dev.* | *Mean* | *St. dev.* | *Mean* | *St. dev.* |
|---|---|---|---|---|---|---|
| **Shopping Behavior** | | | | | | |
| I buy more than I need in the store where I usually shop – through attractive promotions (e.g. Two products for the price of 1) | 3.22 | 1.17 | 3.21 | 1.29 | 3.21 | 1.22 |
| My behavior and actions it happen that I regularly make a detour to go to a particular store for shopping | 3.39 | 0.98 | 3.36 | 1.25 | 3.38 | 1.11 |

*Source:* Own elaboration.
**p* < 0,001, ***p* < 0,05

represent a more neutral attitude toward the opinion: *I have a feeling that the stores shape my eating habits in a positive way*. Polish respondents probably perceived themselves as more independent, and believe, that their consumption style is not shaped by retailers. It can also be noticed that Croatians are more optimistic (however, it is still close to neutral value) about better eating habits owing to retailers. To sum up, retailers overestimate their positive impact on rational and sustainable consumption and – on the other side – consumers are not fully aware of the impact of retailers on their general consumption habits.

In the second stage of our research, the analysis of correlations among SI and knowledge, feelings and shopping behavior of consumers were conducted. To do it, the following indices based on statistically valid differences between analyzed countries were created:

- SI (items no 1, 2, 3, and 6 from Table 10.3);
- knowledge (items no 1, 2, 3, and 4 from Table 10.4);
- feelings (items no 2, 3, and 5 from Table 10.4);
- shopping behavior (items 1 and 2 from Table 10.4).

Since the normal distribution was confirmed, the Pearson correlation coefficients were estimated (Table 10.5).

*Table 10.5* Pearson correlation coefficients between SI and CAC model components

| | *Social impact* | | |
|---|---|---|---|
| | *All* | *Croatia* | *Poland* |
| Knowledge | 0.258** | 0.330** | 0.189** |
| Feelings | 0.297** | 0.368** | 0.267** |
| Shopping behavior | 0.348** | 0.415** | 0.277** |

*Source:* Own elaboration.
***p* < 0,01

The analysis confirmed much stronger relationship between SI and customer knowledge, feelings, and behavior in the Croatian group. This led to the conclusion that they are convinced more than Polish respondents about the impact of retail organizations in all three spheres: on their knowledge, attitude, and behavior. A stronger impact is observed in the sphere of shopping behavior.

## Discussion

The respondents of our research are rather cautious in expressing their opinions. Their assessment of retailers' impact on their lives does not differ between countries as far as knowledge, attitude, or behavior are concerned. The respondents are perceived as much more experienced in ICT and autonomous, proficient internet users than previous generations, who learn from the internet (Cirilli & Nicolini, 2019). Both respondents from Croatia and Poland represent gen Z and Y. They are immersed in the virtual world, while brick-and-mortar stores are a distant option – everything can be bought via the internet, especially during the COVID-19 pandemic. The differences in averages (Tables 10.3 and 10.4) between respondents from both countries generally are not high, mostly with respect to knowledge, where Croatians are more open to absorbing suggestions from retailers. However, there is the question about the skepticism of Polish respondents and its origin – that can be the direction of future research.

The general conclusion is that retailers educate consumers and build their awareness about sustainable consumption and inform them about it in CSR or SD reports (Stefańska, 2014). They assert a significant role in shaping consumer behavior and promoting responsible consumption through education and creating shopping experiences. However, the actual social impact they claim doesn't always align with the content of their social responsibility or sustainable development reports. This discrepancy raises concerns, as it suggests a gap between their professed commitments and tangible actions. Moreover, prevalent irregularities within the industry contribute to consumer skepticism, often leading to retailers' image crises and boycotts. The critical inquiry centers around the genuine contribution of retailers to the anticipated social impact related to sustainable consumption and development. It prompts an examination of how effectively and sincerely these entities implement initiatives that align with their stated values. Consequently, understanding the extent to which retailers genuinely foster responsible consumer behavior becomes pivotal in evaluating their true impact on sustainable development. The question about determining the intentions behind exerting social influence remains open. Probably, as Dal Mas et al. (2021) noticed, clear and extensive communication and translation of CSR initiatives are necessary to raise the awareness of sustainability and achieve a positive impact on retail business performance at the same time. The fact that consumers are the subject of social influence, but they also contribute to it through their attitudes and behaviors is another aspect of retailers' social influence which is worth emphasizing.

In light of retailers' goals, it is crucial to underscore that their primary objectives revolve around maximizing sales and generating profits. This is achieved by creating value and addressing consumers' needs in terms of location, time, quantity, quality, and the diversity of offerings. Although social objectives are not the primary goals, retailers often highlight them in their communication strategies as part of their socially responsible company image. Economic goals take precedence in for-profit organizations to ensure present and future stability and value. Social goals typically exist within a separate strategy, notably CSR. These goals materialize through implemented solutions engaging such stakeholders as employees and consumers, resulting in social or common value creation. The examples include employee volunteering, actions improving workplace safety in distribution channels, enhancing skills of business partners' employees, launching social campaigns for consumer engagement or charity involvement, and philanthropic activities such as sponsoring events or institutions (Muethel, Hoegl & Parboteeah, 2011; Breitsohl & Ehrig, 2017). The need to be engaged in the pursuit of social goals is reflected in the creation of separate entities, such as foundations or associations by large retail organizations, which, thanks to delegated resources and the appropriate competencies of employees, can achieve their intended strategic social goals more efficiently and effectively. Readers can learn about the positive effects of their efforts both offline and online.

Our research signals that the declared retailers' impact may be overestimated, i.e. its scope and actual results may be weaker than expected. This may result from a few phenomena observed in the last years in communication technology. First, retailers have no longer strong direct contact with consumers. In many stores, self-service is provided. Employees support the process of payment but no longer are informed in detail about products or services. What is more, it is not expected by consumers, who first check all information online, then buy or go to the store to pick up an order or to check the physical features of the product. As a result, the impact of the store is often limited to visual stimuli – for example, lower, promotional prices. However, prices are often integrated with sales promotion (buying more pieces or larger packaging), which leads to increased consumption and often waste production.

In conclusion, the integration of SDGs into organizational strategies has emphasized the importance of social goals alongside economic objectives. However, a critical area needing refinement lies in defining and measuring SI, selecting appropriate metrics, and establishing reference points. Measurement of SI is hard because reducing human experience to numbers fails to capture some part of it (Henriques, 2010). Social impact can be measured in terms of the changes that a business brings to society, such as reducing poverty, improving health, and promoting equality (IIC, 2023). The implementation of social goals must align with primary economic objectives in for-profit organizations.

According to Mackey et al. (2007), the supply of and demand for these investment opportunities determine socially responsible activities since they may change the present value of a firm's cash flows and will be positively or negatively related to future firm's market value. This leads to the conclusion that social and economic goals can reinforce each other and create a synergistic effect, provided that the latter do not compromise the well-being of stakeholders or the natural environment (Hansmann, Mieg & Frischknecht, 2012).

In the context of retailers, their responsibility extends to providing services for suppliers, aligning with economic, environmental, and social goals, which can have a positive impact on other stakeholders. However, expanding retailers' responsibility to the products they offer complicates their SI. This complexity includes positive aspects, like promoting environmentally friendly or Fairtrade products (Stefańska & Nestorowicz, 2015) and encouraging healthy consumption behaviors. On the other hand, it may involve negative aspects, such as selling products that contribute to health issues, generate more waste, or promote consumerism, leading to adverse social consequences.

Our chapter fits into the discussion on SI (Rawhouser, Cummings & Newbert, 2019). The considerations focus on the influence of retailers on a specific group of stakeholders. Retailers, as the final link in the product distribution chain, affect consumption by determining where, when, in what quantities, in what structure, and under what conditions customers can meet their needs. Currently, they are facing challenges related to the climate crisis, energy crisis, the effects of the COVID-19 pandemic, as well as changes in the purchasing behavior of younger generations, which are more diverse in terms of consumption style and ways of meeting their needs. At the same time, building a competitive advantage requires an effective combination of cost and differentiation strategies, but integrated with SDGs.

Such studies on the SI of retailers and their perception by consumers have not been conducted yet for several reasons. Firstly, there was a greater demand for measuring economic impact (for owners) and environmental impact (due to prevailing regulations or expectations from specific stakeholder groups – e.g., legislators, local authorities, business partners, and international organizations). What is more, customers declare that they are interested in sustainable and responsible consumption while also they want to purchase goods at attractive price levels. Even though environmental issues are important to them, they place their own needs, safety, and personal development much higher in their value system and expectations. They are willing to forgo environmental actions when their incomes are insufficient. This leads to the conclusion that although consumers feel the need to behave and consume according to the sustainability concept – they are not enough supported in that style of consumption.

To conclude, consumers face challenges in resisting excessive consumption of the items detrimental to health and social life. Widespread sales promotions further encourage buying in larger quantities, including unhealthy products. Retailers, affecting consumer choices, can steer consumption patterns. With growing emphasis on social responsibility and consumerism trends, retailers face external pressures to promote positive behaviors and adopt environmentally and socially responsible strategies. This shifts retailers into a constrained sphere, driven by external factors to reinforce favorable consumer conduct.

Considering the specifics of retailers' activities, they have the greatest opportunities for frequent, regular, and direct interactions with consumers, compared to other market participants. This interaction can bring positive as well as negative consequences – for society and the planet.

## References

Alvarado-Herrera, A., Bigne, A., Aldas-Manzano, J., & Curras-Perez, R. (2017). A scale for measuring consumer perceptions of corporate social responsibility following the sustainable development paradigm. *Journal of Business Ethics*, *140*(2), 243–262. https://doi.org/10.1007/s10551-015-2654-9

Bentley, M., Fien, J., & Neil, C. (2004). Sustainable consumption: Young Australians as agents of change. *Final Report, National Youth Affairs Research Scheme, Modern Economy*, *13*(12), 1–156.

Benton, Jr, R. (2015). Reduce, reuse, recycle…and refuse. *Journal of Macromarketing*, *35*(1), 111–122. http://doi.org/10.1177/02761467145346

Borusiak, B. (2021). Sustainable consumption. In M. Stefańska (Ed.), *Sustainability and sustainable development*, 35–41. PUEB Publishing House, Poznan. http://doi.org/10.18559/978-83-8211-074-6/I3

Breitsohl, H., & Ehrig, N. (2017). Commitment through employee volunteering: Accounting for the motives of inter-organisational volunteers. *Applied Psychology: An International Review*, *66*(2), 260–289. https://doi.org/10.1111/apps.12092

Cirilli, E., & Nicolini, P. (2019). Digital skills and profile of each generation: A review. *International Journal of Developmental and Educational Psychology*, *3*(1), 487–496. https://doi.org/10.17060/ijodaep.2019.n1.v3.1525

Dal Mas, F., Tucker, W., Massaro, M., & Bagnoli, C. (2021). Corporate social responsibility in the retail business. A case study. *Corporate Social Responsibility and Environmental Management*, *29*. https://doi.org/10.1002/csr.2198.

Fien, J., Neil, C., & Bentley, M. (2008). Youth can lead the way to sustainable consumption. *Journal of Education for Sustainable Development*, *2*(1), 51–60. https://doi.org/10.1177/097340820800200111

Hansmann, R., Mieg, H.A., & Frischknecht, P.M. (2012). Principal sustainability components: An empirical analysis of synergies between the three pillars of sustainability. *International Journal of Sustainable Development & World Ecology*, *19*, 451–459.

Henriques, A. (2010). *Corporate impact measuring and managing your social footprint*. Routledge, Earthscan.

Hume, M. (2010). Compassion without action: Examining the young consumers consumption and attitude to sustainable consumption. *Journal of World Business*, *45*(4), 385–394.

IIC. (2023). *Social value and social impact: Understanding the differences*. Retrieved from https://investorsincommunity.org

Knežević, B., Knego, N., & Delić, M. (2014). The retail concentration and changes of the grocery retail structure. *Journal for the International and European Law, Economics and Market Integrations*, *1*(2), 37–51.

Kuchinka, D.G.J., Balazs, S., Gavriletea, M.D., & Djokic, B.-B. (2018). Consumer attitudes toward sustainable development and risk to brand loyalty. *Sustainability, 10*(4), 997. https://doi.org/10.3390/su10040997

Lampert, E. (2024). *The world's top ecommerce companies* (and Top Fastest-Growing Companies) (2023). Retrieved January 3, 2024, from https://www.similarweb.com/blog/sales/selling-to-ecommerce/top-ecommerce-companies/

Latané, B. (1981). The psychology of social impact. *American Psychologist*, *36*(4), 343–356. https://doi.org/10.1037/0003-066X.36.4.343

Mackey, A., Mackey, T.B., & Barney, J.B. (2007). Corporate social responsibility and firm performance: Investor preferences and corporate strategies. *The Academy of Management Review*, *32*(3), 817–835. http://www.jstor.org/stable/20159337

Muethel, M., Hoegl, M., & Parboteeah, K. (2011). National business ideology and employees' prosocial values. *Journal of International Business Studies*, *42*, 183–201. https://doi.org/10.1057/jibs.2010.47

Palmeira, M., & Musso, F. (2020). 3Rs of sustainability values for retailing customers as factors of influence on consumer behavior. In F. Musso, E. Druica (Ed.), *Handbook of research on retailing techniques for optimal consumer engagement and experiences*, 421–444.

Rawhouser, H., Cummings, M., & Newbert, S.L. (2019). Social impact measurement: Current approaches and future directions for social entrepreneurship research. *Entrepreneurship Theory and Practice*, *43*(1), 82–115. https://doi.org/10.1177/1042258717727718

Scherer, A.G., & Palazzo, G. (2011). The new political role of business in a globalized world: A review of a new perspective on CSR and its implications for the firm, governance, and democracy. *Journal of Management Studies*, *48*, 899–931. https://doi.org/10.1111/j.1467-6486.2010.00950.x

Singhapakdi, A., Vitell, S.J., Rallapalli, K.C., & Kraft, K.L. (1996). The perceived role of ethics and social responsibility: A scale development. *Journal of Business Ethics*, *15*, 1131–1140.

Špička, J. (2016). Market concentration and profitability of the grocery retailers in Central Europe. *Central European Business Review, 5*(3), 5–24. https://doi.org/10.18267/j.cebr.155

Stefańska, M. (2014). *Rola społecznej odpowiedzialności w tworzeniu przewagi konkurencyjnej przedsiębiorstw handlu detalicznego*. Wydawnictwo Uniwersytetu Ekonomicznego w Poznaniu.

Stefańska, M., & Nestorowicz, R. (2015). Development of the fair trade idea in Europe and the United States. In M. Stefańska & R. Nestorowicz (Ed.), *Fair trade in CSR strategy of global retailers,* 35–64, 204. Palgrave Macmillan.

Stephan, U., Patterson, M., Kelly, C., & Mair, J. (2016). Organizations driving positive social change: A review and an integrative framework of change processes. *Journal of Management*, *42*(5), 1250–1281. https://doi.org/10.1177/0149206316633268

Vadakkepatt, G.G., Winterich, K.P., Mittal, V., Zinn, W., Beitelspacher, L., Aloysius, J., Ginger, J., & Reilman, J. (2021). Sustainable retailing. *Journal of Retailing*, *97*(1), 62–80. https://doi.org/10.1016/j.jretai.2020.10.008
Vanclay, F. (2020). Reflections on social impact assessment in the 21st century. *Impact Assessment and Project Appraisal, 38*(2), 126–131. https://doi.org/10.1080/14615517.2019.1685807
Vanclay, F. (2003). International principles for social impact assessment. *Impact Assessment and Project Appraisal*, *21*(1), 5–12. https://doi.org/10.3152/147154603781766491
Vanclay, F., Esteves, A.M., Aucamp, I., Research, E., & Franks, D.M. (2015). Social impact assessment: Guidance for assessing and managing the social impact of projects (p. 107). *International Association for Impact Assessment*. Retrieved from https://www.iaia.org/uploads/pdf/SIA_Guidance_Document_IAIA.pdf.
Webb, D.J., Mohr, L.A., & Harris, K.E. (2008). A re-examination of socially responsible consumption and its measurement. *Journal of Business Research*, *61*, 91–98. https://doi.org/10.1016/j.jbusres.2007.05.00

# 11 Areas of social impact of top-listed universities worldwide

*Magdalena Rojek-Nowosielska, Bogusława Drelich-Skulska and Anna H. Jankowiak*

## Introduction

Universities have historically played a key role in the development of societies, but their role has undergone some changes over the centuries. The core activities of European universities usually include two key missions: teaching and research. In recent years, a third mission has been added, namely activities that will facilitate the building and fostering of relationships with the local community and the business sector. The term "third mission" is not explicitly defined in the literature on the subject. In Europe and the United States, the "third mission" is usually understood as "all activities concerned with the generation, use, application and exploitation of knowledge and other university capabilities outside academic environments" (Carrión et al., 2012). In Latin American countries, on the other hand, the concept of a "Triple Helix" model of university-industry-government relations is well-known and widespread (Leydesdorff & Etzkowitz, 1996). The third-mission activities of universities can be clarified through analogy with the following social roles (Betts & Lee, 2005; Rubens et al., 2017):

- Trainer – providing to the local economy an ample supply of skilled young graduates;
- Innovator – delivering and commercializing academic knowledge;
- Partner – providing technical know-how;
- Regional talent magnet – making the region more attractive by using the presence of a university to attract talented academics, entrepreneurs, and engineers;
- Facilitator – facilitating networking between the private and public sectors.

This list does not exhaust the possible social roles of the university but gives a rough idea of its potential involvement.

Interest in the concept of "university social responsibility" has been growing, especially over the past ten years (Jorge & Peña, 2017; Meseguer-Sánchez

DOI: 10.4324/9781003480952-14

et al., 2020). In the literature, there are four main areas of interest that comprise this concept (Chen & Vanclay, 2021). The first area concerns the fundamental purpose of universities (Boyer, 1996; Vasilescu et al., 2010). Another is studies related to the concept of corporate social responsibility (CSR) and the idea that CSR, human rights, and international ESG standards apply to all organizations, including public and private, for-profit and not-for-profit (Brdulak et al., 2020; Nejati et al., 2011; Vanclay & Hanna, 2019; United Nations, 2011). A third area relates to the concept of campus sustainability, eco-campuses, and green universities (Posner & Stuart, 2013). The final area involves studies related to the notion that universities should participate in and contribute to the communities in which they are located (Chile & Black, 2015; Mtawa et al., 2016; Winter et al., 2006).

When explaining the concept of "sustainability in higher education," it should be made clear that the idea does not just involve integrating environmental issues into the university's operations by, for example, having environmentally friendly facilities, campus greening, or teaching about sustainability (Lozano et al., 2013; Shriberg, 2002). Other important issues include a good relationship with local residents (Chen & Vanclay, 2020), ensuring human rights in supply chains (Vanclay & Hanna, 2019), and contributing to community development (Mbah, 2019) and community engagement (Chile & Black, 2015). Like many other organizations, universities are expected to meet various international standards and to contribute to achieving the United Nations Sustainable Development Goals (SDGs) (Filho, 2020). Some researchers believe HEIs have a moral responsibility to support social missions in their communities (Maurrasse, 2001). To do this, universities need to build upon traditional knowledge production activities to deliver social impact education, engage diverse learners, and provide space for other members of society (including local organizations and community members) to come together to achieve shared goals for their place (Urquilla, 2016). Universities and their campuses influence the economy both indirectly and directly, through retail growth, providing skilled workers to the job market, and creating new communities of student housing and consumers in a specific place.

To summarize the discussion so far, it is important to note the evolution of the role of modern universities, which was initiated by the desire to incorporate the third mission, and which continues today with the application/implementation of the concept of social impact. The definition of social impact (referred to here as university social impact) was defined and presented in Chapter 1 of this monograph. Thus, the social impact of a university is

> The consequences for human populations of any public or private actions that alter the ways in which people live, work, play, relate to one another, organize to meet their needs, and generally cope as members of society. The term also includes cultural impacts involving changes to the norms, values, and beliefs that guide and rationalize their cognition of themselves and their society.
>
> (Guidelines and Principles For Social Impact Assessment, 1994)

The social impact that universities have or can have must be considered in terms of the outcomes that contribute to improving various aspects of a community's life but can also cause adverse repercussions. The assessment of social impact depends on the broader context, such as the demographic and health characteristics of the community, the degree of economic, legal, and institutional development, or the geographic features of the area inhabited by the community.

## Materials and methods

In order to answer the research questions, we used an exploratory approach. The study described in this chapter falls into the category of secondary, descriptive, and quantitative research. The analysis uses the Times Higher Education Impact Rankings, which report on the performance of universities in meeting the United Nations' SDGs. The rankings are open to any university that completes a survey on each of the 17 SDGs and provides evidence of real commitment to the goals. For a particular university to be listed in the overall ranking, data must be provided for at least four goals, one of which must be Goal 17 (Partnerships for the Goals). If this condition is not fulfilled, the university will not be included in the ranking, but its data will be displayed in the summary of university achievements for the specific goal.

The first report was compiled in 2019, but because the scope of the data provided was limited and it was therefore impossible to make comparisons with data from subsequent years, the 2019 data were not included in this study. Consequently, the subject of the secondary analysis is the data from 2020 to 2023. The analysis was based on the published reports for the four years, downloaded from https://www.timeshighereducation.com/impactrankings. The breakdowns and calculations in the following section (the average of the scoring results and the number of sets) were carried out using MS Excel spreadsheet tools (pivot table).

The chapter aims to introduce the key areas of universities' social impact out of the Times Higher Education Impact Rankings. We analyze the top 10 universities, starting from 2020. In the ranking, the universities' impact is assessed by its achievements in the Sustainable Development Goals. To reach the aim, we adopted detailed research questions: (1) Is there a leading university that has maintained a high position since it first appeared in the ranking? (2) In which countries are the top 10 universities located? (3) Which goals are least often indicated by the top 10 universities? (4) In which SDGs did the top 10 universities achieve the highest score?

## Results

The analysis of the figures in the reports revealed that the number of universities participating in the ranking, and thus the number of countries where the universities are based, is steadily rising. In 2020, 768 universities from 85 countries took part in the ranking, while in 2021, there were 1,118 universities from 94 countries. Thus, there was a year-on-year (YOY) increase in both the number of universities (by more than 45%) and the number of countries covered by the ranking (a 10% increase). In the following year (2022), 1,406 universities (a 25% YOY increase) from 106 countries (a 12% YOY increase) entered the ranking; in 2023, there was a total of 1,705 universities (a 21% YOY increase) from 116 countries (a 9% YOY increase). Thus, we can note a steady upward trend in the number of universities joining the ranking and of the countries in which they are located during the study period.

In each of the four years covered by the survey, the top 10 applicants with the highest rate of achievement of the SDGs overall were qualified for the analysis. The only exception is the year 2023, in which 11 universities were qualified, as the final indicator for achieving the SDGs had the same value. In the end, 22 institutions based in 11 countries were analyzed (Table 11.1).

Considering whether a given university participated in successive editions of the ranking and how many goals it submitted for review, we can see that only

*Table 11.1* Institutions analyzed and the number of goals, 2020–2023

| *Institution* | *Country* | *Number of goals reported in the year* | | | |
|---|---|---|---|---|---|
| | | *2020* | *2021* | *2022* | *2023* |
| Aalborg University | Denmark | | 17 | | 17 |
| Arizona State University (Tempe) | United States | 17 | 17 | 17 | 17 |
| Hokkaido University | Japan | | | 12 | |
| King Abdulaziz University | Saudi Arabia | | | 17 | |
| King's College London | United Kingdom | 17 | | | |
| La Trobe University | Australia | 11 | 14 | | |
| Newcastle University | United Kingdom | | | 17 | |
| Queen's University | Canada | | 17 | 17 | 17 |
| RMIT University | Australia | 8 | 8 | | 9 |
| Universiti Sains Malaysia | Malaysia | | | 17 | 17 |
| University College Cork | Ireland | | 15 | | |
| University of Alberta | Canada | | | | 17 |
| University of Auckland | New Zealand | 15 | 17 | 17 | |
| University of Bologna | Italy | 10 | | | |
| University of British Columbia | Canada | 17 | | | |
| University of Manchester | United Kingdom | 17 | 17 | 17 | 17 |
| University of Sydney | Australia | 13 | 14 | | |
| University of Tasmania | Australia | | | | 17 |
| University of Victoria | Canada | | | | 17 |
| University of Wollongong | Australia | | 16 | | |
| Western Sydney University | Australia | 17 | | 17 | 17 |
| Western University | Canada | | | 17 | 17 |

*Source:* Own elaboration.

two universities participated in the ranking in each year under review and reported data for all 17 Sustainability Goals. These were Arizona State University (Tempe) and the University of Manchester. However, if we take into account the overall SDGs achievement index, which ranks universities according to the highest number of points earned (data shown on www.timeshighereducation.com/impactrankings), Western Sydney University most often ranked first (twice, in 2022 and 2023).

As for the second research question, the two countries that dominated the ranking were Australia and Canada. Between 2020 and 2023, there were six universities from Australia and five from Canada, which demonstrates that universities located in these countries attach great importance to achieving the SDGs and fulfilling the third mission. The UK came next with three universities; the other leading universities in the top 10 were from Denmark, Ireland, Italy, Japan, Malaysia, New Zealand, Saudi Arabia, and the USA (one each).

Answering the third research question on the Sustainability Goals that were least frequently reported by the participating universities and taking into account data from all four years considered for the study, we can say that the least frequently reported goal was no. 2, namely zero hunger (Table 11.2).

Table 11.2 shows the number of institutions that reported a specific sustainability goal for the ranking in a given year. By arranging the results in order from least to most frequently reported, we obtained a hierarchy of the frequency of reporting Sustainability Goals. Looking at the overall picture, based on data from 2020 to 2023, we can see that goals no. 1 (no poverty), no. 14 (life below water), and no. 7 (affordable and clean energy) were the least frequently reported by universities in the THE Impact Ranking.

The summary in Table 11.3 makes it possible to answer the fourth research question: In which SDGs did the top 10 universities achieve the highest score? The order of the goals in the table is based on the number of points obtained by each SDG, calculated as a simple arithmetic average (those goals that were not submitted by the institutions were eliminated, which reduced the divisor in calculating the given average accordingly). Number 1 in the first column on the left indicates the highest position in the hierarchy.

From 2000 to 2023, the highest ranked goals (except for no. 17) were, respectively, no. 11 (sustainable cities and communities), no. 15 (life on the land), and no. 16 (peace, justice, and strong institutions). Surprisingly, goal no. 4 (quality education) ranked lowest among all goals reported by the higher education institutions.

## Discussion

When looking at the activities of the world's leading universities, one gets the impression that enacting the third mission is becoming a key task for higher education institutions. This is because social impact is the cornerstone for carrying

*Table 11.2* Hierarchy of Sustainable Development Goals according to their implementation by the institutions

| *2020* | | *2021* | | *2022* | | *2023* | | *Total number of times the goal was reported between 2020 and 2023* | |
|---|---|---|---|---|---|---|---|---|---|
| *Goal no.* | *Number of universities reporting the goal* | *Goal no.* | *Number of universities reporting the goal* | *Goal no.* | *Number of universities reporting the goal* | *Goal no.* | *Number of universities reporting the goal* | *Goal no.* | *Number of universities reporting the goal* |
| 6 | 7 | 2 | 7 | 5 | 9 | 9 | 10 | **2** | **34** |
| 14 | 7 | 5 | 8 | 10 | 9 | 1 | 10 | **1** | **35** |
| 7 | 7 | 7 | 8 | 8 | 9 | 2 | 10 | **14** | **35** |
| 2 | 7 | 14 | 8 | 4 | 9 | 3 | 10 | **7** | **36** |
| 13 | 7 | 1 | 8 | 1 | 9 | 4 | 10 | 9 | 37 |
| 9 | 8 | 9 | 9 | 9 | 10 | 14 | 10 | 16 | 37 |
| 12 | 8 | 10 | 9 | 12 | 10 | 16 | 10 | 15 | 37 |
| 1 | 8 | 4 | 9 | 7 | 10 | 15 | 10 | 4 | 37 |
| 16 | 8 | 3 | 9 | 13 | 10 | 10 | 11 | 5 | 37 |
| 15 | 8 | 13 | 9 | 3 | 10 | 13 | 11 | 13 | 37 |
| 4 | 9 | 16 | 9 | 14 | 10 | 7 | 11 | 6 | 38 |
| 3 | 9 | 15 | 9 | 11 | 10 | 11 | 11 | 3 | 38 |
| 5 | 9 | 12 | 10 | 15 | 10 | 8 | 11 | 10 | 39 |
| 10 | 10 | 8 | 10 | 6 | 10 | 6 | 11 | 12 | 39 |
| 11 | 10 | 11 | 10 | 16 | 10 | 5 | 11 | 8 | 40 |
| 8 | 10 | 6 | 10 | 2 | 10 | 12 | 11 | 11 | 41 |
| 17 | 10 | 17 | 10 | 17 | 10 | 17 | 11 | 17 | 41 |

*Source:* Own elaboration.

*Table 11.3* Hierarchy of Sustainable Development Goals by average number of points scored in each goal, 2020–2023

| | *2020* | *2021* | *2022* | *2023* | *On average between 2020 and 2023* |
|---|---|---|---|---|---|
| *Hierarchy of goals* | *Goal no.* | *Goal no.* | *Goal no.* | *Goal no.* | *Goal no.* |
| I | 17 | 17 | 17 | 17 | 17 |
| II | 15 | 9 | 11 | 11 | 11 |
| III | 3 | 11 | 16 | 14 | 15 |
| IV | 16 | 16 | 1 | 15 | 16 |
| V | 11 | 15 | 12 | 12 | 12 |
| VI | 12 | 8 | 5 | 16 | 14 |
| VII | 5 | 12 | 15 | 6 | 3 |
| VIII | 14 | 1 | 3 | 3 | 1 |
| IX | 7 | 6 | 14 | 8 | 8 |
| X | 9 | 14 | 2 | 2 | 6 |
| XI | 1 | 3 | 6 | 5 | 5 |
| XII | 10 | 10 | 8 | 10 | 9 |
| XII | 8 | 2 | 9 | 7 | 2 |
| XIV | 2 | 7 | 13 | 1 | 10 |
| XV | 6 | 5 | 10 | 13 | 7 |
| XVI | 4 | 4 | 7 | 9 | 13 |
| XVII | 13 | 13 | 4 | 4 | 4 |

*Source:* Own elaboration.

out research, educating students, and influencing the university community. Researchers incorporate elements related to SDGs into their studies, their lectures, and student assignments, and serving society is becoming a natural university activity. Many universities have introduced elements of SDGs into their missions, by promoting sustainable development, training responsible leaders, or developing green campuses. These activities are echoed in the rankings of the universities from different parts of the world that together want to change the environment in which they operate. The steadily growing number of universities in the THE Impact Ranking shows that meeting SDGs is gaining in importance. It is safe to assume that this trend will continue in the future, as the role of universities has long since moved beyond doing research and educating professionals.

The findings we presented in this chapter suggest that leading global universities are striving to achieve all or a significant number of SDGs. This is an ambitious task, but one that is difficult to accomplish because both universities and SDGs can be highly diverse. As a result, some goals are met to a significant degree, while others are met only at a basic level. It seems desirable, therefore, that individual universities should specialize in SDGs that can be fulfilled to a considerable degree. If individual universities choose the SDGs consciously when they are defining their missions and values, they will be able to carry out these activities purposefully and increase social impact in selected aspects. Setting a limited number of only three or four goals may bring more benefits to the local area, as the restricted financial resources available to universities regardless of their location will then be used more efficiently. Universities will also be able to enter into collaboration with partners, especially NGOs, to jointly realize their mission and goals and to carry out prosocial activities. It should be reiterated that such activities prevent social exclusion, marginalization, discrimination, and other negative social phenomena. They will also help a given academic community to engage in and concentrate on collectively selected activities. It is crucial to involve students in the university's implementation of the SDGs, as development that is in line with the idea of social impact will contribute to promoting these values in everyday life, raise the students' level of satisfaction, and shape appropriate work standards in the future. Specialization, however, may entail new rankings based only on individual SDGs, as opposed to rankings of all goals combined.

An analysis of the THE Impact Ranking and the Top 10 survey has led to some surprising conclusions. The first one is the low position of goal no. 4 (quality education). Pursuing this very goal seems natural for higher education institutions, whose "first" mission is to educate future professionals to the highest standards. Another surprising fact is the low number of American universities featured in the ranking. The data in Table 11.1 shows that only one US university received a rating as a leader in achieving the SDGs (Arizona State University, Tempe). Social impact is one of the factors reviewed by bodies accrediting US universities (e.g., AACSB), so the absence of leading US universities from the ranking may be surprising and is likely to be corrected in future years. Although there were 50 American universities in the 2023 ranking, the vast majority of them (34 universities) were placed in the 200+ positions in the 2023 ranking. We must conclude that, at present, the universities from Australia and Canada are clearly leading the way for global universities in achieving the SDGs.

## References

Betts, J.R., & Lee, C. (2005). Universities as drivers of regional and national innovation: An assessment of the linkages from universities to innovation and economic growth. In C.M. Beach, R.W. Boadway, & R. Marvin McInnis (Eds.), *Higher education in Canada*, 113–157. McGill-Queens University Press.

Boyer, E. (1996). The scholarship of engagement. *Bulletin of the American Academy of Arts and Sciences, 49*(7), 18–33.

Brdulak, H., Dąbrowski, T., Jastrzębska, E., & Legutko-Kobus, P. (2020). Social responsibility of Universities and colleges: The view of SGH Warsaw School of economics stakeholders. In K. Bachnik, M. Kaźmierczak, M. Rojek-Nowosielska, M. Stefańska, & J. Szumniak-Samolej (Eds.), *CSR in contemporary Poland institutional perspectives and stakeholder experiences,* 85–102. Palgrave Macmillan. https://doi.org/10.1007/978-3-030-42277-6

Carrión, A., García-Gutierrez, V.R., Bas, M.C., & Carot, J.M. (2012). A new methodology for measuring third mission activities of Universities. *Proceedings of 6th International Technology, Education and Development Conference Inted 2012*, 1218–1223.

Chen, C., & Vanclay, F. (2021). Transnational universities, host communities and local residents: Social impacts, university social responsibility and campus sustainability. *International Journal of Sustainability in Higher Education, 22*(8), 88–107. https://doi.org/10.1108/IJSHE-10-2020-0397

Chen, C., & Vanclay, F. (2020). University social responsibility in the context of economic displacement from the proposed upgrading of a higher education institution: The case of the University of Groningen Yantai campus. *International Journal of Educational Development, 78*(June), 1–7. https://doi.org/10.1016/j.ijedudev.2020.102268

Chile, L.M., & Black, X.M. (2015). University-community engagement: Case study of university social responsibility. *Education, Citizenship and Social Justice, 10*(3), 234–253.

Filho, W.L. (2020). Viewpoint: Accelerating the implementation of the SDGs. *International Journal of Sustainability in Higher Education, 21*(3), 507–511.

Larrán Jorge, M., & Andrades Peña, F. (2017). Analysing the literature on university social responsibility: A review of selected higher education journals. *Higher Education Quarterly, 71*(4), 302–319.

Leydesdorff, L., & Etzkowitz, H. (1996). Emergence of a Triple Helix of University-Industry- Government relations. *Science and Public Policy, 23*, 279–286.

Lozano, R., Lukman, R., Lozano, F., Huisingh, D., & Lambrechts, W. (2013). Declarations for sustainability in higher education: Becoming better leaders, through addressing the university system. *Journal of Cleaner Production, 48*, 10–19.

Maurrasse, D. (2001). *Beyond the campus: How colleges and universities form partnerships with their communities*. Routledge. https://doi.org/10.4324/9780203904350

Mbah, M. (2019). Can local knowledge make the difference? Rethinking universities' community engagement and prospect for sustainable community development. *The Journal of Environmental Education, 50*(1), 11–22.

Meseguer-Sánchez, V., Abad-Segura, E., Belmonte-Ureña, L., & Molina-Moreno, V. (2020). Examining the research evolution on the socio-economic and environmental dimensions on university social responsibility. *International Journal of Environmental Research and Public Health, 17*(13), 4729.

Mtawa, N.N., Fongwa, S.N., & Wangenge-Ouma, G. (2016). The scholarship of university-community engagement: Interrogating Boyer's model. *International Journal of Educational Development, 49*, 126–133.

Nejati, M., Shafaei, A., Salamzadeh, Y., & Daraei, M. (2011). Corporate social responsibility and universities: A study of top 10 world universities' websites. *African Journal of Business Management, 5*(2), 440–447.

Posner, S., & Stuart, R. (2013). Understanding and advancing campus sustainability using a systems framework. *International Journal of Sustainability in Higher Education, 14*(3), 264–277.

Rubens, A., Spigarelli, F., Cavicchi, A., & Rinaldi, C. (2017). Universities' third mission and the entrepreneurial university and the challenges they bring to higher education institutions. *Journal of Enterprising Communities, 11*(3), 354–372. https://doi.org/10.1108/JEC-01-2017-0006

Shriberg, M. (2002). Institutional assessment tools for sustainability in higher education: Strengths, weaknesses, and implications for practice and theory. *International Journal of Sustainability in Higher Education*, *3*(3), 254–270.

The Interorganizational Committee on Guidelines and Principles for Social Impact Assessment. (1994). *Guidelines and principles for social impact assessment.*

United Nations. (2011). *Guiding principles on business and human rights: Implementing the UN 'respect, protect and remedy' framework, united nations. Geneva.* Retrieved from www.ohchr.org/ Documents/Publications/GuidingPrinciplesBusinessHR_EN.pdf

Urquilla, M. (2016). To build leaders for social impact, universities must adapt. *Stanford Social Innovation Review*. Retrieved from https://ssir.org/articles/entry/to_build_leaders_for_social_impact_universities_must_adapt#

Vanclay, F., & Hanna, P. (2019). Conceptualizing company response to community protest: Principles to achieve a social license to operate. *Land*, *8*(6), 101.

Vasilescu, R., Barna, C., Epure, M., & Baicu, C. (2010). Developing university social responsibility: A model for the challenges of the new civil society. *Procedia – Social and Behavioral Sciences*, *2*(2), 4177–4182.

Winter, A., Wiseman, J., & Muirhead, B. (2006). University-community engagement in Australia: Practice, policy and public good. *Education, Citizenship and Social Justice*, *1*(3), 211–230.

# 12 Social impact of universities of third age on seniors

*Iwona Olejnik, Pavel Kotyza and Magdalena Stefańska*

## Introduction

Population aging observed in developed countries confirms a real need to create and improve living conditions, protect the environment, and implement tools that help achieve expected quality of life and well-being in society, especially for seniors. Therefore, the needs of this segment are more and more often included in the strategies of organizations and institutions from various industries, in particular those related to health care, tourism, sports and recreation (Santos et al., 2014), new technologies, and financial services, including savings for old age (Peacock & Künemund, 2007; Khosravi, Rezvani, & Wiewiora, 2016; Olejnik & Stefańska, 2020), as well as education (Noble et al., 2021).

The aim of the chapter is to explain the social impact of organizations such as universities of the third age (U3A) on seniors. It seems obvious that the conclusions of our research are of interest for the achievement of the United Nations Sustainable Development Goals, specifically goal three, i.e., ensuring healthy lives and promoting well-being for all at all ages. Due to the fact that seniors are retired, and their physical or mental health is weaker than few decades ago, they are often not visible on the market and are neglected because of lower financial status than during the time they were active on the labor market. However, many researchers indicate that their engagement in society and social life as well as productive activities are associated with positive outcomes on a variety of widely interpreted health indicators.

The chapter will discuss social impact of universities of the third age within the Czech University of Life Sciences Prague (CULS) and Erga Omnes from Poznań University of Economics and Business in Poland.

## Literature review

One of the earliest definitions of SI indicates that social impact is the consequence to human populations of any public and private actions that alter the ways in which people live, work, play, relate to one another, organize to meet

DOI: 10.4324/9781003480952-15

their needs, and generally cope as members of society (Interorganizational Committee on Guidelines and Principles for Social Impact Assessment, 1994). It means that the source of impact may come both from individuals and any type of organization, and that the results of the impact will rely on changes in knowledge, emotions, and behavior. Such a broadly interpreted definition may lead to the conclusion that the change evoked by activities results in changes in norms, values, and beliefs of the target group.

For centuries, universities have been primarily responsible for educating future generations and conducting conceptual and practically implemented research. These areas constituted the two main pillars of their contribution to society. Recent decades have observed the expansion of expectations targeted at this type of institution to include a third pillar, i.e., social impact. Certainly, this influence has always existed, but it has not been identified, measured, or shaped in a planned way. The dilemmas caused by the fact of reporting social impact, at least for its conscious shaping, increased the need to explain the essence of social impact in the activities of universities, including its addressees, as well as the methods and techniques of its measurement. Social expectations toward universities therefore concern their "greater efficiency, effectiveness and relevance for society" (Meyer & Sporn, 2018).

As Godonoga and Sporn indicate (2023): "university's contribution to society is not only a moral duty but has also become a key element of its mission, strategy and performance". Social impact is therefore an element of the so-called third mission of universities, which emphasizes not only the need for a greater impact of scientific research on society but also the increased need to expand the educational offer in order to provide common benefits to society (Scott, 2006). On the other hand, Johnson (2020) indicates that social impact of university is "an effect on, change or benefit to the economy, society, culture, public policy or services, health, the environment or quality of life, beyond academia". As Vanclay (2002) emphasizes, the interpretive understanding of the issue of social impact is continuously evolving.

Social impact is also consistent with another context – the social responsibility of universities, which basically concerns three areas. Firstly, social responsibility of universities includes the exchange of knowledge between scientists and business practitioners, aimed at generating new knowledge and finding practical solutions to contemporary challenges (Carl & Menter, 2021). Secondly, social responsibility of universities also comprises volunteering activities, including those related to the involvement of employees and students, as well as partnerships with external stakeholders (Godonoga & Sarrico, 2019). Finally, as Miotto, Blanco-González, and Castillo-Feito (2018) emphasize, social responsibility of universities engages a wider range of stakeholders in their activities, when offering services to a non-traditional segment of customers, such as mature people, seniors, or people who prefer flexible ways of learning (Godonoga & Sporn, 2023).

As regards the latter area, universities, especially in developed countries, consider the ongoing demographic changes when shaping their educational offer. They begin to notice not only youth and working people but also pensioners. Older people have a lot of free time and can therefore be an important target segment for many entities. The literature study is dedicated to social impact, and seniors emphasize such topics as change of attitude, mental condition, and physical health. However, programs of organizations dedicated to seniors are not fully recognized and estimated due to expenses and lack of identified long-term benefits. The research on various dimensions of aging also includes issues related to lifelong learning. Nevertheless, relatively little attention is paid to analyzing the impact of learning older individuals on their life satisfaction (Formosa, 2014) and overall well-being (Ricardo & Porcarelli, 2019), as well as its impact on the environment.

Many authors emphasize that learning-related activities positively influence seniors, particularly contributing to the extension of the period preceding the occurrence of health issues in older individuals (Ondrakova, 2014). However, when analyzing, for example, OECD or EUROSTAT statistical data on participation in lifelong learning, it can be noticed that the participation of adults is scarce.[1] The perspective of lifelong learning is a fundamental element of the concept of active and successful aging, especially in societies where life expectancy is increasing (Günder, 2014). The universities of third age are one of the responses to these changes (U3A).

As noted by Ricardo and Porcarelli (2019), U3As are part of informal learning, enabling older individuals to participate in education and socialization. They offer activities that seniors were previously unable to be engaged in during their lives for various reasons. Formosa (2010) emphasizes that helping older people to integrate with society, develop their intellectual potential, shape a sense of belonging to society and a sense of personal fulfillment, as well as psychological support, including increased self-acceptance, is the role of the universities of third age.

U3As fulfill various roles, and the literature indicates the following among the most important:

- Social meeting place: their primary role is to counteract the isolation and loneliness of older individuals, providing a venue for social interactions;
- Extension of the period before health issues occurs: these universities contribute to prolonging the period preceding the occurrence of health problems in older individuals;

- Facilitation of integration: they offer new possibilities for better integration, shaping family relationships (e.g., with grandchildren), connections with the local community, and interactions with peers;
- Promotion of physical, intellectual, and social activity: they contribute to the increased physical, intellectual, and social activity of seniors, thereby enhancing the quality of their lives in terms of knowledge, culture, and more.

U3A may therefore contribute to improving the quality of life in each of the areas that determine this quality. According to the Council for Third Age (2012), decent quality of life for seniors includes six aspects, i.e., physical, social, emotional, spiritual, intellectual, as well as vocational wellness. Also, as defined by Statistics Poland (2023), "The effect of the operation of universities of the third age is therefore multidimensional – it allows the implementation of the students' individual needs and, in the social dimension, prevents the exclusion of elderly people in various spheres of life". However, statistical research conducted by this institution shows that universities' activities are aimed not only at older people. Universities and seniors using their services also implement social activities for those in need. The groups of recipients of these activities include other seniors but also children and youth (25%), sick and disabled persons, and the poor. They also conduct activities for local communities, victims of natural disasters and accidents, natural environment, animals as well as institutions (cultural, associations, parish), etc.

Their representatives also regularly participate in social consultations organized by local government or central administration or are involved in advocacy, representing interests of the elderly. Therefore, it can be stated that there is a diffusion of social capital from seniors to other beneficiaries (Zgliczyński, 2012).

In the light of the above considerations, the question arises of how the created social value is understood, who it affects, what social effects universities of the third age bring, and what the scope of the created social value is. Research on this topic is conducted both among people involved in the organization and operation of such universities (Strunga, 2015), as well as seniors participating in classes. Considering research among seniors, special attention of researchers is focused on the quality of life of seniors participating in U3A activities, although research does not always focus on the impact of U3A on this quality of life (Zielińska- Więczkowska et al., 2012; Kobylarek et al., 2022). However, research aimed at verifying the impact of participation in U3A activities on the lives of seniors is increasingly often conducted. For example, Sahin et al. (2023) assessed the quality of life and related factors among seniors, comparing this quality among people who participated in U3A classes and those who are just starting such education. In turn, Kozieł and Trafiałek (2016) compared the quality of life of seniors studying at U3A with the control group, i.e., people who have not undertaken such activities at all.

Summing up, research on the social impact of U3A focuses primarily on assessing the relationship between seniors' participation in classes at such universities and the quality of their life. Therefore, a cognitive gap related to the comprehensive assessment of the social impact of such universities is noticeable. The conducted research is an attempt to identify social values and impact by indicating the interactions and their effects occurring between U3A participants.

## Methodology

Primary research was conducted to identify the social impact of U3A on seniors. To assess the perceived impact of U3A on seniors, two groups of stakeholders were studied, i.e., university representatives involved in organizing and teaching at such universities, as well as the service recipients, i.e., seniors participating in classes. Qualitative studies were conducted in which the method of individual-in-depth-interviews was applied. They were followed by semi-structured interviews and field notetaking, using two versions of the scenario – one for the organizers, the other version for seniors. The study was conducted for four months in 2023. Participants were selected through purposive sampling method. This kind of sampling was found appropriate to obtain the best insights about the social impact of the organization on seniors. Purposive sampling is useful in qualitative research, particularly among populations, where there may be limitations when performing quantitative research, which are difficult to access, and when the research issues may be perceived by the respondents as difficult and sensitive (Stefańska & Olejnik, 2021). Therefore, participation in the research presented below was obviously determined by being involved in organizing classes at U3A or being a student of such a university.

In the case of research among organizers, coordinators, and teachers, there were 12 respondents in the survey (Table 12.1): coordinators (CEO), local U3A organizer, and U3A administrative staff as well as teachers conducting classes with seniors at such universities (including teachers of economics, foreign languages, running workshops on photography, as well as yoga and Nordic walking).

Three men and nine women participated in the survey. They represented two universities of the third age: "ERGA OMNES" Open University of Economics operating at the Poznań University of Economics and Business (Poland) and U3A operating at the Life Science University in Prague (Czech Republic).

Interviews with organizers covered the following topics:

- Social impact of U3A;
- Changes in seniors as a result of the activities;
- Perception of seniors before and after courses;
- Adaptation of courses for seniors (compared to courses for students);
- Unexpected aspects of classes with seniors;
- Seniors' perception of courses – perspectives of organizers and teachers.

*Table 12.1* Characteristics of the respondents

| *no* | *Gender* | *Teacher/administrative role/ coordinator (CEO)* | *Age* | *Time of the courses (semester/one time)* |
|---|---|---|---|---|
| 1PL | Men | Coordinator (CEO) | 50+ | Long time contact |
| 2PL | Women | Administrative | 35–50 | Long time contact |
| 3PL | Men | Teacher (behavioral economy) | > 35 | Temporary (one lecture) |
| 4PL | Women | Teacher (workshop of photography) | 35–50 | Long time contact |
| 5PL | Women | Teacher (language) | 50+ | Long time contact |
| 6PL | Women | Teacher (language) | 50+ | Long time contact |
| 7PL | Women | Teacher (yoga and Nordic walking) | 35–50 | Long time contact |
| 1CZ | Women | Teacher and coordinator of standard studies | 50+ | Temporary (one lecture) + Long term contract |
| 2CZ | Women | Coordinator of Virtual Studies | 35–50 | Long time contact |
| 3CZ | Women | Coordinator of Virtual Studies | 35–50 | Long time contact |
| 4CZ | Women | Teacher | > 35 | Temporary (one lecture) |
| 5CZ | Men | Coordinator of Virtual Studies | 35–50 | Long time contact |

Respondents: PL – from Poland, CZ – from the Czech Republic

*Source:* Own elaboration.

On the other hand, in the studies conducted among seniors from both universities, 36 semi-structured individual in-depth interviews were conducted in Poznań and 39 in Prague.

Discussions with seniors included an assessment of changes in various aspects of life caused by the participation in U3A activities. It should be added here that in order to assess the areas and level of social impact of universities, during the interviews, seniors completed a mini questionnaire based on a literature review and interviews previously conducted with the organizers of such universities. The questions were scaled on a 5-point Likert scale as presented in Table 12.2.

Analyzing the characteristics of respondents participating in the studied sample of seniors, it is worth noting that 29 women and seven men participated in the Polish study. All individuals had higher education, and the average age of the respondents was 69 years, with the youngest senior being 61 years old and the oldest 80. It should be added that 56% of retirees (20 individuals) declared they had grandchildren. On the other hand, in the Czech study, 85% of respondents were women. The youngest U3A student was 63 years old, and the oldest was 85. Furthermore, 39% of individuals declared having higher education, and 87% of seniors had grandchildren.

*Table 12.2* Declared impact of U3A on seniors

| | *Total* | | *Poland* | | *Czech Republic* | | *F* | *Sig.* |
|---|---|---|---|---|---|---|---|---|
| | *Mean* | *SD* | *Mean* | *SD* | *Mean* | *SD* | | |
| Participating in classes at U3A causes changes in my life | 4.27 | 0.918 | 4.25 | 0.874 | 4.33 | 1.047 | 0.086 | 0.771 |
| I am more active | 4.20 | 0.811 | 4.25 | 0.806 | 4.16 | 0.823 | 0.236 | 0.628 |
| I go to museums, theaters, cinemas, and other cultural places more often | 3.63 | 1.010 | 3.53 | 0.845 | 3.74 | 1.163 | 0.736 | 0.394 |
| I understand the world around me better | 3.96 | 0.842 | 3.97 | 0.810 | 3.94 | 0.886 | 0.023 | 0.879 |
| I have discovered a new passion as a way to spend leisure time | 3.99 | 0.954 | 3.94 | 0.924 | 4.03 | 0.999 | 0.138 | 0.711 |
| I feel that my existing knowledge and life experience can be useful to someone; I can share them with others | 4.00 | 0.943 | 3.75 | 1.052 | 4.24 | 0.760 | 5.292 | 0.024 |
| I feel healthier | 3.85 | 0.957 | 3.75 | 0.874 | 3.97 | 1.048 | 0.860 | 0.357 |
| My brain works better; I feel that my intellectual abilities have increased | 3.89 | 0.859 | 3.94 | 0.860 | 3.84 | 0.866 | 0.278 | 0.600 |
| I feel better physically | 3.86 | 0.946 | 3.75 | 0.967 | 3.97 | 0.923 | 0.973 | 0.327 |
| I am a more conscious consumer – I sort waste better, manage money better | 3.44 | 1.197 | 3.08 | 0.906 | 3.81 | 1.348 | 7.114 | 0.009 |
| I definitely speak positively about the university | 4.68 | 0.619 | 4.42 | 0.732 | 4.92 | 0.354 | 14.901 | 0.000 |
| I adopt healthier dietary habits | 3.35 | 1.122 | 3.28 | 1.003 | 3.42 | 1.251 | 0.290 | 0.592 |
| I would like my grandchildren/the grandchildren of my friends to study at this university | 4.05 | 1.104 | 3.89 | 1.008 | 4.22 | 1.182 | 1.617 | 0.208 |

*Source:* Own elaboration.

The analysis of the content of the collected material was performed according to the principles developed by Miles and Huberman (1984) and with the use of the descriptive, attribute and process coding of statements in accordance with Saldan's recommendations (2009).

## Results

### *The impact of U3A on seniors in the opinions of the organizers*

The impact of U3A can be examined in relation to the following entities:

- Seniors;
- Teachers conducting activities;
- Universities;
- Families of participants;
- Families of instructors;
- The broader community and environment.

The conducted studies reveal that this impact can be perceived as both positive and, which is interesting, negative. Initiating the analysis of the influence of U3A on the participants of these activities, the opinions of coordinators and teachers will be presented first.

Identifying the impact of U3A on seniors, coordinators, and teachers highlighted elements that can be attributed to two aspects: socialization and well-being. Regarding socialization, coordinators and teachers primarily emphasized the importance and main purpose of the activities – meeting other people. According to them, the most significant aspects are social contacts, meetings with people, the opportunity to get to know other individuals/friends of the same age, talk, and share experiences. U3A activities are also a good reason to leave the house, to develop social relationships, communication skills, and factors that increase tolerance and empathy toward others.

Respondents also indicate that with participation in the activities, seniors' openness increases, and initial uncertainty is replaced by warmth and willingness to help others. This leads to the creation of a friendly community that cares for its members, as well as an increase in engagement in social issues and prevention of withdrawal.

In addition to the undisputable improvement in socialization, U3A organizers also indicate changes in seniors' well-being, especially in the following areas:

- Improving physical condition;
- Increase in mental well-being, elimination of the feeling of loneliness;
- Self-esteem – a sense of prestige – because "I'm doing something" and it is at university;
- Increase in knowledge and skills in various fields, and the very learning, the transfer and acquisition of new knowledge, occurs somehow incidentally, and not as the most important goal of such universities;
- Greater independence in searching for information, awareness of one's rights;
- Improving memory and motor skills;

- Better preparation for old age;
- Better coping with the financial situation;
- Counteracting theft, fraud, and domestic violence – better awareness of proper lifestyle.

On the other hand, when analyzing the perceived impact of U3A on teachers, the lecturers primarily indicated that lectures and workshops with seniors bring them great satisfaction. As one of the Czech teachers states: "*I receive a lot of positive energy from seniors, they have a lot of enthusiasm, they are very grateful people*". Teachers, especially the younger ones, note that classes at U3A motivate and develop their teaching work and also allow them to "*tame the generational barrier*". As one of the Polish teachers states:

> Lectures with seniors are completely different from classes with students, quoting the words of Forest Gump: "they are like a box of chocolates – you never know what you will get." These are more "human" classes, interesting and worth conducting, even though they are more demanding, it is worth working at the university for such lectures.

Moreover, classes with seniors enable conducting scientific research, especially if this society group is the subject of interest of a given scientist.

Running U3A by a university also brings certain effects for the university. Firstly, the organizers and lecturers indicate that U3A enables the fulfillment of the third mission of the university and allows for activities in the field of social responsibility of the university. People involved in organizing classes with seniors also believe that U3A is primarily an opportunity for intergenerational cooperation. On the one hand, not only academic teachers but also traditional students, graduates, PhD students, and companies cooperating with the university engage in organizing and conducting classes, and on the other hand, seniors also motivate their loved ones (children, grandchildren) to cooperate (e.g. study) with a given university. In the latter case, the existence of word-of-mouth marketing is a very important issue from the university's point of view. A good opinion of seniors about the university shapes its positive image, and thus can help attract new students (regular students, students of postgraduate studies and courses organized at the university, or U3A students). Seniors therefore help shape the prestige of a given university and build its position as an institution where you can meet and conduct debates regardless of age. Finally, when analyzing the impact of U3A on universities, it is interesting to look at the relationships between scientific research and teaching activities conducted among seniors. Although U3As allow for conducting scientific research on this group of people, it is not a popular target group for scientific research.

Seniors' participation in U3A activities also affects seniors' families. According to university representatives, by participating in classes, seniors increase their current knowledge, so "*they have something to talk about with their children and grandchildren*". Thus, "*the joy and pride of the family that their loved ones – seniors are studying, is noticed, which is especially observed during the graduates' diploma award ceremony – we can then see whole families (including grandchildren)*". Participating in classes also helps keep seniors in good mental condition and thus reduces the potential burden on family members. At the same time, there is a possible negative impact of seniors' participation in U3A activities on family relationships. It may be related, for example, to the dissatisfaction of relatives with the senior, limiting the time they devote to the family – the seniors cannot, for example, take care of their grandchildren. The fears of family members related to the senior possibly meeting a new life partner is another example.

Summing up, U3A organizers generally indicate the positive impact of these universities on seniors. The main effects include:

- Helping seniors adapt to changes taking place in society;
- Increasing the population's participation in lifelong learning;
- Development of closer relationships between older people and the community, including the involvement of seniors in social consultations organized by local government and senior volunteering (e.g., by reading books to children, participating in the organization of local events);
- Lower social costs of caring for seniors;
- Increasing seniors' awareness of many potential threats in the modern world and thus contributing to seniors becoming a more difficult target for thieves, fraudsters, etc.

***The impact of U3A on seniors in their opinions***

Before we proceed to assessment of the social impact of U3A on seniors in their eyes, it seems valuable to start by presenting the reasons for choosing the university. Seniors indicate that the most important reasons include the desire for learning or expanding knowledge, especially in economics but also in foreign languages, either new ones or those they were familiar with before. Another significant factor is the desire to maintain contact with other people – seniors recognize it as an important activity that contributes to maintaining good mental and physical health, particularly considering the range of physical activities offered. It is worth noting that some individuals decided to participate in U3A activities out of sentiment – either because they or their close ones studied at this university before.

When assessing the changes in life resulting from participation in U3A classes, Polish and Czech seniors are very similar in their opinions, with Czechs being slightly more positive. Seniors declare that participating in U3A classes caused some changes in their life. First of all, they indicate that when they tell other people about the university they attend, they do it in a positive way and they would very much like their grandchildren or other young people they know to also study at that university. When considering the impact of the university on them, they notice that they are more active in general, including, for example, discovering new passions and ways of spending free time and better understanding of the world around them. They believe that their brain works better, and they feel physically and mentally healthier. Participation in U3A classes resulted in relatively smaller changes among seniors in terms of the frequency of using the services of cultural institutions, better nutrition, or being a more conscious consumer (e.g., in terms of sorting garbage or better money management). However, seniors add that considering the latter issues (nutrition or managing the household budget), they have not changed significantly because they were already conscious consumers in this respect before enrolling in U3A.

Additionally, during the interviews, in the context of the changes caused by participation in classes at U3A, Polish seniors especially emphasized the increase in their foreign language competences (thanks to which they feel more confident during trips abroad and in contacts with foreigners), as well as the ability to take good photographs. In turn, Czech seniors emphasized particularly strongly that, thanks to classes at U3A, they look at some aspects of life from a different perspective – the classes broadened their thinking horizons and opinions on many topics. Moreover, they indicated greater sensitivity and responsibility toward the environment and a more positive perception of old age.

However, all seniors indicate that getting to know other people, making new friends, meeting new friends that they also meet outside the classes, as well as better communication with other people are one of the greatest positive effects of participating in U3A classes. For them, participating in classes is "time well spent" but also "less free time".

## Discussion

The key role of universities of the third age is to improve the quality of life of seniors through active aging. The results of our own research confirm that U3As play a significant role not only in the context of the formal need for universities to implement the third mission. The social impact of U3A on all stakeholders, i.e., not only seniors but also their families, friends, teachers conducting classes at these universities and the universities themselves is noticeable. The results of our research are consistent with the research by Nováková and Lorenzová (2020), among others. They show that the desire to continue learning and the need to spend free time actively are the main motives for starting studies at U3A. Research also shows that U3A has a positive effect on the health of seniors. This is also consistent with the research of Sahin et al. (2023). The authors indicate that participation in U3A activities has a positive impact on health, both mental and physical, compared to seniors who do not participate in such activities. However, research by Kozieł and Trafiałek (2016) shows that in terms of the assessment of global quality of life and the perception of general health and mental functioning, there are no statistically significant differences between seniors participating and not participating in U3A activities. However, according to their research, such differences are noticeable in terms of physical quality of life, level of independence, environmental functioning, and spirituality. Our research also confirms, similarly to the research of Ricardo and Porcarelli (2019), that U3A has an important socialization function – it is a space for social meetings, creating new social networks, and counteracting the isolation of older people.

However, it should be highlighted that, according to our research, seniors do not want to conduct classes as teachers, i.e., share their experience with others. It should be emphasized that sharing knowledge is at the core of the assumptions of the U3A role in active aging – so that when finishing their professional career and leaving the labor market, seniors continue to share their knowledge and experience with others (Günder, 2014).

According to the authors, the importance of universities of the third age in developed countries will increase significantly in the coming years. This is caused by several reasons. On the one hand, universities are expected to show social impact. Recently, university rankings that consider their involvement in the implementation of sustainable development goals have been conducted (Impact Rankings, 2023). Given the pace at which the number of participants in these rankings is increasing, it can be assumed that the importance of U3A in universities' social responsibility strategies will also become greater, increasingly noticed, and exposed by them to emphasize their role in society. However, as Strunga (2015) notes, it is necessary for universities from different countries to exchange best practices in organizing U3A.

Secondly, attention should be paid to the ongoing aging processes of many populations, especially in developed countries, and thus also to the progressive increase in the number of seniors. Moreover, the generation of seniors is definitely changing. The modern senior is different, better educated, and focused on self-development as much as possible. They do not always want to play the traditional role of grandchildren's childminder, which is assigned to them in multigenerational families. For example, both seniors in Poland and the Czech Republic lived most of their professional lives in capitalist conditions, hence they have different requirements, needs, lifestyles, and prefer other forms of spending their free time.

Thirdly, the systemic support provided and, finally, the growing importance and understanding of the concept of lifelong learning and open education also contribute to the increasing importance of U3As and the need to study their social impact.

Summing up, from the point of view of an aging society, U3A is:

- A place for social meetings, the important purpose of which is to prevent isolation and loneliness of older people;
- A solution that helps extend the period before seniors' health problems occur;
- A solution with great development potential, enabling better integration of seniors not only with their peers but also with the local community and better opportunities to shape family relationships (e.g., by developing seniors' ICT competences – the ability to find a "common language" with grandchildren or their children);
- A place that enables seniors to increase their physical, intellectual, and social activity and thus contributes to improving the quality of life.

In turn, from the perspective of an institution organizing activities for seniors, U3A is a place and a way of:

- Implementation of the third mission of universities and creation of social capital;
- Activation of university lecturers;
- Implementation of sustainable development goals, in particular inclusiveness and care about the sustainable development of societies as well as integration of generations;
- Creation of empathy for people with various types of disabilities;
- Development of innovative ideas to meet the needs of older generations;
- Sharing knowledge.

It should be noted, however, that active aging by engaging in the lifelong learning process requires the senior students to overcome certain barriers, such as a sense of uncertainty, lack of faith in their abilities in old age, and reluctance to leave the comfort and safety zone they have developed. Older people are more afraid of something unknown, hence the role of people they know and trust is to encourage this and other forms of older people's activation.

In the future, it can be expected that the number of entities offering activities for older people will increase, but the offer targeted at and adapted to this group of recipients will also be expanded. The concept of universities of the fourth age appears in the discourse. As Pavelková (2019) notes, it is necessary to expand the offer of educational and activation activities aimed at older people living not in their homes but in care facilities. Moreover, it will be necessary to accelerate the education of seniors in the use of technological achievements that allow them to overcome a number of physical barriers and health-related limitations.

In the light of the above reflections, the question arises about social impact assessment (SIA), which is about the processes of managing the social issues associated with planned interventions (Vanclay, 2005). The impact analysis may be based on such criteria as duration, timing, intensity, severity, frequency, scale, extent, and durability of each impact (Esteves, Vanclay, Morardi, Sairinen, & Sauer, 2010). These criteria may indicate further research on the social impact of U3A.

## Note

According to EUROSTAT (2023) in 2021, the adult participation rate in lifelong learning was 11% in the EU, whereas according to OECD data (2022), participation of people aged 55–64 in non-formal education and training is 7%, with most older people studying in Scandinavian countries: Sweden 24%, Finland 17%, Denmark 15%, and also in Netherlands – 16%.

## References


Carl, J., & Menter, M. (2021). The social impact of universities: Assessing the effects of the three university missions on social engagement. *Studies in Higher Education, 46*(5), 965–976. https://doi.org/ 10.1080/03075079.2021.1896803

Council for Third Age. (2012). An intergenerational learning program in Singapore. *Journal of Intergenerational Relationships, 10*(1), 86–92. https://doi.org/ 10.1080/ 15350770.2012.646566

Esteves, A.M., Vanclay, F., Morardi, B., Sairinen, R., & Sauer, A. (2010). International experiences with social impact assessment at the project level. In T. Auwers (Ed.), *Strengthening social mainstreaming in the EU. Round up of discussions on social impact assessment during the Belgiaņ Presidency of the Council of the European Union,* 1–48. *Brussels*. Belgium: Belgian Federal Public Service Social Security.

Eurostat. (2023). *Participation in lifelong learning increases in 2021.* Retrieved from https://ec.europa.eu/eurostat/web/products-eurostat-news/-/edn-20230130-1

Formosa, M. (2014). Four decades of universities of the third age: Past, present, future. *Ageing and Society, 34*, 42–66. https://doi.org/10.1017/S0144686X12000797

Formosa, M. (2010). Universities of the third age: A rationale for transformative education in later life. *Journal of Transformative Education, 8*(3), 197–219.

Godonoga, A., & Sarrico, C.S. (2019). Civic and social engagement of higher education. In Susan Faircloth (Ed.), *Oxford bibliographies in education.* New York: Oxford University Press.

Godonoga, A., & Sporn, B. (2023). The conceptualization of socially responsible universities in higher education research: A systematic literature review. *Studies in Higher Education, 48*(3), 445–459. https://doi.org/ 10.1080/03075079.2022.2145462

Günder, E.E. (2014). Third age perspectives on lifelong learning: Third age university, 5th World Conference on Educational Sciences -–WCES 2013. *Procedia - Social and Behavioral Sciences, 116*, 1165–1169.

Impact Rankings 2023. (2023). Retrieved from https://www.timeshighereducation.com

IOCGP, Interorganizational Committee on Principles and Guidelines for Social Impact Assessment (1993). Guidelines and Principles for Social Impact Assessment, US Department of Commerce NOAA Tech Memo NMFS-F/SPO-16, reprinted in Impact Assessment, *12*(2), 107–152.

Johnson, M.T. (2022). The knowledge exchange framework: Understanding parameters and the capacity for transformative engagement. *Studies in Higher Education, 47*(1), 194–211. https://doi.org/10.1080/03075079.2020.1735333

Khosravi, P., Rezvani, A., & Wiewiora, A. (2016). The impact of technology on older adults' social isolation. *Computers in Human Behavior, 63*, 594–603.

Kobylarek, A., Błaszczyński, K., Ślósarz, L., Madej, M., Carmo, A., Hlad, Ľ., Králik, R., Akimjak, A., Judák, V., Maturkanič, P., Biryukova, Y.T., Martin, J.G., & Petrikoviˇcová, L. (2022). The quality of life among University of the third age students in Poland, Ukraine and Belarus. *Sustainability. 14*(4), 2049. https://doi.org/10.3390/su14042049

Kozieł, D., & Trafiałek, E. (2016). Assessing the influence of studying at the University of the Third Age on life satisfaction of elderly people. *Gerontologia Polska 15*(3), 104–108.

Meyer, M., & Sporn, B. (2018). Leaving the Ivory Tower: Universities' third mission and the search for legitimacy. *Zeitschrift für Hochschulentwicklung 13*(2), 41–60. https://doi.org/ 10.3217/zfhe-13-02/02.

Miles, M., Huberman, A.M. (1984). *Qualitative Data Analysis*. London: Sage.

Miotto, G., Blanco-González, A., & Castillo Feito, C. (2018). Social responsibility: A tool for legitimation in Spanish Universities' strategic plans. *Trípodos, 42*, 59–79. http://www.tripodos.com/index.php/Facultat_Comunicacio_Blanquerna/article/view/522

Noble, C., Medin, D., Quail, Z., Young, C., & Carter, M. (2021). How does participation in formal education or learning for older people affect wellbeing and cognition? A systematic literature review and meta-analysis. *Gerontology and Geriatric Medicine, 7*, 233372142098602. https://doi.org/10.1177/2333721420986027

Nováková, D., & Lorenzová, J. (2020). Motivation of seniors to learn at the Universities of the Third Age. *Social Education, 8*(2), 71–83. https://doi.org/10.7441/soced.2020.08.02.05

OECD. (2022). *Education at a glance 2022: OECD indicators*. Retrieved from https://www.oecd-ilibrary.org/sites/4585016b-en/index.html?itemId=/content/component/4585016b-en#tablegrp-d1e9400

Olejnik, I., & Stefańska, M. (2020). Integration of the employee pension programs with CSR. In K. Bachnik et al. (Eds.), *CSR in contemporary Poland*, 183–195. Springer Books. https://doi.org/10.1007/978-3-030-42277-6_13

Ondrakova, J. (2014). *Education of seniors at universities of the third age, psychology and psychiatry, sociology and healthcare, education*, 3, International Multidisciplinary Scientific Conferences on Social Sciences and Arts, 257–264.

Pavelková, J. (2019). University of the fourth age as one of the new possibilities of pedagogical. *Educational and Activation Activities for Seniors in Residential Facilities, Zdravotnícke štúdie, 2*, 6–8. https://www.ceeol.com/search/article-detail?id=969378

Peacock, S., & Künemund, H. (2007). Senior citizens and Internet technology. *European Journal of Ageing, 4*, 191–200. https://doi.org/10.1007/s10433-007-0067-z

Ricardo, R., & Porcarelli, A. (2019). Education and socialization in later life: The case of a University of Third Age in Portugal, *European Journal for Research on the Education and Learning of Adults, 10*(3), 247–260.

Sahin, S., Kocakoc, N., Arayici, M.E., Baybas, B.K., Boyacioglu, H., & Akcicek S.F. (2023). Evaluation of the quality of life in the university of third age students: A cross-sectional study. *European Geriatric Medicine, 14*, 389–396. https://doi.org/10.1007/s41999-023-00764-3

Santos, B.R.D., Pavarini, S.C.I., Brigola, A.G., Orlandi, F.D.S., & Inouye, K. (2014). Factors associated with quality of life in elderly undertaking literacy programs. *Dementia & Neuropsychologia*, *8*(2), 169–174. https://doi.org/10.1590/s1980-57642014dn82000013

Scott, J.C. (2006). The mission of the university: Medieval to postmodern transformations. *The Journal of Higher Education, 77*(1), 1–39. https://doi.org/10.1080/00221546.2006.11778917

Statistics Poland. (2023). *Universities of the third age in the 2021/2022 academic year*. Warszawa, Gdańsk. http://stat.gov.pl/obszary-tematyczne/edukacja/

Stefańska, M., & Olejnik, I. (2021). Dobór próby i analiza wyników w badaniach jakościowych. In M. Rószkiewicz, K. Mazurek-Łopacińska, & A. Sagan (Eds.), *Dobór próby we współczesnych badaniach marketingowych. Podejścia ilościowe, jakościowe i mieszane*), 59–74. Rozprawy i Studia - Uniwersytet Szczeciński, *1311*(1237. Szczecin, Uniwersytet Szczeciński.

Strunga, A.C. (2015). The role of university in seniors' education: A Romanian perspective. *Social Sciences and Education Research Review, 1*, 81–90.

Vanclay, F. (2002). Conceptualizing social impacts. *Environmental Impact Assessment Review*, *22*(3), 183–211. https://doi.org/10.1016/S0195-9255(01)00105-6

Vanclay, F. (2005). Principles for social impact assessment: A critical comparison between the international and US documents. *Environmental Impact Assessment Review*, *26*(1), 3–14. https://doi.org/10.1016/j.eiar.2005.05.002

Zgliczyński, W.S. (2012). Aktywność społeczna osób starych w Polsce w ramach wolontariatu i uniwersytetów trzeciego wieku. *Studia BAS*, *2*, 129–150.

Zielińska-Więczkowska, H., Muszalik, M., & Kędziora-Kornatowska, K. (2012). The analysis of aging and elderly age quality in empirical research: Data based on University of the Third Age (U3A) students. *Archives of Gerontology and Geriatrics*, *55*(1), 195–199. https://doi.org/10.1016/j.archger.2011.07.011

# 13 NGOs in delivering social impact

*Sergiusz Prokurat*

## Introduction

Contemporary economics tends to ignore the influence of economic development on institutional changes and factors, while actively emphasizing the role of mathematical algorithms in shaping expectations instead. The problem with this approach is that it does not recognize the role of actors, social forces, the set of institutions on which a given system is built, as well as its path dependence, and the psychological and social aspects and consequences of decision-making by people. Contemporary economics treats behavior as rational or irrational, which ignores the role of context and diversity in the decision-making process. Neoinstitutional economics deals with decision-making and incentives that are influenced by non-economic factors: historical, legal, political, and social (North, 1990; Rutherford, 1994; Field, 1999; Furubotn & Richter, 2005). It includes theories of public choice, rational choice principles, and shows mechanisms that highlight the causes of making decisions and what leads to choices that affect the subsequent behavior of individuals and the entire societies. Social phenomena, including so-called social economics, are inherent in the research of economic sciences.

Social economy is a concept that has many different definitions in the literature (Evers, 1995, 1998; Castells, 1998; Pestoff, 1998; Van Til, 2000; Evers & Laville, 2004; Mendell, 2009). It offers an alternative conceptual understanding of social systems as dynamic, open system, grounded in complex institutional networks. A social enterprise is in particular an organization that meets most of the following criteria: (1) economic dimension, especially production of goods or services; (2) social dimension: community benefits as the main statutory goal; (3) participatory management: high level of autonomy, decision-making power is in the hands of community members (Borzaga & Defourny, 2001; Defourny & Nyssens, 2012). There are three sectors of contemporary society: (1) business sector, focused on profit, (2) public sector, and (3) the third sector consisting of organizations which are not focused on profit and are autonomous from the state. The latter one, which includes non-governmental organizations (NGOs), social purpose organizations (SPOs), in order to achieve their statutory goals,

DOI: 10.4324/9781003480952-16

especially in the field of providing social services, must cooperate with public administration and private entities (Evers, 1998). They also need this cooperation to obtain funds for financing their activities. However, if they decide blindly to perform tasks assigned to them by public administration, they lose their independence and become an instrument of the state in conducting public policy or, in case of thoughtless cooperation with market organizations (corporations), an extension of private or shareholder interests. Therefore, the social economy has important benefits for non-governmental organizations or more broadly for social entrepreneurship. It allows to go beyond the discussion of market versus state (Pestoff, 1998) and consists of theoretical and empirical concerns about the role of the third sector in mediating the relationship between state, society, and economy (Gonzales, 2007; Defourny, 1992). Despite numerous empirical studies on the phenomenon of social economy, its formed theory is quite fresh and developmental (Nicholls & Murdock, 2012; OECD, 2019; Rawhouser et al., 2019).

Social entrepreneurship is a key element of the social economy (Evers, 2004; Evers & Laville, 2004). Its function is not only to produce specific goods and services but also to mobilize social capital, generate social dynamics in the work that could lead to innovations, and inclusion of previously excluded people. Although social entrepreneurship works as a part of the market economy, it places its mission and goals outside the market (Laville, 2001). The main actors within social entrepreneurship are NGOs/SPOs that attach the greatest importance to supporting society while not giving up their activities, sometimes generating profits. All these aspects of the functioning of social economy entities result in negative or positive effects but certainly different from those brought by standard instruments used by market entities. Therefore, there is a need to apply identification and measurement (KPI) of efficiency that measures their economic and social impact. In the latter case, the concept that will be discussed in this chapter is social impact. The aim of this study is to indicate the theoretical foundation and identification of potential added value, social and economic, produced by organizations from the third sector – NGOs/SPOs, in social economy, along with examples and practical possibilities of applying added value management of measurements.

### *Social impact and its importance in the context of NGOs/SPOs*

In the process of the functioning of third-sector organizations around the world, three main directions can be identified. The first is the increasing interest of citizens and stakeholders in the transparency of financial information presented by NGOs/SPOs (Tejedo-Romero & Araujo, 2023). Transparency is associated with positive openness and the concept of public accountability (Bovens et al., 2014). Organizations face greater pressure to make information about fundraising and expenditures, resources, management methods, and finally results achieved through entrusted funds as transparent as possible (Ebrahim & Weisband, 2007). By accepting financial support from their donors, organizations commit to carrying out certain actions and thus accept the moral and legal responsibility arising from the challenge undertaken. The second direction concerns shifting the scope of reporting activities from legal responsibility to a specific concept of social impact measurement, which becomes crucial from the point of view of this chapter. Organizations are required to demonstrate specific goal-oriented results in solving complex social problems such as poverty, hunger, and social inequalities. The third direction is the growing influence and visibility of NGOs/SPOs in today's economies (Lage & Brandt, 2008). This is happening due to easier access to data and promotion of activism through the Internet and social media.

Social impact is related to the consequences of human action. Under this concept, there are often different conceptual constructs, phenomena, dependencies (Datta & Gailey, 2012; Stephan et al., 2016). Numerous attempts are made to precisely define the concept of social impact (Reisman & Giennap, 2004; Choi & Majumdar, 2012; Epstein & Yuthas, 2014; Stephan et al., 2016 Rawhouser et al., 2019). OECD (2019) generally defines social impact as positive and negative, primary and secondary long-term effects caused by a development intervention, directly or indirectly, intended or unintended. A more insightful definition is given by Burdge and Vanclay (1995, p. 59):

> Social impacts include all social and cultural consequences to human populations of any public or private actions that alter the ways in which people live, work, play, relate to one another, organize to meet their needs, and generally cope as members of society.

Originally, social impact was understood as the effect of actions, activities, projects, or programs affecting people and communities (Latané in 1981). It is variable and modeled over time (short term, medium term, long term) and identified with a change in the situation of people as a result of specific actions, understood as a positive effect – an increase in positive external effects with no or presence of negative results (Stephan et al., 2016), or a reduction in negative social external effects of various phenomena or actions (Rawhouser et al., 2019), applicable to NGOs/SPOs, social enterprises. The broad definition and constantly redefined concepts in different ways make both theoretical and practical work in this area difficult (Maas & Liket, 2011). It also contributes to numerous problems with precise quantification and building a coherent theory of social impact. This poses a challenge for both scientists dealing with this topic and practitioners.

## Methods of measuring economic and social added value

Economic impact is easier to determine, as there are specific methods and tools for measuring the financial value of goods and services produced by entities in the economy. The EVA (economic value added) indicator is used to measure strictly economic concept of added value. It is defined as the excess of adjusted operating profit reduced by taxation over the costs of capital involved in achieving it. Added value can also be determined using economic profit, which measures the economic value that a company generated in a given year, as well as using the MVA (market added value) indicator. In addition, market organizations utilize other key indicators, including ROI (return on investment); EBIT/EBITDA (earnings before interest and taxes; earnings before interest, taxes, depreciation, and amortization) or CBA (cost-benefit analysis), which are used to assess total costs in relation to total expected benefits, in order to determine whether the benefits outweigh the costs.

Social impact is usually understood as an additional benefit for society (and in some approaches also for the natural environment) resulting from a given action (Moss et al., 2011). It is therefore added value that goes beyond the direct benefits that beneficiaries receive. This concept is particularly visible in the form of social value, which is wrongly placed in opposition to purely economic value (Harlock, 2013). There are attempts to measure actions using the concept of SAV (social added value), which is used in literature, and understood as a measurable dimension of social impact. Produced social added value is defined as a positive result for the people, the environment, or for the local community during the creation of certain products or services. This results from the fact that social enterprises were established to achieve certain social goals, not economic ones.

The measurement of the social impact by using traditional indicators to assess the effectiveness of social enterprises does not produce proper comparable results, as they focus only on measuring value expressed in money. To assess the effects of social impact that comes from NGOs/SPOs, tools are needed that measure not only the financial value of actions undertaken but also added value expressed by external benefits generated by an entity directly for the society. Important aspects that should be taken into account in social impact analysis include the time of occurrence of the effects of a specific action or the consequences of an action (short, medium, long term) and the level of analysis (Rawhouser et al., 2019). If the analysis boundaries are set too narrowly, it may result in losing sight of the full range of social impact of specific actions. This is particularly important in situations where unaccounted results outweigh those taken into account in the analysis, especially when the accounted results have a positive character and the unaccounted, negative.

There are many ways to measure economic phenomena such as economic and social impact, which can be useful for NGOs/SPOs. The first method, which indirectly illustrates the social value added, is multipliers. The noun "multiplier" defines the mechanism of action of the method. For example, according to John Maynard Keynes's theory, the investment multiplier shows how increasing investment expenditures contributes to the growth of employment, national income, and consumption and thus welfare. In the case of J.M. Keynes's investment multiplier, we are dealing with welfare in the macroeconomic sense (this is an element of economic impact), while multipliers can also try to measure phenomena from the social impact area. The original social impact theory applies multiplier to the effects of social variables – strength, immediacy, and number of sources (Latané, 1981). However, it did not account for the nature of these influencing processes. Newer approaches try to approach this complex problem in a different way. For example, the Local Multiplier3 (LM3) includes nature of the influencing origins, while putting more emphasis on the economic aspects than on the social aspect of an entity's activity (Sachs, 2002). It is a tool that enables the financial determination of the impact of an organization on the local economy, showing what part of the money, as a result of the activity of a given entity, remains in its immediate vicinity. The money introduced into the economy stimulates demand for goods and services, depending on which part of the initial funds remains in the local economy and which part is transferred outside. The multiplier used by the LM3 method examines the size of additional local expenditures generated by the initial cash flow and can be applied to tourism, cultural events (concerts, festivals), or investments (Vaughan et al., 2000; Pacaud et al., 2007). Initially, the total amount of income of a given organization is calculated. In the second stage, the expenditure of money in a given local area is examined in detail. The third phase consists of further analysis of how money is spent by subsequent entities. In a fairly simple way, through financial measures, it determines how strongly an entity is rooted in the local environment.

The second proposed method for NGOs/SPOs is social return on investment (SROI), developed originally in 1996 as a tool to evaluate grant requests (Gair, 2002). The SROI model was developed and structured as a specific blended value-accounting method. It has worked as an impact assessment tool and has been defined as a framework for measuring and accounting for the much broader concept of value. It seeks to reduce inequality and environmental degradation and improve individual well-being by incorporating social, environmental, and economic costs and benefits (Nicholls & Murdock, 2012; Hall et al., 2015). This method is based on the ROI (return on investment) indicator often used to measure performance. It allows to measure all the benefits generated by an entity, especially the long-term impact on the local community and environment in which it operates. Its application is particularly important in the case of organizations that are focused on improving the situation of beneficiaries by providing free or partially paid services. The assessment of financial results in such organizations would most likely be negative from a commercial point of view; therefore, this method allows to calculate all the benefits generated by a given organization, including the intangible ones.

Another tool recommended for NGOs is the social audit. It is not a specific measurement method because there is no uniform methodology for its use. Different organizations propose different approaches, which, however, come down to a qualitative analysis of such elements as, among others, resources possessed, organization management methods, analysis of the mission and objectives of activity, types of activities or effects achieved. The result of the audit is a report along with a scorecard that shows stakeholders the effects of the analysis conducted. An example of such a tool is social impact assessment (SIA), which refers rather to the assessment of non-economic results and thus concerns the impact of an organization that goes beyond purely economic character (Vanclay, 2003). In this case, the concept of social impact refers not only to the impact on people or communities but also goals such as poverty reduction or social exclusion (Spear et al., 2001). Becker and Vanclay (2003) define SIA as a process of identifying potential future consequences of current actions or proposed initiatives related to individuals, organizations, or even macroeconomic events.

Another framework that can be used by NGO/SPO is Five Dimensions of Impact (5DOI), developed in 2019, which is a ready-to-serve framework model that identifies five dimensions of impact –what, who, how much, contribution, and risk – and provides mean values to make impacts benchmarked and measured (IRIS+, 2019). 5DOI is enterprise-centric and allows to apply the aforementioned five dimensions to processes: define, measure, assess, and communicate its impact (define the problem, identify the indicators, collect raw data, analyze the data, assess the impact).

As the literature on the subject shows, social impact is an important part of the phenomenon of social entrepreneurship. Attempts to measure social impact are made in various ways (Rawhouser et al., 2019). Not only through multipliers, social return/social return on investment (Emerson, 2003), assessments/audits but also using concepts such as social performance (Nicholls, 2008), social accounting (Nicholls, 2009), and impact scorecards (So & Staskevicius, 2015). There are also other more general ways of measuring social impact: economists use various measures of well-being, such as happiness, life satisfaction, and quality of life, based on surveys, to assess the social impact of outcomes of interventions or investments.

***Why NGO/SPO should try to measure social impact?***

Non-governmental organizations were established to achieve certain important social goals. But how do we know that organizations are really contributing to solving social problems? What have they achieved? Are they effective? What are the results from their actions? In the case of NGOs/SPOs and measuring the social impact of such entities, the problem of measuring social impact most often concerns organizations that operate at the interface between the business sector (for profit) and governmental sector. The techniques used to assess social impact have evolved in parallel with the perspective and vision of the need for assessments to function in a social context. The context is changing, because measuring social impact results from different needs, and various benefits are perceived as new normal. It is important to be able to understand multidimensional phenomena and obtain quantitative and qualitative sources that allow for a better understanding of the mechanisms leading to a specific measurable result. For stakeholders, the efficiency and effectiveness of actions implemented by NGOs/SPOs are crucial, and the measuring of their impact is intended to formulate recommendations for improving future actions. Measuring added social value primarily allows us to obtain information needed for making decisions about future directions of action and resource allocation. Thanks to them, the organization also builds its credibility toward stakeholders and donors. Documented information plays an extremely important role in the process of determining target groups, community members, or investors. The organization can build its activity and attract new customers by knowing exactly the value of its products and services. Measuring social impact is a way of attributing positive social change to an organization's actions. It can help NGOs/SPOs to prove and improve their effectiveness, accountability, and attractiveness to funders and stakeholders. It can also help them gather data and create stories for their marketing and communication and drive positive change in their business systems.

Measuring social impact allows organizations to obtain information necessary to make decisions about future directions of action and resource allocation. They also build their credibility with stakeholders. Documented information plays an extremely important role in the process of identifying target groups, community members, or investors. Organizations can build their business and attract new customers by knowing the exact value of their products and services. Measuring social impact is a way of attributing positive social change to an organization's actions. It can help NGOs/SPOs to prove its worth and further improve effectiveness, accountability, and attractiveness to donors, funders, and stakeholders. It can also help to gather data and create stories for their marketing and communication and to drive positive change in day-to-day business.

### *Difficulties with measuring social impact*

The process of measuring social impact is difficult to carry out because there are no repeatable indicators that can be used to verify the quality of work of NGO/SPO organizations. Ready-made methodologies, including various measurement tools and techniques, are rather difficult to implement in practice. Most often, organizations design their own indicators for the purpose of measuring social impact (based on their own activities: input-output; outcome). The lack of knowledge of existing clear and universal frameworks for the functioning of social impact theory increases the difficulty in linking the effects of change with their actions. Thus, building a measurement system from scratch for every organization is a long and costly process. Non-profit organizations suffer from a lack of funds for employees dealing with administration (including reporting) and a lack of defined time frames for the functioning of activities. Measuring social impact requires consistent and dedicated work, often over several years to provide comparable results. For many third-sector entities, system/framework and tools can be difficult to develop. Especially, this is the case of smaller non-profit organizations. Moreover, the elements that make up the concept of social impact are often difficult to measure.

Even defining social impact does not directly lead to a simple solution to the problem of assessing and measuring this phenomenon. It should also be remembered that social impact refers to changes that are the result of the activities of a wide range of entities, as well as being determined by external conditions that may facilitate (or hinder) the achievement of a specific goal. Maas and Liket (2011) identified four main obstacles that cause such a situation: (1) social impact usually has a qualitative character and is difficult to describe using quantitative indicators; (2) entities can achieve both positive and negative social impact, which can also be created in different areas; (3) social impact includes both short- and long-term social effects, and the latter are difficult to assess due to the time interval between the investment/intervention being carried out and the effect that the actions achieved; (4) many different factors can contribute to achieving a social effect, and sometimes, it is difficult to isolate the social impact of a specific organization or project.

Another problem regarding social impact analysis is the issue of results arising from a given action. These results can be direct (easier to measure) and indirect (more difficult to measure). In the case of indirect results, problems arise when actions or the lack of actions affect groups not covered by the action (excluded on purpose, or accidentally). This may require analysis at many levels (individual, company, industry, community, region, or country) and at different time intervals, assuming very rigorous analysis frameworks (Davidsson & Wiklund, 2001; Rauch, Frese & Utsch, 2005; Baron & Ensley, 2006). In research on the functioning of organizations, the analysis period is often the result of an accepted theory or method of measuring the impact of these entities (Zaheer et al., 1999). In many cases, measuring results in a rigidly defined time interval is impossible. Moreover, a broad approach to the areas in which social impact is sought raises problems with comparability of different research results on this phenomenon (Rawhouser et al., 2019).

***Crafting a unique methodology based on given framework***

To fully understand the concept of social impact, it is necessary to move from a process perspective, which focuses primarily on the implementation of specific actions, to a results perspective, which emphasizes the effects of these actions. Organizations such as NGOs/SPOs know that the characteristic of the results perspective is the systematic approach to the actions taken and effects them within two categories: product or service (output) and result (outcome). Outputs are the direct and measurable effects of an organization's activities, either product or service (e.g., the number of trained people, the percentage of new employees in employment, etc.). Outcomes are results, benefits, and knowledge that are triggered by delivering a product or service in the medium and long term (e.g., reducing social exclusion). There is a chance that NGO/SPO can use own specific metrics or previously developed generic metrics. Such metrics help to

*Table 13.1* Logic model of outputs and outcomes

| Branch | What problem(s) are addressed? | How do you measure your outputs/your impact? | How do you measure your outcomes/your impact? | What existing system of indicators, measure systems can fit? |
|---|---|---|---|---|
| | **Challenge** | **Outputs (KPI apply)** | **Outcomes (KPI apply)** | **Potential framework system** |
| Healthcare | To improve healthcare system<br>Health improvement of local residents | Number of hours doctors volunteered in healthcare<br>Number of applied vaccinations | Improved health for members of served community<br>Improved quality of life for members of served community | Social return on investment (SROI).<br>SIA<br>Well-being measures (survey)<br>Five Dimensions of Impact.<br>Impact Scorecards |
| Food industry | To combat against hunger<br>Nutrition improvement program for local residents | Number of meals provided<br>Number of people fed | Reduction of food insecurity<br>Sustained reduction of poverty in the community at large<br>Reduction of hunger<br>Percent of communities impacted within the state | Local Multiplier3<br>Social return on investment (SROI).<br>SIA<br>Well-being measures (survey)<br>Five Dimensions of Impact. |
| Education | Improve education among the local community | Percent of community attending education session<br>Number of people educated<br>Number of hosted education sessions | Reduction of gaps in knowledge<br>Increase in awareness of education needs<br>Increase in labor participation<br>Percent of communities impacted within the state/region | SIA<br>Well-being measures (survey)<br>Five dimensions of Impact.<br>Impact Scorecards |

*Source:* Own elaboration.

track and measure NGOs/SPOs actions and programs. To design custom metrics, the basic logic model (framework) of outputs and outcomes can be followed (Table 13.1).

## Conclusion

Overall, social impact measurement and reporting can play an important role in helping NGO/SPO to achieve their goals and make a positive impact on society. It is important for such organizations to develop a learning culture where impact measurement is truly integrated into their operations, producing data that matters and is inclusive of the voices of the people who are impacted. To illustrate the practicality of this topic, below are described two cases of NGOs/SPOs that have successfully implemented social impact measurement practices and reporting.

Investisseurs & Partenaires (I&P) is a social impact fund focused on supporting small and fast-growing African enterprises, with a high social and/or environmental impact. Since it started measuring social impact, thanks to the definition of clear objectives and indicators, their work could be better monitored and improved. Also, they discovered that it served to align their team internally on the impact objectives. For each of its impact funds, the I&P team uses Impact Screening Scorecards. They intended to establish an impact on local entrepreneurship (entrepreneur location); impact on employees (creation of decent jobs); impact on clients (local and essential needs); impact on local suppliers and distributors, environment (EVPA, 2018).

Reach for Change is an NGO/SPO focusing on improving the lives of children. Over the years, they have understood the importance of measuring impact to explain what NGO is doing for its investors, to identify successes. A very precise impact measurement and management system, to monitor KPI quantitatively and qualitatively, has been developed to track and evaluate both the direct impact on social ventures and the indirect impact on children. Outcome and output assume the use of KPI metrics, e.g., reports on the number of children supported (EVPA, 2018).

However, it should be noted that social impact is a category that eludes unambiguous and precise definitions. It usually concerns the social effects of various types of actions taken by various entities. Social effects are understood very broadly – as any changes affecting the situation of individuals, groups of individuals, local communities, and society, both in positive and negative ways. The challenge is not only to determine what is a social impact but also how to unify the approach to the topic of measuring social impact, taking into account the fact that some effects are difficult to measure, dependent on the industry and periods of time.

NGOs/SPOs can use social impact measurement and its reporting to improve their effectiveness, accountability, and transparency (O'Leary, 2015). Some of the benefits are demonstrating value to donors and funders, improving performance and accountability, transparency, team-work, and team motivation, while positively influencing the environment. Social impact measurement can help to secure more fundings and organize support for work that is carried out. For scientific NGOs/SPOs, social impact measurement can help to evaluate the effectiveness of the research and thus demonstrate contributions to society or community. Measuring can help NGOs/SPOs to set realistic objectives, monitor and improve their activities, prioritize decisions, and access funding. At a larger scale, social impact measurement can help organizations working on similar social issues or in similar geographic areas to better understand the aggregate impacts of their work and collaborate to achieve greater change.

## References


Baron, R.A., & Ensley, M.D. (2006). Opportunity recognition as the detection of meaningful patterns: Evidence from comparisons of novice and experienced entrepreneurs. *Management Science*, *52*(9), 1331–1344. https://doi.org/10.1287/mnsc.1060.0538

Becker, H., & Vanclay, F. (2003). *The international handbook of social impact assessment conceptual and methodological advances*. Edward Elgar Publishing.

Borzaga, C., & Defourny, J. (Eds.) (2001). *The emergence of social enterprise* (1st ed.). Routledge. https://doi.org/10.4324/9780203164679

Bovens, M., Goodin, R.E., & Schillemans, T. (2014). Public accountability. In M. Bovens, R.E. Goodin, & T. Schillemans (Eds.), *The Oxford handbook of public accountability*, 1–20. Oxford University Press.

Burdge, R.J., & Vanclay, F. (1995). Social impact assessment: A contribution to the state of the art series. *Environmental and Social Impact Assessment*, *14*(1), 59–86. https://doi.org/10.1080/07349165.1996.9725886

Castells, M. (1998). *End of millennium, the information age: Economy, society and culture*. Blackwell.

Choi, N., & Majumdar, S. (2012). Social entrepreneurship as an essentially contested concept: Opening a new avenue for systematic future research. *Journal of Business Venturing*, *29*(3), 363–376. https://doi.org/10.1016/j.jbusvent.2013.05.001

Datta, P.B., & Gailey, R. (2012). Empowering women through social entrepreneurship: Case study of a women's cooperative in India. *Entrepreneurship Theory and Practice*, *36*(3), 569–587. https://doi.org/10.1111/j.1540-6520.2012.0050

Davidsson, P., & Wiklund, J. (2001). Levels of analysis in entrepreneurship research: Current research practice and suggestions for the future. *Entrepreneurship: Theory & Practice*, *25*(4), 81–100.

Defourny, J. (1992). The origins forms and role of a third major sector. In J. Defourny & J. Campos (Eds.), *Econmie sociale.entre economie capitaliste et economie publique*, 27–49. De BoeckWesmael.

Defourny, J., & Nyssens, M. (2012). Conceptions of social enterprise in Europe: A comparative perspective with the United States. In B. Gidron & Y. Hasenfeld (Eds.), *Social enterprises: An organizational perspective*, 71–90. Palgrave Macmillan.

Ebrahim, A.S., & Weisband, E. (2007). *Global accountabilities: Participation pluralism and public ethics*. Cambridge University Press.

Emerson, J. (2003). The blended value proposition: Integrating social and financial results. *California Management Review*, *45*(4), 35–51.

Epstein, M., & Yuthas, K. (2014). *Measuring and improving social impacts a guide for nonprofits companies and impact investors*. Berrett-Koehler.

Evers, A. (2004). Social services by social enterprises: On the possible contributions of hybrid organizations and a civil society. In A. Evers & J.-L. Laville (Eds.), *The third sector in Europe*, 237–255. Edward Elgar.

Evers, A. (1998). The constant challenge of defining public good: How do third sector organizations contribute to it? *Voluntas: International Journal of Voluntary and Nonprofit Organizations*, *10*(4), 371–379.

Evers, A. (1995). Part of the welfare mix: The third sector as an intermediate area between the market economy, state, and community. *Voluntas: International Journal of Voluntary and Nonprofit Organizations*, *6*, 159–182.

EVPA. (2018). *Impact strategies, how investors drive social impact*. Retrieved from https://www.evpa.ngo/sites/www.evpa.ngo/files/publications/EVPA_Impact_Strategies_2018.pdf

Field, A.J. (1999). New economic history and law and economics. In: G. De Geest G. & C. Nagel (Eds.), *Elgar Encyclopedia of law and economics*, 728–753. E. E. Elgar.

Furubotn, E.G., & Richter, R. (2005). *Institutions and economic theory: The contribution of the new institutional economics*. University of Michigan Press.

Gair, C. (2002). *A report from the good ship SROI, San Francisco*. The Roberts Foundation. Retrieved from http://www.socialreturns.org/docs/good_ship_sroi_gair.pdf

Gonzales, V. (2007). Globalization. Welfare reform and the social economy: Developing an alternative approach to analyzing social welfare systems in the post-industrial era. *The Journal of Sociology & Social Welfare*, *34*(2), 225–251.

Hall, M., Millo, Y., & Barman, E. (2015). Who and what really counts? Stakeholder prioritization and accounting for social value. *Journal of Management Studies*, *52*(7), 907–934. https://doi.org/10.1111/joms.12146

Harlock, J. (2013). *Impact measurement practice in the UK third sector: A review of emerging evidence*. Working Paper. University of Birmingham.

IRIS+ (2019). *Five dimensions of impact*. Retrieved from https://s3.amazonaws.com/giin-web-assets/iris/assets/files/guidance/IRIS-five-dimensions_June-2020

Lage, D., & Brandt, L. (2008). The growing influence of non-governmental organizations: Chances and risks. *Anuário Brasileiro de Direito Internacional, 3*(1), 79–93.

Latané, B. (1981). The psychology of social impact. *American Psychologist*, *36*(4), 343–356.

Laville, J. (2001). The social enterprise: Towards a theoretical socioeconomic approach. In J. Defourny (Ed.), *The emergence of social enterprise*, 312–322. Routledge.

Maas, K.E.H., & Liket, K.C. (2011). Talk the walk: Measuring the impact of corporate philanthropy. *Journal of Business Ethics*, *100*, 445–464.

Mendell, M. (2009). The three pillars of the social economy: The Quebec experience. In A. Amin (Ed.), *The social economy. International perspective on economic solidarity*, 176–207. Zed Books.

Moss, T.W., Short, J.C., Payne, G.T., & Lumpkin, G.T. (2011). Dual identities in social ventures: An exploratory study. *Entrepreneurship: Theory and Practice*, *35*(4), 805–830. https://doi.org/10.1111/j.1540-6520.2010.00372.x

Nicholls, A. (2009). 'We do good things, don't we?': Blended Value Accounting in social entrepreneurship. *Accounting Organizations and Society*, *34*(6–7), 755–769. https://doi.org/10.1016/j.aos.2009.04.008

Nicholls, A. (2008). Capturing the performance of the socially entrepreneurial organisation (SEO): An organisational legitimacy approach. In J. Robinson, J. Mair, & K. Hockerts (Eds.), *International perspectives on social entrepreneurship research*, 27–74. Palgrave Macmillan.

Nicholls, A., & Murdock, A. (2012). *Social innovation*. Palgrave Macmillan.

North, D. (1990). *Institutions, institutional change, and economic performance*. Cambridge University Press.

OECD. (2019). *Social impact investment: The impact imperative for sustainable development*. OECD Publishing. https://doi.org/10.1787/9789264311299-en

O'Leary, D.E. (2015). Armchair auditors: Crowdsourcing analysis of government expenditures. *Journal of Emerging Technologies in Accounting*, *12*(1), 71–91.

Pacaud, L., Vollet, D., & Angeon, V. (2007). Impact of tourism infrastructure on regional development: The implantation of a Center Parcs resort in northern France. *Tourism Economics, 13*(3), 389–406.

Pestoff, V.A. (1998). *Beyond the market and state: Social enterprises and civil democracy in a welfare state*. Ashgate.

Rauch, A., Frese, M., & Utsch, A. (2005). Effects of human capital and long-term human resources development and utilization on employment growth of small-scale businesses: A causal analysis. *Entrepreneurship Theory and Practice, 29*(6), 681–698.

Rawhouser, H., Cummings, M., & Newbert, S.L. (2019). Social impact measurement: Current approaches and future directions for social entrepreneurship research. *Entrepreneurship Theory and Practice, 43*(1), 82–115. https://doi.org/10.1177/104225871772771

Reisman, J., & Giennap, A. (2004). *Theory of change: A practical tool for action, results and learning*. The Netherlands: Organizational Research Services, Erasmus University. http://www.aecf.org/m/resourcedoc/aecftheoryofchange-2004.pdf

Rutherford, M. (1994). *Institutions in economics—the old and new institutionalism*. Cambridge University Press.

Sachs, J. (2002). *The Money trail: Measuring your impact on the local economy using LM3*. New Economics Foundation. https://neweconomics.org/uploads/files/money-trial.pdf

So, I., & Staskevicius, A. (2015). *Measuring the "impact" in impact investing*. Harvard Business School. https://www.hbs.edu/socialenterprise/wp-content/uploads/2021/09/MeasuringImpact-1.pdf

Spear, R., Defourny, J., Favreau, L., & Laville, J. (Eds.) (2001). *Tackling social exclusion in Europe: The contribution of the social economy*. Aldershot.

Stephan, U., Patterson, M., Kelly, C., & Mair, J. (2016). Organizations driving positive social change a review and an integrative framework of change processes. *Journal of Management, 42*(5), 1250–1281. https://doi.org/10.1177/0149206316633268

Tejedo-Romero, F., & Araujo, F. (2023). Critical factors influencing information disclosure in public organisations. *Humanities and Social Sciences Communications, 10*, 1–12. https://doi.org/10.1057/s41599-023-01814-8

Van Til, J. (2000). *Growing civil society: From nonprofit sector to third space*. Indiana University Press.

Vanclay, F. (2003). International principles for social impact assessment. *Impact Assessment and Project Appraisal, 21*(1), 5–11.

Vaughan, D.R., Farr, H., & Slee, W. (2000). Estimating and interpreting the local economic benefits of visitor spending: An explanation. *Leisure Studies, 19*, 95–118.

Zaheer, A., Albert, S., & Zaheer, A. (1999). Time scales and organizational theory. *Academy of Management Review, 24*, 725–741.

# 14 Trends and future perspectives on social impact generation

*Katarzyna Bachnik, Magdalena Kaźmierczak, Magdalena Rojek-Nowosielska, Magdalena Stefańska and Justyna Szumniak-Samolej*

## Introduction

An organization's social impact is one of the three dimensions of the organization's impact (social, environmental, economic) on the environment in the context of sustainable development and is also an area that generates much more difficulty in defining, categorizing, and measuring than the other two. Extensive knowledge of the economic impact of organizations and methods for measuring this impact is provided by economic science, with tools and data for measuring environmental impact provided by natural and engineering sciences. The social impact of organizations, on the other hand, seems to be much more elusive, fuzzy, interdisciplinary, as well as hitherto more overlooked in analyses. Significant difficulties in diagnosing social impact versus environmental impact are set out in the *Final report on social taxonomy* (European Commission, 2022). Firstly, it was noted that while environmental objectives can be based on science, social taxonomy should be based on international authoritative standards of topical relevance, such as the International Bill of Human Rights. Secondly, it was suggested that most economic activities have a negative impact on the environment, although at the same time by their very nature have some positive social impact (e.g., creation of decent jobs, payment of taxes, and production of socially beneficial goods and services). In measuring social impact, the challenge is therefore to distinguish such intrinsic impact from additional social benefits that directly contribute to the realization of human rights, such as improving access to quality health care or providing decent work (European Commission, 2022). Creating frameworks for the social impact of organizations as a practical tool to help investors identify opportunities to contribute to social objectives, in particular support the equitable transformation of the economy through appropriate redirection of capital, and for management and employees to confirm that the organization is moving in the right direction, is therefore an extremely difficult task.

This monograph is an attempt to understand the above challenge, our contribution to a better understanding of the determinants of social impact, how it can

DOI: 10.4324/9781003480952-17

be measured and, most importantly, how organizations can create better social strategies and actions.

The following chapter concludes the publication and aims to join the discussion about the future of social impact of organizations, providing conclusive observations, identifying recurring themes across the chapters, highlighting more universally applicable findings and practices, and indicating the paths for further research on social impact within the broader context of corporate social responsibility, business, and society.

The objectives of this chapter are as follows:

- To verify, based on an analysis of the literature, the areas of research within the scope of management and economics that can be identified as future trends in the social impact of organizations;
- To analyze and synthesize the content of the chapters of this monograph, identifying the main conclusions and resulting areas for further research in the field of the social impact of organizations.

## Literature review

The first purpose of this chapter is to try to identify directions for future research on the social impact of organizations within the management sciences, with a particular focus on the issue of corporate social responsibility based on literature review. For this purpose, the scientific literature cataloged in Scopus and Web of Science (WoS) databases was reviewed. The social impact of organizations and future trends were taken as keywords. In addition, it was limited to Business, Management and Accounting and Economics, Econometrics and Finance, with the years 2000–2023 adopted as the timeframe. The result is the selection of 144 publications in the Scopus database.

The selection of publications allowed for a very interesting research review, leading to the following conclusions. Firstly, Figure 14.1 indicates the current and future five areas of interest to researchers – two focus on macro issues, and three indicate researchers' grasp of the micro, organizational perspective. The first two clusters include social security and demographic phenomena, related to structural changes in societies, particularly the aging population. Another three clusters, with which the bridges (integrators) are the topics of employment and the economy, concern sustainable development and sustainability, followed by social responsibility. It can be noted that the database of 144 publications includes 366 authors who are united by the study of the following issues: sustainable development and sustainability, decision-making, social impact, corporate social responsibility, artificial intelligence, globalization, and pandemics. These publications, usually compiled by several authors, cover narrow issues, and the analysis indicates poor keyword repetition, in addition to those mentioned. The most

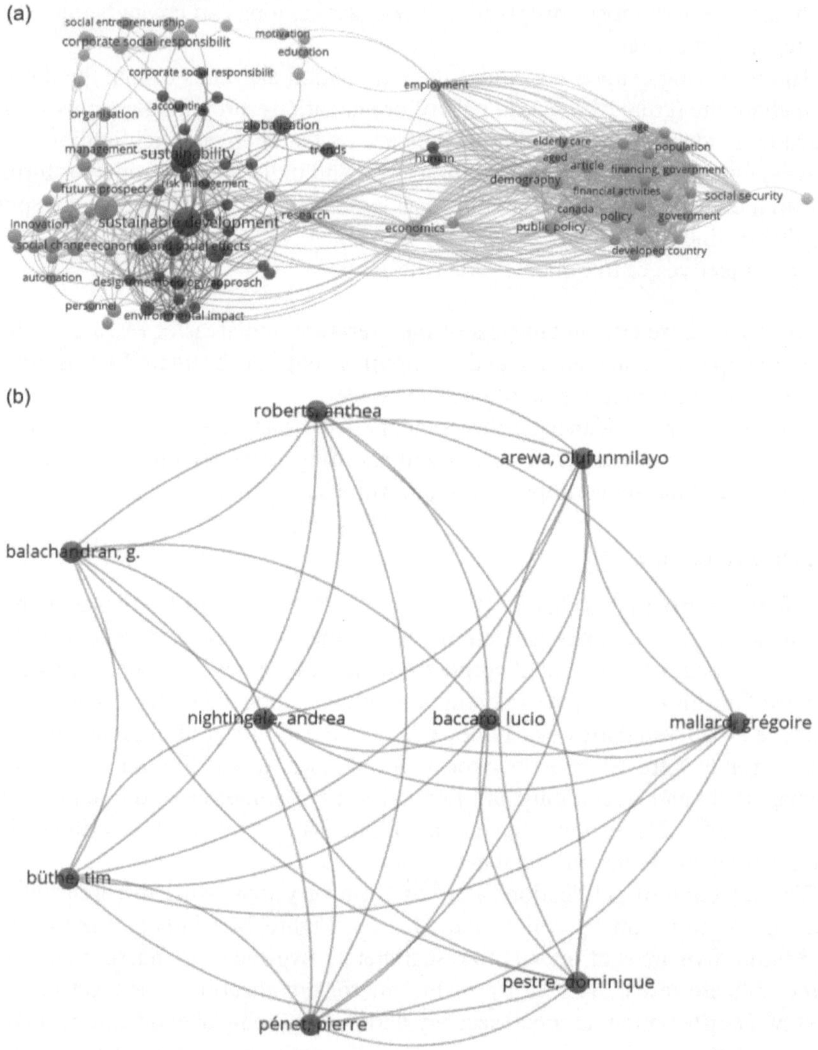


*Figure 14.1* Scopus – results of analysis

*Source:* Own elaboration.

cited publications covered issues of human resource management, logistics, product innovation, and crisis management in the tourism services sector.

Slightly different results were obtained from the analysis of the WoS database – assuming the same restrictions as for the literature review in the Scopus database, it resulted in 163 publications (see Figure 14.2), with six overlapping research areas emerging. These were:

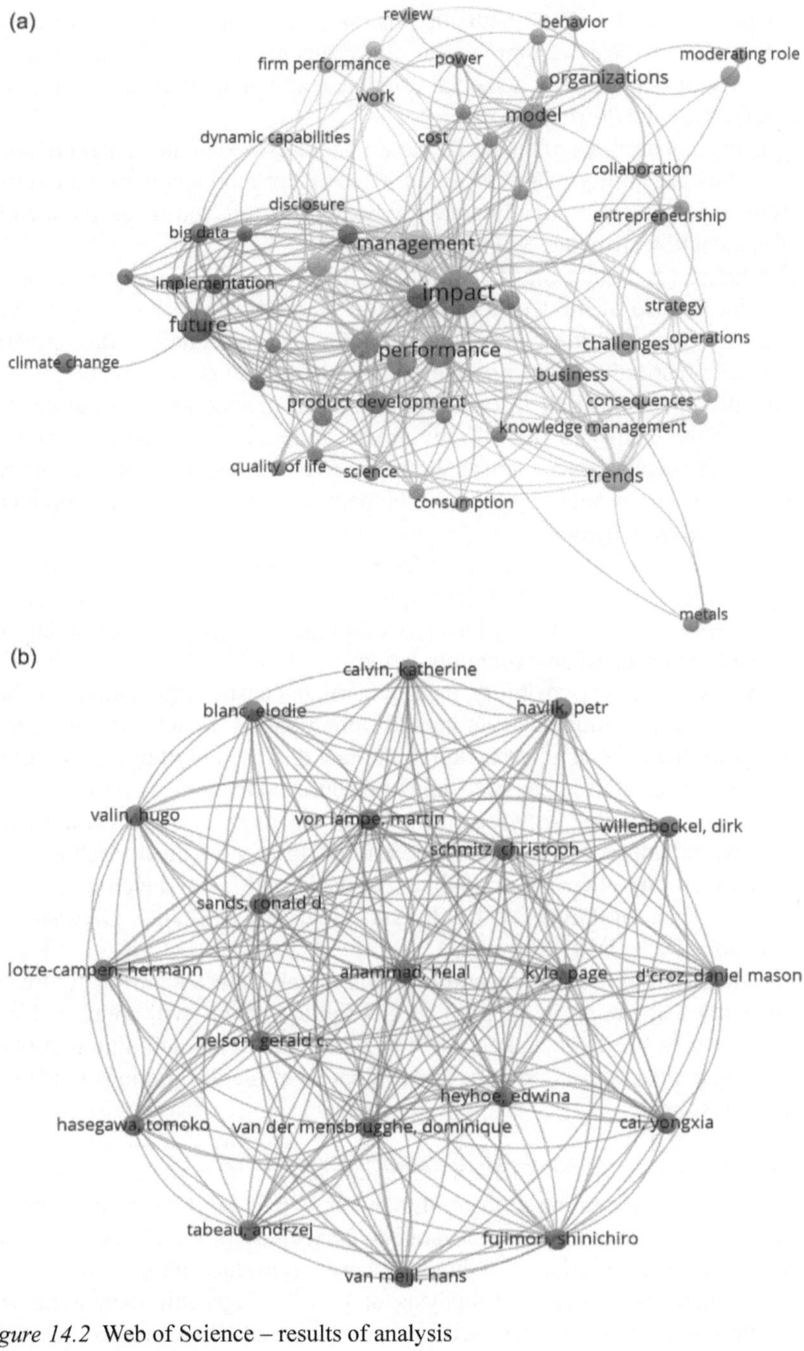


*Figure 14.2* Web of Science – results of analysis

*Source:* Own elaboration.

- Cooperation and entrepreneurship. In the future, increasing social impact will require a creative approach to doing business, especially in NGOs, as third-sector entities have a special role in social impact that stems from their organizational culture and mission;
- Dynamic capabilities of the organization – understood in the context of social impact as the ability of the organization to adapt to changes in the environment, especially of a social nature, by pursuing goals that foster the creation of value and well-being of employees;
- The future (including big data, industry 4.0) – is a direction of changes involving the use of modern technology in identifying and implementing solutions to improve the quality of life. They can be related to the operation of public institutions that provide services to residents, the creation of sustainable cities and their infrastructure, or the introduction of solutions that improve the quality of life of individuals. Undoubtedly, in the technological field, huge social consequences, both positive and negative, but not entirely predictable, are brought by the development and increasingly widespread use of artificial intelligence;
- Change and quality of life, strategies and consequences – adaptation of the organization's strategies and development of offers in response to changing social needs, such as caring for the well-being of employees, or taking into account the needs of an aging population;
- Corporate social responsibility, including related costs, organizational behavior, and business models – the increase in emphasis on activities in accordance with the CSR concept is due to the fact that the next few years will see increased interest in sustainable human resource management. Advancing demographic processes, growing awareness of the diversity of people in various aspects, and unprecedented intergenerational differences due to technological changes, among other factors, will drive organizations to develop new solutions for ensuring Diversity, Equity and Inclusion, or Equity, Diversity and Inclusion (DEI/EDI);
- Consumption and its social and environmental impact – in the future, organizations operating in supply and distribution chains will come under increasing pressure from stakeholders to report social impact, although based on more precise measurements, and to document the declarations made with actual results.

Of the 153 selected authors of WoS publications, those that are most often mentioned are those concerning industry 4.0 and its impact on the environment, followed by those concerning the relevance to agriculture of the impact of climate change on water circulation, and those concerning product innovation.

Summarizing the conducted analysis of two bibliographic databases, with rather narrowly defined subject areas, it can be noted that there are not many publications focusing directly on social impact. The issues mentioned indicate that researchers conduct analyses in rather narrow areas, that they note the social impact of the issues they study but it is not the direct focus of the researchers. Social impact happens indirectly, through activities in organizations in the area of human resource management or the development of innovative products, or by introducing new solutions in logistics.

In addition, the research does not indicate cooperation between them, except in a small number of bodies. However, it would undoubtedly be valuable for researchers to join forces in revealing social influence and its implications as one of the many outcomes of an organization's behavior under study.

In general terms, such issues as demographic trends and social security, impact on an organization's human resources, impact on the economy, sustainable development and sustainability, and measurement of social impact are emerging as the main directions for further research in scientific work. The authors of the analyzed publications highlight the existence of an ecosystem – the intertwining of economy, society, and environment and the need to look to the future.

To conclude this part of the analysis, it is worth referring to the FSG report,[1] which indicates trends for the upcoming year. According to the report, the future of SI in 2024 means (FSG, 2023):

- Corporate changemakers will be key to advancing impact;
- Ensuring job quality in the future of work;
- A rising commitment to place;
- Leveraging government action and regulations for climate justice;
- Advancing health equity in a post-pandemic world.

## Methods

The analysis and synthesis of the content of the chapters collected in this monograph, the identification of the main conclusions of the research presented, and the resulting further development of concepts in the social impact of organizations are the second issue addressed in this chapter. After Ritchey (1991), we assume that analysis and synthesis, as scientific methods, always go hand in hand, that they complement one another. Each synthesis is built upon the results of the preceding analysis, and every analysis requires a subsequent synthesis to verify and correct its results.

In order to present them clearly, reference was made to the division of the chapters into three main parts made by the monograph editors: identification of the social impact scope, social impact on internal stakeholders, and social impact on external stakeholders. Part 1 introduces the reader to the issue of social impact, while Part 2 and Part 3 analyze the various areas of social impact (toward a wide range of stakeholders) of an organization. In order to summarize the main conclusions of the chapters and at the same time embed them in a broader framework for social impact, the authors created a framework indicating possible

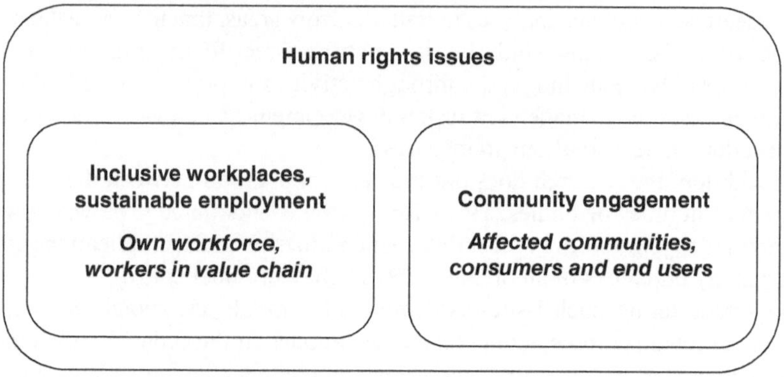


*Figure 14.3* Framework of possible areas of an organization's social impact

*Source:* Own elaboration, based on Business in the Community Ireland, 2023; European Commission, 2023a.

dimensions of an organization's social impact activities (see Figure 14.3). The framework is the result of a compilation of the European Union's Sustainability Reporting Standards (ESRS), and social metrics and key themes under the social pillar proposed by a non-profit advisory body, Business in the Community Ireland.

## ESRS

In our monograph, Part 2 and Part 3 explicitly refer to the areas of social impact metrics that are in place in the EU, with the European Union's aspiration to be the first climate-neutral continent being unprecedented in the world (European Commission, n.d.c), resulting in a number of legislative solutions covering entities operating in the EU and also cooperating with them. The solutions being implemented also address the measurement and reporting of environmental, social, and governance impacts.

In the area of social impact in the EU, an important document was the report on social taxonomy published in February 2022 by the EU Platform on Sustainable Finance (European Commission, n.d.b).[2] Based on the public consultation carried out, it was proposed to create a classification system for economic activities that contribute significantly to social objectives, along the lines of the existing environmental taxonomy (European Commission, 2022). This study became the starting point for the formulation of the EU social impact metrics published on 31 July 2023 by the European Commission, called European Union's Sustainability Reporting Standards (ESRS) (European Commission, 2023b).

Among the ESRS were 12 metrics covering the range of sustainability issues. The first two are cross-cutting: General Requirements (ESRS1) and General Disclosures (ESRS2). Then, there are five environmental ones (ESRS E1 to E5):

climate; pollution; water and marine resources; biodiversity and ecosystems; resource use and circular economy. The other four concern social issues (ESRS S1 to S4): own workforce, workers in the value chain, affected communities, consumers and end users, and one on governance (ESRS G1): business conduct (European Commission, 2023a).

ESRS are extremely important, as they must be applied by all companies affected by the Corporate Sustainability Reporting Directive (CSRD), i.e., a legislative document implementing ESG reporting obligations by EU businesses (including qualifying EU subsidiaries of non-EU companies) starting from 1 January 2024 (IBM, n.d.).

In our monograph Part 2 overlaps with the areas of ESRS metrics S1 and S2 (own workforce, workers in the value chain), while Part 3 overlaps with ESRS metrics S3 and S4 (affected communities, consumers, and end users).

#### *Social pillars*

Business in the Community Ireland (BITCI) published a *2023 Sustainability handbook* (Business in the Community Ireland, 2023), which is a part of a wider project to identify and take the necessary steps toward transformation to a low-carbon and inclusive society. In compiling this handbook, an extensive range of relevant resources was used. For the BITCI network to measure progress toward true sustainability, it is necessary to focus on three basic pillars: economic, environmental, and social, which will be underpinned by governance. All of these pillars make up BITCI's proposed EESG framework.

Given the subject matter of this monograph, we will focus on the social pillar only. BITCI addressed four key themes under the social pillar: inclusive workplaces, sustainable employment, community engagement, and human rights.

#### *Framework of possible dimensions of an organization's social impact activities*

Overlaying the key themes under the social pillar according to BITCI and social ESRS, we obtain the following framework indicating possible areas of social impact in an organization's activities (see Figure 14.3):

- Inclusive workplaces and sustainable employment in the context of own workforce and workers in the value chain;
- Community engagement in the context of affected communities, consumers, and end users.

Human rights is a cross-cutting issue – it affects both internal and external stakeholders and relates to all previously mentioned social pillar themes. We therefore decided to address human rights in the context of each dimension. Human right issues in business are distinguished according to the Business & Human

Rights Navigator UN Global Compact: child labor, forced labor, discrimination, freedom of association, occupational safety and health, living wage, working time, gender equality, migrant workers, indigenous people (UN Global Compact, n.d.).

The vast majority of human right issues in business relate to the workplace (own and in the value chain), although companies also have the opportunity to play an important role in coping with human rights issues in the context of affected communities, consumers, and end users. This includes cooperation with NGOs and international organizations in the area of social projects focused on solving human rights issues, responsible communication strategies and campaigns (including social marketing), or designing and offering socially responsible products and services that address human rights challenges. With regard to consumers and end users, the human rights aspect also refers to a responsible and social impact-oriented corporate response to social expectations resulting from increasingly conscious and sustainable consumption (Edelman Trust Institute, 2023).

## Results

The main conclusion concerning social impact that resounds both from the literature review conducted in Chapter 1 and from virtually all the other chapters in this monograph is that social impact is a topic that is still new, presenting researchers and organizations with many challenges that are still to be discovered. There are many definitions and ambiguities and no common approaches or methods of measurement. Organizations are only just learning how to measure, report, and thus better create this impact.

The conclusions of the opening Chapter 1, which attempts to define and classify social impact as the key term for the publication, clearly indicate that this is a hard task. The recurring observation is that it is very difficult to find articles talking about this concept in general (without reference to a sector or specific context) and that there is currently a lack of consensus on the meaning of social impact, which results in a lack of a single and commonly accepted definition. The multiplicity of definitions consequently leads to a variety of approaches to assessing and measuring social impact and consequently a variety of measurement methods. Finally, reflecting on the areas of changes resulting from the social initiatives undertaken by enterprises, the authors propose a classification of the changes in terms of their focus and scale of potential impact distinguishing: micro-scale and inward-focused, meso-scale and outward focus, and macro-scale with an outward focus.

In Chapter 2, the authors address the topic of measuring social impact from the perspective of startups. They point out that in the literature the main focus is given to startup activity, and still little is known about the ways and tools to assess their factual performance with regard to social impact. As a result of their research, they propose an impact assessing framework for startups, a set of metrics to assess startup outcomes with regard to the implementation of UN Sustainable Development Goals.

In contrast, the author of the next chapter (Chapter 3) draws attention to the new category of social impact, which looks at its negative facet, i.e., the negative consequences of companies' actions. They distinguish between the concepts of social irresponsibility and negative impact, which, although complimentary to some extent, are also disconnected. While social irresponsibility implies the decision-making process and all stages of irresponsible action, negative social impact focuses more on the effect that negative actions bring. Making small enterprises measure the two will transmit into uncovering opportunities and challenges that might enormously impact their development in the long term.

From Part 2, which is devoted to social impact on internal stakeholders, it clearly resounds that the next years will bring an increased interest in responsible leadership, sustainable human resource management, as well as the topics of equity, diversity, and inclusion, which dovetails perfectly with the area of inclusive workplaces and sustainable employment (own workforce and workers in the value chain) on our framework (see Figure 14.3). According to BITCI, sustainable employment consists of strategic workforce planning, organizational change management, compelling employee proposition, and enhancing employee engagement (Business in the Community Ireland, 2023).

Making organizational changes toward a better future requires responsible and committed leaders. As shown in Chapter 4, leadership is important, as it inspires, motivates, and sets an example for people to accomplish positive changes in the company and therefore in the world. Leaders, while running their businesses, should seek to tackle the world's most difficult challenges in order to create a positive social impact. This means that the focus on social impact requires a good leader with an ethical mindset. But unfortunately, as the analysis shows, for the moment, there is lack of quantitative research, comparative studies and long-run analyses, investigating the role of ethical leadership for social impact.

Chapter 5 refers to another element of sustainable employment, which is the compelling employee proposition, and deals with the inclusion of employee interests, discussing them in the context of the company's social impact for the benefit of workforce. This is an important aspect of social impact, since, as the authors of the BITCI report referenced in the design of our framework write, the employee proposition goes beyond compensation and rewards. "It's about: being respected and valued, having equal opportunities for personal and professional development, having a sense of purpose achieved through work and engagement with colleagues" (Business in the Community Ireland, 2023).

Chapters 6 and 7 analyze the impact on employees of the Covid-19 pandemic and the actions taken by managers in response to it. Chapter 6 assesses work-life balance and job security in the context of the pandemic and discusses the evolution of the terms over time. In contrast, Chapter 7 analyzes the effects of solutions implemented by managers in response to the pandemic on employee well-being and work performance. Given that an organization's environment is characterized by increasing levels of volatility, uncertainty, complexity, and ambiguity (VUCA) (Bennett & Lemoine, 2014), the ability to spot sudden and unexpected phenomena (such as the next pandemic, war, or groundbreaking technology), respond to them, and measure the social impact of actions taken is undoubtedly an extremely important area for improving the organization in the future.

The topic discussed in Chapters 8 and 9 within the context of the inclusive workplace is DEI management. DEI/EDI concerns (diversity, equity, and inclusion or equality, diversity, and inclusion) are also some of the most important issues addressed by the UN in the context of human rights (Global Compact Network Poland, n.d.b) and are reflected in the Sustainable Development Goals (SDGs). Openness to diversity encompasses all differences that exist between people, including but not limited to gender, age, nationality, language, race, ethnicity, religion, and socioeconomic status, as well as those that have been talked about relatively recently such as neurodiversity, or sexual orientation and/or gender identity (LGBTQIA). It is through the active inclusion of all employees in the organizational structures of companies that the scale of inequality and prejudice in societies can be reduced (Kostrzewa et al., 2023). This may sound promising, but according to the Global Gender Gap Report (2023) published by the World Economic Forum, at the current rate of DEI/EDI development by companies, it will still take 131 years to achieve full equality in work environments (Kostrzewa et al., 2023). There is no doubt, therefore, that this is a key topic for organizations consciously creating their social impact.

In Chapter 8, it is set out that companies and organizations' DEI/EDI/D&I/I&D policies can lead them to growth and success. However, in order to properly utilize diversity, the organization must be inclusive with the Management by Values (MBV) strategy embedded in the company culture. In order to benefit from differences in the workplace, people must feel included, as such inclusion creates a well-being environment and open atmosphere where everyone feels important and their opinion matters. What might be surprising is the fact that one of the most significant advantages of a diverse workforce is the increased creativity and innovation in the workplace – two key skills and mindsets both sought after in the job market and applicable in any dimension of organizational operations.

Gender equality is a basic human right. According to the Global Gender Gap Index, the global gap defining the level of equality of opportunity between men and women in 2022 was 68.1%, with the global share of women in leadership positions at only 31% (Global Compact Network Poland, n.d.a). Achieving gender equality and empowerment of women is undoubtedly an important area for social impact, as results from the wording of SDG No. 5. Nevertheless, Chapter 9 raises an issue that is not obvious in this context. The authors try to determine the perception of gender equity management in the workplace by men, with the study suggesting the surprising conclusion that there are salient needs among men who have been discriminated against in the workplace or feel threatened by practices solely oriented at women that should be addressed in diversity management practice. From the practical perspective, HR experts would be well advised to look for ways to make diversity management more attractive to men by communicating the advantages of diversity management and gender equality for them.

The content discussed in Part 2 of this monograph refers specifically to the aspects of social impact (inclusive workplaces and sustainable employment) in the area of own workforce. Undoubtedly, the topic of social impact in the value chain needs further analysis, with particular focus on social impact in key areas of human rights in the value chain. This is undoubtedly a trend of the future, as indicated, among other things, by the fact that the EU is in the process of drafting the final version of the Corporate Sustainability Due Diligence Directive (CSDD), which will require EU and non-EU companies to conduct environmental and human rights due diligence across their operations, subsidiaries, and value chains. As the European Commission states:

> The aim of this Directive is to foster sustainable and responsible corporate behavior and to anchor human rights and environmental considerations in companies' operations and corporate governance. The new rules will ensure that businesses address adverse impacts of their actions, including in their value chains inside and outside Europe.
>
> (European Commission, n.d.a)

As announced, implementation of the directive is expected to bring benefits for citizens (e.g. increased trust in businesses), for companies (e.g. better awareness of companies' negative environmental and human rights impacts, higher attention to innovation, better access to finance), and for developing countries (e.g. better protection of human rights and the environment, improved sustainability-related practices, or improved living conditions for people) (European Commission, n.d.a).

Part 3 analyzes the social impact of an organization on external stakeholders. In the framework in question (see Figure 14.3), this area is called "community engagement (affected communities, consumers and end users)."

In Chapter 10, the authors highlight the role that retail chains play in shaping consumption. In the future, organizations operating in supply and distribution chains might come under increasing pressure from stakeholders to report social impact, but based on more precise measurements, and also evidence the declarations made with actual results. Purchasers' attitudes indicate that they consciously shape their consumption, which retail chains can facilitate. However, the narrative used in communication often creates a false picture of what is good for the consumer. Therefore, greater transparency in communications is necessary for creating both a strong reputation as a responsible organization and a positive social impact on consumers.

The chapter's conclusions are consistent with analyses of global changes in consumer behavior, such as that consumers are putting brands under more scrutiny, are more concerned about a brand's impact, reward brands they trust with purchase, loyalty, and advocacy, and are more likely to buy brands that take action. The latter observation is particularly interesting in the context of the social impact, as consumers indicate that they are more likely to buy from brands that commit to such issues as improving healthcare access, addressing climate change, ending racism, promoting gender equality, retraining workers, and combating misinformation (Edelman Trust Institute, 2023). The relevance of community engagement to consumers and end users was also confirmed in the studies cited above, with a conclusion that consumers want ongoing engagement with brands, and that brand engagement builds trust in the product and the brand. Consumers indicate that through their interactions with the brand, they gain confidence that the brand is competent, ethical, and relevant (Edelman Trust Institute, 2023).

The area of affected communities from the framework in question is referred to in Chapters 11, 12, and 13 of this monograph.

Chapters 11 and 12 emphasize the importance of universities – both as places to educate managers who will be responsible in the future for decisions that result in social and environmental changes brought about by organizations, and also as a place to create value for people who have left the labor market but still want to develop and continue their education. The trend of developing offers for those who have left the labor market will intensify in the Global North as a consequence of aging populations and declining birth rates. Concern for the well-being of seniors will be expressed with offers tailored to the capabilities of both intellectual and physical representatives of this age group. Ensuring the inclusiveness of seniors, their longer professional and social activity brings a number of psychological, as well as social and economic benefits.

The last chapter deals with entities from the third sector, whose importance in creating social impact (including in the area of human rights) is indisputable. These organizations usually have social and environmental objectives incorporated in the core of their activities, and they are of paramount importance. Chapter 13 aims to indicate the theoretical foundation and identification of added value, both social and economic, realized by entities from the third sector – NGOs/SPOs. The author claims that it is important for these organizations to develop a learning culture, where impact measurement is truly integrated into their operations, producing data that matters and is inclusive of the voices of the people who are impacted. Additionally, available frameworks can immediately help organizations working on similar social issues or with similar goal areas to better understand how to aggregate social impacts of their work and collaborate to achieve better outcomes.

The need for a partnership indicated in Chapter 13 relates to the "cooperation and entrepreneurship" research area that emerged from the analysis of the WoS base conducted at the outset of this chapter and also clearly overlaps with SDG No. 17: Revitalize the global partnership for sustainable development. The pursuit of sustainable development, including greater positive social impact, requires inclusive and collaborative partnerships between governments, the private sector, and civil society at the global, regional, national, and local level (UN, n.d.).

## Discussion and conclusion

The analysis carried out shows that the future of the social impact concept seems to be extremely promising, with the topic of corporate social impact increasingly resonating in the consciousness of the public, although it must be clearly emphasized that it is still in the early stages of development. This is particularly evident in the area of research, where there is still a lack of consistency in approach, definitions, and especially the research itself on the social impact of business, which all the more reinforces our belief that this monograph is needed and fits into an apparent research gap.

One can clearly see a growing interest in the topic of social impact among academics and practitioners, as shown in the literature analysis conducted in Chapter 1 of this monograph. This can also be seen in publications issued by international organizations (EU, UN), NGOs, research agencies, or consulting firms. In part, this is likely due to the high level of interest in the SDGs, and now, in particular, in trying to account for progress on their implementation. In addition, there is growing legislative pressure on enterprises (particularly without precedence within the EU) in the area of the need for ESG reporting, including, most definitely, social impact. The purpose is to encourage informed measurement of current social impact and ultimately design processes, projects, and activities that are more thoughtful, responsible, and will have a greater positive impact in the future. Undoubtedly, this is and will present a major challenge for enterprises given the complexity and holistic nature of the topic of social impact, or the difficulties associated with measuring the right impact (research methods, access to data). This is certainly a very important area for future cross-sector research and cooperation between the university, business, and the third sector.

Not only the study of social impact but also the implementation of real social change requires extremely urgent action, as the outlook for the world is not optimistic. In terms of achieving the objectives of Agenda 2030, all SDGs are currently "off track" (Sustainable Development Report, n.d.). Over the past three years, following the Covid-19 pandemic and subsequent crises (e.g., the war in Ukraine, commodity crisis, inflation), SDG progress has stalled globally (Sustainable Development Report, n.d.). According to research analyzing the impact of megatrends and trends on the SDGs (Hatalska, 2022), the megatrends slowing down the realization of the SDGs the most are: health crises, loss of social cohesion, and a mirror world.[3] And within the trends having the biggest negative impact on the realization of the SDGs, they are techno-power accumulation, digital inequality, the commodity crisis, disrupted supply chains, disillusionment with democracy, polarization, and anti-science. However, there are also positive aspects. Trends such as invisible technology, giga-connectivity, clean energy, conscious consumption, closed-loop economy, social economy, inclusivity and diversity, and women's empowerment have the greatest positive impact on the realization of the SDGs. The area with the greatest chance of realization as envisioned by Agenda 2030 is related to economic growth, which includes such SDGs as economic growth, decent work and innovation, industry, and infrastructure. The lowest indicator in terms of the chance of implementation as envisioned by the Agenda was given to the area of dignity, which includes such goals as an end to poverty, zero hunger, less inequality, and gender equality. This is a clear signal that humanity, including business, still has plenty of work to do in these social areas.

According to the author of the cited research, today simply undertaking activities to support or counter trends in order to achieve the SDGs is insufficient. What is needed is a change at a deeper socio-cultural level that includes: the ability to think about the future, the ability to think systemically, cooperation and solidarity, and a change in the understanding of the definition of progress (Hatalska, 2022). The recipients and creators of this change must all become important participants in socioeconomic life, among others: business, policy makers, social activists, scientists, or educators. As Hutchinson, Novacek, Chin, and Falco (2023) argue, it is possible for a business to become socially transformative, that is, one that will build smart social impact that nurtures resilience and long-term advantage (Hutchinson, Novacek, Chin & Falco, 2023). Crucial elements of a successful approach to socially transformative business include dedicated leadership, substantive authenticity, clear communication, and innovation. (Hutchinson, Novacek, Chin & Falco, 2023). In order to design and implement the necessary changes as humanity, we need conscious, responsible, ambitious, and courageous leaders who are ready to challenge existing patterns. Educating such leaders today is a huge task and responsibility for universities, among others. The role of universities in the context of social impact seems to be invaluable, as they not only shape the attitudes and values of future leaders and participants in socioeconomic life, but through their research projects, they point out areas in need of urgent action, propose tools and methods, and themselves exert a social impact locally.

In conclusion, we trust that in a polarized world, where clickbait wins, algorithms lock us into bubbles, and bad news sells far better than good news, at a time of constantly emerging new and global threats, doubt and depression (including climate-related one), an organization's measurable and communicated social impact in the public space is proof that positive social and environmental change is possible, meaning that there is hope for a better future. And hope is extremely important, as it gives significance to our activities and motivates us to continue despite uncertainties (Solnit, 2022). Thus understood, social impact, in addition to describing the positive effects of actions taken by organizations in the present, provides an impetus for innovation and activity in changes for a better future. By monitoring social impact trends and implementing innovative and socially engaged organizational management strategies, it is possible to create a more just and sustainable world that serves everyone.

## Notes

1 FSG is a global nonprofit consulting firm that partners with foundations and corporations to create equitable systems change.
2 The EU Platform on Sustainable Finance gathers preeminent sustainability experts representing diverse stakeholder groups, including private entities from financial, non-financial, and business sectors, NGOs and civil society, academia and think tanks, individual experts, as well as public and international institutions.
3 The mirror world means the intensive and constant transfer of life at all possible levels to the digital world (Hatalska, n.d.).

## References

Bennett, N., & Lemoine, G.J. (2014). *What VUCA really means for you*. Retrieved from https://hbr.org/2014/01/what-vuca-really-means-for-you?tpcc=intlcontent_strategy&gad_source=1

Business in the Community Ireland. (2023). *Sustainability handbook*. Retrieved from https://www.bitc.ie/wp-content/uploads/2023/05/BITC-Sustainability-Handbook.pdf

Edelman Trust Institute. (2023). *Edelman trust barometer*. Global report. Retrieved from https://www.edelman.com/sites/g/files/aatuss191/files/2023-03/2023%20Edelman%20Trust%20Barometer%20Global%20Report%20FINAL.pdf

European Commission. (n.d.a). *Corporate sustainability due diligence. Fostering sustainability in corporate governance and management systems*. Retrieved from https://commission.europa.eu/business-economy-euro/doing-business-eu/corporate-sustainability-due-diligence_en

European Commission. (n.d.b). *Platform on sustainable finance*. Retrieved from https://finance.ec.europa.eu/sustainable-finance/overview-sustainable-finance/platform-sustainable-finance_en

European Commission. (n.d.c). *The European green deal. Striving to be the first climate-neutral continent*. Retrieved from https://commission.europa.eu/strategy-and-policy/priorities-2019-2024/european-green-deal_en

European Commission. (2023a). *Questions and answers on the adoption of European sustainability reporting standards*. Retrieved from https://ec.europa.eu/commission/presscorner/detail/en/qanda_23_4043

European Commission. (2023b). *The commission adopts the European sustainability reporting standards*. Retrieved from https://finance.ec.europa.eu/news/commission-adopts-european-sustainability-reporting-standards-2023-07-31_en

European Commission. (2022). *Final report on social taxonomy*. Platform on sustainable finance. Retrieved from https://commission.europa.eu/system/files/2022-03/280222-sustainable-finance-platform-finance-report-social-taxonomy.pdf

FSG. (2023). *Future of social impact: What to watch for in 2024*. Retrieved from https://www.fsg.org/blog/future-of-social-impact-2024/

Global Compact Network Poland (n.d.a). "*Business and Human Rights – Together for Sustainable Development" report*. Retrieved from https://ungc.org.pl/raport-biznes-i-prawa-czlowieka-razem-dla-zrownowazonego-rozwoju/

Global Compact Network Poland. (n.d.b). *On the road to DEI*. Retrieved from https://ungc.org.pl/raport-dei/

Hatalska. (n.d). *The mirror world – the intensive and constant transfer of life at all possible levels to the digital world*. Retrieved from https://hatalska.com/2023/02/21/mapa-trendow-2023/

Hatalska. (2022). *The impact of trends on the Sustainable Development Goals*. Retrieved from https://infuture.institute/raporty/wplyw-trendow-na-cele-zrownowazonego-rozwoju-sdg-2023

Hutchinson, R., Novacek, G., Chin, V., & Falco, G. (2023). Socially transformative business is smart business. *BCG*. Retrieved from https://www.bcg.com/publications/2023/socially-transformative-business-is-smart-business

IBM. (n.d.). *What is the Corporate Sustainability Reporting Directive (CSRD)?* Retrieved from https://www.ibm.com/topics/csrd

Kostrzewa, A., Wasilewski, J., Leszczyńska, Z., & Brand Republic (Eds.) (2023). On the road to DEI. *UN Global Compact Network Poland*. Retrieved from https://ungc.org.pl/wp-content/uploads/2023/11/Raport-22W-drodze-do-DEI22.pdf

Ritchey, T. (1991). Analysis and synthesis. On scientific method – Based on a study by Bernhard Riemann. *Systems Research, 8*(4), 21–41. ISSN 0731 Revised version, 1996. https://www.swemorph.com/method/anaeng-r.pdf

Solnit, R. (2022). Climate despair is a luxury. *The New Statesman*, October.

Sustainable Development Report. (n.d.). *Executive summary. Summary of key findings and recommendations*. Retrieved from https://dashboards.sdgindex.org/chapters/executive-summary

UN. (n.d.). *Goal 17: Strengthen the means of implementation and revitalize the Global Partnership for Sustainable Development*. Retrieved from https://www.un.org.pl/cel17

UN Global Compact. (n.d.). *Business & human rights navigator*. Retrieved from https://bhr-navigator.unglobalcompact.org/

# Index